Language Structure and Language Use

Language Structure and Language Use

Essays by Charles A. Ferguson

Selected and Introduced by Anwar S. Dil

Stanford University Press, Stanford, California

Language Science and National Development

A Series Sponsored by the
Linguistic Research Group of Pakistan

General Editor: Anwar S. Dil

Stanford University Press
Stanford, California
© 1971 by the Board of Trustees of the
Leland Stanford Junior University
Printed in the United States of America
ISBN 0-8047-0780-4
Original edition 1971
Last figure below indicates year of this printing:
85   84   83   82   81   80   79   78   77   76

Contents

Acknowledgments

The Linguistic Research Group of Pakistan and the Editor of the Language Science and National Development Series are deeply grateful to Professor Charles A. Ferguson, Chairman of the Committee on Linguistics of Stanford University and Honorary Life Member of the LRGP, for giving us the privilege of presenting his selected writings as the inaugural volume in our series established in response to the general appeal of the Secretary-General of the United Nations and the Director-General of Unesco to scholars and academic institutions to dedicate 1970 as the International Education Year.

The Editor completed work on this volume during 1969-70, while he was in residence as Visiting Scholar with the Committee on Linguistics, Stanford University. He received financial assistance during the period from the Center for Research in International Studies, Stanford University.

We are indebted to the editors and publishers of the following publications. The ready permission on the part of the holders of the copyrights, acknowledged in each case, is a proof of the existing international cooperation and goodwill that gives hope for better collaboration among scholars of all nations for international exchange of knowledge.

Diglossia. Word 15. 325-40 (1959). By permission of the Linguistic Circle of New York.

Linguistic Diversity in South Asia. International Journal of American Linguistics 26:3. 1-8 (1960).

By permission of the co-author Professor John J. Gumperz, and the Editor of IJAL.

The Language Factor in National Development. Anthropological Linguistics 4.23-27 (1962). By permission of the Editor.

Background to Second Language Problems. Study of the Role of Second Languages in Asia, Africa, and Latin America, ed. by Frank A. Rice (Washington, D.C.: Center for Applied Linguistics, 1962), pp. 1-7. By permission of the Editor and the Center for Applied Linguistics.

Problems of Teaching Languages with Diglossia. Georgetown University Monograph Series on Languages and Linguistics: Monograph No. 15, Report of the Thirteenth Annual Round Table Meeting, Georgetown University Press, Washington, D.C., 1962, pp. 165-77. By permission of the School of Languages and Linguistics, Georgetown University.

Assumptions about Nasals: A Sample Study in Phonological Universals. Universals of Language, ed. by Joseph H. Greenberg (Cambridge, Massachusetts: The M.I.T. Press, 1963), pp. 53-60. By permission of the M.I.T. Press, Cambridge, Massachusetts.

Linguistic Theory and Language Learning. Georgetown University Monograph Series on Languages and Linguistics: Monograph No. 16, Report of the Fourteenth Annual Round Table Meeting, Georgetown University Press, Washington, D.C., 1963, pp. 115-24. By permission of the School of Languages and Linguistics Georgetown University.

Baby Talk in Six Languages. American Anthropologist 66:6.2.103-14 (1964). By permission of the American Anthropological Association.

Applied Linguistics. Language Teaching:
Broader Contexts, ed. by Robert G. Mead, Jr. (Menasha, Wisconsin: The Northeast Conference on the
Teaching of Foreign Languages, 1966), pp. 50-58. By
permission of The Northeast Conference on the Teaching
of Foreign Languages.

Sociolinguistically Oriented Language Surveys.
The Linguistic Reporter 8:4. 1-3 (1966). By permission of the Center for Applied Linguistics.

National Sociolinguistic Profile Formulas.
Sociolinguistics, ed. by William Bright (The Hague:
Mouton & Co., 1967), pp. 309-24. By permission of
Mouton & Co.

Sentence Deviance in Linguistics and Language
Teaching. A Common Purpose, ed. by James R.
Squire (Champaign, Illinois: National Council of
Teachers of English, 1966), pp. 61-69. By permission
of the National Council of Teachers of English.

St. Stefan of Perm and Applied Linguistics.
For Roman Jakobson, ed. by Morris Halle (The Hague:
Mouton & Co., 1967), pp. 643-53. By permission
of Mouton & Co.

Language Development. Language Problems of
Developing Nations, ed. by Joshua A. Fishman, J.
Das Gupta and Charles A. Ferguson (New York:
John Wiley & Sons, 1968), pp. 27-35. By permission
of John Wiley & Sons, Inc.

Contrastive Analysis and Language Development.
Georgetown University Monograph Series on Language
and Linguistics: Monograph No. 21, Report of the
Nineteenth Annual Round Table Meeting, Georgetown
University Press, 1968, pp. 101-12. By permission

of the School of the School of Languages and Linguistics, Georgetown University.

Contrasting Patterns of Literacy Acquisition in a Multilingual Nation. Language Use and Social Change, ed. by W. H. Whiteley (London: International African Institute, in press), pp. 234-53. By permission of the International African Institute.

Absence of Copula and the Notion of Simplicity: A Study of Normal Speech, Baby Talk, Foreigner Talk, and Pidgins. To appear in Social Factors in Pidginization and Creolization, ed. by Dell Hymes (New York: Cambridge University Press, in press). By permission of the Cambridge University Press.

The Role of Arabic in Ethiopia: A Sociolinguistic Perspective. Georgetown University Monograph Series on Languages and Linguistics: Monograph No. 23, Report of the Twenty First Annual Round Table Meeting, Georgetown University Press, 1970, pp. 355-68. By permission of the School of Languages and Linguistics, Georgetown University.

The Editor also wishes to record his thanks to Professors Joseph H. Greenberg, John J. Gumperz, Einar Haugen, Wallace E. Lambert, Joshua A. Fishman, and other language scholars who have sent us materials for our forthcoming volumes. Professor Munier Chowdhury of the University of Dacca, Professor Afia Dil of the Education Extension Centre for West Pakistan, and Mr. L. E. Seltzer of Stanford University Press deserve our gratitude for encouragement and advice. Saeqa Dil of the Massachusetts Institute of Technology, has done a good job of typing the manuscript for which she deserves a special word of appreciation. Thanks are also due to Mrs. Jean Beeson who has been helpful in compiling Dr. Ferguson's list of publications and Mr. James J. Duran who assisted in proof reading.

Introduction

Charles A. Ferguson was born in Philadelphia in
1921. He was educated at the University of Pennsylvania,
where he received a Ph. D. degree in Oriental Studies in 1945.
His doctoral dissertation was on the phonology and morphology
of Standard Colloquial Bengali. From 1946 to 1955 he analyzed
and taught languages at the Foreign Service Institute in
Washington, D. C. In 1955 he joined the Center for Middle
Eastern Studies at Harvard University as lecturer in linguistics.

In 1959, when the Center for Applied Linguistics
was established under the auspices of the Modern Language
Association of America, Charles Ferguson was appointed its
first director. When he left the Center in 1967 to take up a
full-time teaching and research position at Stanford University,
the Center had become an independent institution, with a staff
of about a hundred, and from an unknown position it had gained
international stature. Among the continuing activities of the
Center with which the name of Ferguson is closely associated,
mention should be made here of its promoting the teaching and
testing of English as a second language, cooperating with the
Latin American linguistic programs, increasing the flow of

linguistic information at the international level, and establishing programs in sociolinguistics and psycholinguistics.

From 1964 to 1970, Ferguson served as chairman of the Committee on Sociolinguistics of the Social Science Research Council. Among other activities, the Committee has sponsored the Conference on Language Problems of Developing Nations (1966), the Conference on Pidginization and Creolization of Languages (1968), and the Summer Workshop in Sociolinguistics (1968). The Committee has sponsored the publication of an international journal, Language in Society, beginning in 1972.

Professor Ferguson has taught at the universities of Georgetown, Michigan, Washington, Indiana, Pennsylvania, and at the Deccan College, Poona, India. He has attended numerous national and international conferences, and has visited major centers of linguistic activity in many parts of the world. In January, 1964, the Linguistic Research Group of Pakistan (LRGP) invited him to participate in the Second Pakistan Conference of Linguists at Lahore. In the inaugural session of the conference it was my privilege to present Honorary Life Membership of the LRGP to him in recognition of his "outstanding contribution to modern linguistic studies and research." Ferguson's work is of special significance to Pakistani linguistics because of his eminence as a scholar of the Arabic and Bengali languages.

Ferguson has had firsthand contact with a variety of sociolinguistic problems. In 1968-69 he served as the Director of the Language Survey of Ethiopia, part of a five-nation Survey of Language Use and Language Teaching in Eastern Africa. The primary objective of these surveys is to enable national and international agencies to take stock of the sociolinguistic resources of the countries involved, in order to plan for better national development.

In his present position as Chairman of the Committee on Linguistics at Stanford University, Professor Ferguson directs research projects in language universals, child language development, and language planning processes. One project deserving special mention here is concerned with the study of Third World language problems. Attention is being focussed on the use of common national languages, especially in higher education and government, and on the need for competency in languages of wider communication.

Ferguson belongs to that small group of linguists who have been concerned with extending the scope of modern linguistic studies by establishing points of contact with other branches of knowledge. His continuing effort in this direction has helped to bring the work of linguists closer to current research interests in the social sciences and international development, thus making both social scientists and educators more aware of the importance of language.

A second notable feature of Ferguson's work so far, lies in his emphasis on application of linguistic knowledge to practical language problems — to the eventual benefit, I should add, of theoretical linguistics.

Perhaps I can best evaluate Ferguson's contribution to language science if I call him the linguists' linguist. There is in his work a certain quality of suggestiveness, as if he were more interested in opening new areas of linguistic interest for others through his explorations. Ferguson seems to take special delight in trying his hand at problems that do not lend themselves to an easy definition; he is content to pinpoint some of the complexities, and then suggest how they might be handled. It is, therefore, not surprising that some of his studies have inspired subsequent work by others. For example, the article on diglossia (1959) has led to more than a score of important studies of this phenomenon. In this respect Ferguson belongs to that select group of scholars whose real achievement lies in the ideas that they stimulate in others.

The eighteen articles selected for this volume cover the period from 1959 to 1970. They represent the wide range of Ferguson's search for universal features of language structure and language use.

Anwar S. Dil

Stanford International Development
Education Center,
Stanford University
March 1971

EDITOR'S NOTE

These articles have been reprinted from the originals with only minor changes made in the interest of uniformity of style and appearance. A few changes in wording have been made in consultation with the author. In some cases bibliographical entries and notes have been updated. Footnotes marked by asterisks have been added by the Editor.

Language Structure and Language Use

1 | Diglossia

In many speech communities two or more varieties of the same language[1] are used by some speakers under different conditions. Perhaps the most familiar example is the standard language and regional dialect as used, say, in Italian or Persian, where many speakers speak their local dialect at home or among family or friends of the same dialect area but use the standard language in communicating with speakers of other dialects or on public occasions. There are, however, other quite different examples of the use of two varieties of a language in the same speech community. In Baghdad the Christian Arabs speak a "Christian Arabic" dialect when talking among themselves but speak the general Baghdad dialect, "Muslim Arabic," when talking in a mixed group. In recent years there has been a renewed interest in studying the development and characteristics of standardized languages,[2] and it is in following this line of interest that the present study seeks to examine carefully one particular kind of standardization where two varieties of a language exist side by side throughout the community, with each having a definite role to play. The term "diglossia" is introduced here, modeled on the French diglossie, which has been applied to this situation, since there seems to be no word in regular use for this in English; other languages of Europe generally use the word for "bilingualism" in this special sense as well.

It is likely that this particular situation in speech communities is very widespread, although it is rarely mentioned, let alone satisfactorily described. A full explanation of it can be of considerable help in dealing with problems in linguistic description, in historical linguistics, and in language typology. The present study should be regarded as preliminary in that much more assembling of descriptive and historical data is required; its purpose is to characterize diglossia by picking out four speech communities and their languages (hereafter called the defining languages) which clearly belong in this category, and describing features shared by them which seem relevant to the classification. The defining languages selected are Arabic, Modern Greek, Swiss German, Haitian Creole.[3]

Before proceeding to the description it must be pointed out that diglossia is not assumed to be a stage which occurs always and only at a certain point in some kind of evolution, e.g. in the standardization process. Diglossia may develop from various origins and eventuate in different language situations. Of the four defining languages, Arabic diglossia seems to reach as far back as our knowledge of Arabic goes, and the superposed "Classical" language has remained relatively stable, while Greek diglossia has roots going back many centuries, but it became fully developed only at the beginning of the nineteenth century with the renaissance of Greek literature and the creation of a literary language based in large part on previous forms of literary Greek. Swiss German diglossia developed as a result of long religious and political isolation from the centers of German linguistic standardization, while Haitian Creole arose from a creolization of a pidgin French, with standard French later coming to play the role of the super-

posed variety. Some speculation on the possibilities of development will, however, be given at the end of the paper.

For convenience of reference the superposed variety
in diglossia will be called the H ("high") variety or simply H,
and the regional dialects will be called L ("low") varieties or,
collectively, simply L. All the defining languages have names
for H and L, and these are listed in the accompanying table.

ARABIC

	H is called	L is called
Classical (= H)	'al-fushā	'al-^cāmmiyyah, 'ad-dārij
Egyptian (= L)	'il- faṣīh, 'in- naḥawi	'il-^cammiyya

SW. GERMAN

Stand. German (= H)	Schriftsprache	[Schweizer] Dialekt, Schweizerdeutsch
Swiss (= L)	Hoochtüütsch	Schwyzertüütsch

H. CREOLE

French (= H)	français	créole

GREEK

H and L	katharévusa	dhimotikí

It is instructive to note the problems involved in
citing words of these languages in a consistent and accurate
manner. First, should the words be listed in their H form
or in their L form, or in both? Second, if words are cited
in their L form, what kind of L should be chosen? In Greek
and in Haitian Creole, it seems clear that the ordinary conversational language of the educated people of Athens and Port-
au-Prince respectively should be selected. For Arabic and
for Swiss German the choice must be arbitrary, and the ordi-

nary conversational language of educated people of Cairo and
of Zürich city will be used here. Third, what kind of spelling
should be used to represent L ? Since there is in no case a
generally accepted orthography for L, some kind of phonemic
or quasi-phonemic transcription would seem appropriate.
The following choices were made. For Haitian Creole, the
McConnell-Laubach spelling was selected,[4] since it is approxi-
mately phonemic and is typographically simple. For Greek,
the transcription was adopted from the manual Spoken Greek,[5]
since this is intended to be phonemic; a transliteration of the
Greek spelling seems less satisfactory not only because the
spelling is variable but also because it is highly etymologizing
in nature and quite unphonemic. For Swiss German, the spelling backed by Dieth, [6] which, though it fails to indicate
all the phonemic contrasts and in some cases may indicate
allophones, is fairly consistent and seems to be a sensible
systematization, without serious modification, of the spelling
conventions most generally used in writing Swiss German
dialect material. Arabic, like Greek, uses a non-Roman
alphabet, but transliteration is even less feasible than for
Greek, partly again because of the variability of the spelling,
but even more because in writing Egyptian colloquial Arabic
many vowels are not indicated at all and others are often indicated ambiguously; the transcription chosen here sticks closely
to the traditional systems of Semitists, being a modification
for Egyptian of the scheme used by Al-Toma. [7]

The fourth problem is how to represent H. For
Swiss German and Haitian Creole standard German and French
orthography respectively can be used even though this hides
certain resemblances between the sounds of H and L in both
cases. For Greek either the usual spelling in Greek letters
could be used or a transliteration, but since a knowledge of
Modern Greek pronunciation is less widespread than a knowledge of German and French pronunciation, the masking effect

of the orthography is more serious in the Greek case, and we use the phonemic transcription instead. Arabic is the most serious problem. The two most obvious choices are (1) a transliteration of Arabic spelling (with the unwritten vowels supplied by the transcriber) or (2) a phonemic transcription of the Arabic as it would be read by a speaker of Cairo Arabic. Solution (1) has been adopted, again in accordance with Al-Toma's procedure.

1. FUNCTION

One of the most important features of diglossia is the specialization of function for H and L. In one set of situations only H is appropriate and in another only L, with the two sets overlapping only very slightly. As an illustration, a sample listing of possible situations is given, with indication of the variety normally used:

	H	L
Sermon in church or mosque	x	
Instructions to servants, waiters, workmen, clerks		x
Personal letter	x	
Speech in parliament, political speech	x	
University lecture	x	
Conversation with family, friends, colleagues		x
News broadcast	x	
Radio "soap opera"		x
Newspaper editorial, news story, caption on picture	x	
Caption on political cartoon		x
Poetry	x	
Folk literature		x

The importance of using the right variety in the right
situation can hardly be overestimated. An outsider who learns
to speak fluent, accurate L and then uses it in a formal speech
is an object of ridicule. A member of the speech community
who uses H in a purely conversational situation or in an informal activity like shopping is equally an object of ridicule. In
all the defining languages it is typical behavior to have someone read aloud from a newspaper written in H and then proceed to discuss the contents in L. In all the defining languages
it is typical behavior to listen to a formal speech in H and then
discuss it, often with the speaker himself, in L.[8]

The last two situations on the list call for comment.
In all the defining languages some poetry is composed in L,
and a small handful of poets compose in both, but the status
of the two kinds of poetry is very different, and for the speech
community as a whole it is only the poetry in H that is felt to
be "real" poetry.[9] On the other hand, in every one of the
defining languages certain proverbs, politeness formulas,
and the like are in H even when cited in ordinary conversation
by illiterates. It has been estimated that as much as one-
fifth of the proverbs in the active repertory of Arab villagers
are in H.[10]

2. PRESTIGE

In all the defining languages the speakers regard H as
superior to L in a number of respects. Sometimes the feeling
is so strong that H alone is regarded as real and L is reported
"not to exist." Speakers of Arabic, for example, may say (in L)
that so-and-so doesn't know Arabic. This normally means he
doesn't know H, although he may be a fluent, effective speaker
of L. If a non-speaker of Arabic asks an educated Arab for help
in learning to speak Arabic the Arab will normally try to teach
him H forms, insisting that these are the only ones to use.
Very often, educated Arabs will maintain that they never use L

at all, in spite of the fact that direct observation shows that they use it constantly in all ordinary conversation. Similarly, educated speakers of Haitian Creole frequently deny its existence, insisting that they always speak French. This attitude cannot be called a deliberate attempt to deceive the questioner, but seems almost a self-deception. When the speaker in question is replying in good faith, it is often possible to break through these attitudes by asking such questions as what kind of language he uses in speaking to his children, to servants, or to his mother. The very revealing reply is usually something like: "Oh, but they wouldn't understand [the H form, whatever it is called]."

Even where the feeling of the reality and superiority of H is not so strong, there is usually a belief that H is somehow more beautiful, more logical, better able to express important thoughts, and the like. And this belief is held also by speakers whose command of H is quite limited. To those Americans who would like to evaluate speech in terms of effectiveness of communication it comes as a shock to discover that many speakers of a language involved in diglossia characteristically prefer to hear a political speech or an expository lecture or a recitation of poetry in H even though it may be less intelligible to them than it would be in L.

In some cases the superiority of H is connected with religion. In Greek the language of the New Testament is felt to be essentially the same as the katharévusa, and the appearance of a translation of the New Testament in dhimotikí was the occasion for serious rioting in Greece in 1903. Speakers of Haitian Creole are generally accustomed to a French version of the Bible, and even when the Church uses Creole for catechisms, and the like, it resorts to a highly Gallicized spelling. For Arabic, H is the language of the Qur'an and as such is widely believed to constitute the actual words of God and even to be outside the limits of space and time, i.e., to have existed "before" time began with the creation of the world.

3. LITERARY HERITAGE

In every one of the defining languages there is a sizable body of written literature in H which is held in high esteem by the speech community, and contemporary literary production in H by members of the community is felt to be part of this otherwise existing literature. The body of literature may either have been produced long ago in the past history of the community or be in continuous production in another speech community in which H serves as the standard variety of the language. When the body of literature represents a long time span (as in Arabic or Greek) contemporary writers —and readers—tend to regard it as a legitimate practice to utilize words, phrases, or constructions which may have been current only at one period of the literary history and are not in widespread use at the present time. Thus it may be good journalistic usage in writing editorials, or good literary taste in composing poetry, to employ a complicated Classical Greek participial construction or a rare twelfth-century Arabic expression which it can be assumed the average educated reader will not understand without research on his part. One effect of such usage is appreciation on the part of some readers: "So-and-so really knows his Greek [or Arabic]," or "So-and-so's editorial today, or latest poem, is very good Greek [or Arabic]."

4. ACQUISITION

Among speakers of the four defining languages adults use L in speaking to children and children use L in speaking to one another. As a result, L is learned by children in what may be regarded as the "normal" way of learning one's mother tongue. H may be heard by children from time to time, but the actual learning of H is chiefly accomplished by the means of formal education, whether this be traditional Qur'anic schools, modern government schools, or private tutors.

This difference in method of acquisition is very important. The speaker is at home in L to a degree he almost never achieves in H. The grammatical structure of L is learned without explicit discussion of grammatical concepts; the grammar of H is learned in terms of "rules" and norms to be imitated.

It seems unlikely that any change toward full utilization of H could take place without a radical change in this pattern of acquisition. For example, those Arabs who ardently desire to have L replaced by H for all functions can hardly expect this to happen if they are unwilling to speak H to their children.[11]

5. STANDARDIZATION

In all the defining languages there is a strong tradition of grammatical study of the H form of the language. There are grammars, dictionaries, treatises on pronunciation, style, and so on. There is an established norm for pronunciation, grammar, and vocabulary which allows variation only within certain limits. The orthography is well established and has little variation. By contrast, descriptive and normative studies of the L form are either non-existent or relatively recent and slight in quantity. Often they have been carried out first or chiefly by scholars outside the speech community and are written in other languages. There is no settled orthography and there is wide variation in pronunciation, grammar, and vocabulary.

In the case of relatively small speech communities with a single important center of communication (e. g. , Greece, Haiti) a kind of standard L may arise which speakers of other dialects imitate and which tends to spread like any standard variety except that it remains limited to the functions for which L is appropriate.

In speech communities which have no single most important center of communication a number of regional L's may arise. In the Arabic speech community, for example, there is no standard L corresponding to educated Athenian dhimotikí, but regional standards exist in various areas. The Arabic of Cairo, for example, serves as a standard L for Egypt, and educated individuals from Upper Egypt must learn not only H but also, for conversational purposes, an approximation to Cairo L. In the Swiss German speech community there is no single standard, and even the term "regional standard" seems inappropriate, but in several cases the L of a city or town has a strong effect on the surrounding rural L.

6. STABILITY

It might be supposed that diglossia is highly unstable, tending to change into a more stable language situation. This is not so. Diglossia typically persists at least several centuries, and evidence in some cases seems to show that it can last well over a thousand years. The communicative tensions which arise in the diglossia situation may be resolved by the use of relatively uncodified, unstable, intermediate forms of the language (Greek mikti, Arabic al-luġah al-wustā, Haitian créole de salon) and repeated borrowing of vocabulary items from H to L.

In Arabic, for example, a kind of spoken Arabic much used in certain semiformal or cross-dialectal situations has a highly classical vocabulary with few or no inflectional endings, with certain features of classical syntax, but with a fundamentally colloquial base in morphology and syntax, and a

generous admixture of colloquial vocabulary. In Greek a kind
of mixed language has become appropriate for a large part of
the press.

The borrowing of lexical items from H to L is clearly
analogous (or for the periods when actual diglossia was in
effect in these languages, identical) with the learned borrowings
from Latin to Romance languages or the Sanskrit tatsamas in
Middle and New Indo-Aryan.[12]

7. GRAMMAR

One of the most striking differences between H and L
in the defining languages is in the grammatical structure: H
has grammatical categories not present in L and has an inflectional system of nouns and verbs which is much reduced or
totally absent in L. For example, Classical Arabic has three
cases in the noun, marked by endings; colloquial dialects have
none. Standard German has four cases in the noun and two
non-periphrastic indicative tenses in the verb; Swiss German
has three cases in the noun and only one simple indicative
tense. Katharévusa has four cases, dhimotikí three. French
has gender and number in the noun, Creole has neither. Also,
in every one of the defining languages there seem to be several striking differences of word order as well as a thoroughgoing set of differences in the use of introductory and connective particles. It is certainly safe to say that in diglossia
there are always extensive differences between the grammatical structures of H and L. This is true not only for the four
defining languages, but also for every other case of diglossia
examined by the author.

For the defining languages it may be possible to
make a further statement about grammatical differences. It
is always risky to hazard generalizations about grammatical

complexity,[13] but it may be worthwhile to attempt to formulate
a statement applicable to the four defining languages even if
it should turn out to be invalid for other instances of diglossia.

There is probably fairly wide agreement among linguists that the grammatical structure of language A is "simpler" than that of B if, other things being equal,

1. the morphophonemics of A is simpler, i.e. morphemes
   have fewer alternants, alternation is more regular, automatic (e.g., Turkish -lar~-ler is simpler than the
   English plural markers);

2. there are fewer obligatory categories marked by morphemes or concord (e.g., Persian with no gender distinctions in the pronoun is simpler than Egyptian Arabic with
   masculine-feminine distinction in the second and third
   persons singular);

3. paradigms are more symmetrical (e.g., a language with
   all declensions having the same number of case distinctions is simpler than one in which there is variation);

4. concord and rection are stricter (e.g., prepositions all
   take the same case rather than different cases).

If this understanding of grammatical simplicity is accepted,
then we may note that in at least three of the defining languages,
the grammatical structure of any given L variety is simpler
than that of its corresponding H. This seems incontrovertibly
true for Arabic, Greek, and Haitian Creole; a full analysis of
standard German and Swiss German might show this not to be
true in that diglossic situation in view of the extensive morphophonemics of Swiss.

8. LEXICON

Generally speaking, the bulk of the vocabulary of H and L is shared, of course with variations in form and with differences of use and meaning. It is hardly surprising, however, that H should include in its total lexicon technical terms and learned expressions which have no regular L equivalents, since the subjects involved are rarely if ever discussed in pure L. Also, it is not surprising that the L varieties should include in their total lexicons popular expressions and the names of very homely objects or objects of very localized distribution which have no regular H equivalents, since the subjects involved are rarely if ever discussed in pure H. But a striking feature of diglossia is the existence of many paired items, one H one L, referring to fairly common concepts frequently used in both H and L, where the range of meaning of the two items is roughly the same, and the use of one or the other immediately stamps the utterance or written sequence as H or L. For example, in Arabic the H word for 'see' is ra'ā, the L word is šāf. The word ra'ā never occurs in ordinary conversation and šāf is not used in normal written Arabic. If for some reason a remark in which šāf was used is quoted in the press, it is replaced by ra'ā in the written quotation. In Greek the H word for 'wine' is ínos, the L word is krasí. The menu will have ínos written on it, but the diner will ask the waiter for krasí. The nearest American English parallels are such cases as illumination~ light, purchase~ buy, or children~ kids, but in these cases both words may be written and both may be used in ordinary conversation: the gap is not so great as for the corresponding doublets in diglossia. Also, the formal-informal dimension in languages like English is a continuum in which the boundary between the two items in different pairs may not come at the same point, e.g., illumination, purchase, and children are not fully parallel in their formal-informal range of usage.

A dozen or so examples of lexical doublets from three of the sample languages are given below. For each language two nouns, a verb, and two particles are given.

GREEK

H		L
íkos	house	spíti
ídhor	water	neró
éteke	gave birth	eyénise
alá	but	má

ARABIC

hiðā'un	shoe	gazma
'anfun	nose	manaxīr
ðahaba	went	rāh
mā	what	ēh
'al'āna	now	dilwa'ti

CREOLE

homme, gens	person, people	moun[14]
		(not connected
		with monde)
âne	donkey	bourik
donner	give	bay
beaucoup	much, a lot	âpil
maintenant	now	kou-n-yé-a

It would be possible to present such a list of doublets for Swiss German (e.g., nachdem ≅ no 'after,' jemand ≅ öpper 'someone,' etc.), but this would give a false picture. In Swiss German the phonological differences between H and L are very great and the normal form of lexical pairing is regular cognation (klein ≅ chly 'small,' etc.).

9. PHONOLOGY

It may seem difficult to offer any generalization on
the relationships between the phonology of H and L in diglossia
in view of the diversity of data. H and L phonologies may be
quite close, as in Greek; moderately different, as in Arabic
or Haitian Creole; or strikingly divergent, as in Swiss German.
Closer examination, however, shows two statements to be
justified. (Perhaps these will turn out to be unnecessary when
the preceding features are stated so precisely that the statements about phonology can be deduced directly from them.)

(a) The sound systems of H and L constitute a single
phonological structure of which the L phonology is the basic
system and the divergent features of H phonology are either a
subsystem or a parasystem. Given the mixed forms mentioned
above and the corresponding difficulty of identifying a given
word in a given utterance as being definitely H or definitely L,
it seems necessary to assume that the speaker has a single
inventory of distinctive oppositions for the whole H-L complex
and that there is extensive interference in both directions in
terms of the distribution of phonemes in specific lexical items.[15]

(b) If "pure" H items have phonemes not found in
"pure" L items, L phonemes frequently substitute for these in
oral use of H and regularly replace them in tatsamas. For
example, French has a high front rounded vowel phoneme / ü / ;
"pure" Haitian Creole has no such phoneme. Educated speakers
of Creole use this vowel in tatsamas such as Luk (/ lük/ for
the Gospel of St. Luke), while they, like uneducated speakers,
may sometimes use / i/ for it when speaking French. On the
other hand, / i/ is the regular vowel in such tatsamas in
Creole as linèt 'glasses. '

In cases where H represents in large part an earlier stage of L, it is possible that a three-way correspondence will appear. For example, Syrian and Egyptian Arabic frequently use /s/ for /θ/ in oral use of Classical Arabic, and have /s/ in tatsamas, but have /t/ in words regularly descended from earlier Arabic not borrowed from the Classical.[16]

Now that the characteristic features of diglossia have been outlined it is feasible to attempt a fuller definition. DIGLOSSIA is a relatively stable language situation in which, in addition to the primary dialects of the language (which may include a standard or regional standards), there is a very divergent, highly codified (often grammatically more complex) superposed variety, the vehicle of a large and respected body of written literature, either of an earlier period or in another speech community, which is learned largely by formal education and is used for most written and formal spoken purposes but is not used by any sector of the community for ordinary conversation.

With the characterization of diglossia completed we may turn to a brief consideration of three additional questions: How does diglossia differ from the familiar situation of a standard language with regional dialects? How widespread is the phenomenon of diglossia in space, time, and linguistic families? Under what circumstances does diglossia come into being and into what language situations is it likely to develop?

The precise role of the standard variety (or varieties) of a language vis-à-vis regional or social dialects differs from one speech community to another, and some instances of this relation may be close to diglossia or perhaps even better considered as diglossia. As characterized here, diglossia differs from the more widespread standard-with-dialects in that no segment of the speech community in diglossia regularly uses

H as a medium of ordinary conversation, and any attempt to
do so is felt to be either pedantic and artificial (Arabic, Greek)
or else in some sense disloyal to the community (Swiss
German, Creole). In the more usual standard-with-dialects
situation the standard is often similar to the variety of a certain region or social group (e.g., Tehran Persian, Calcutta
Bengali) which is used in ordinary conversation more or less
naturally by members of the group and as a superposed
variety by others.

Diglossia is apparently not limited to any geographical
region or language family.[17] Three examples of diglossia from
other times and places may be cited as illustrations of the
utility of the concept. First, consider Tamil. As used by the
millions of members of the Tamil speech community in India
today, it fits the definition exactly. There is a literary Tamil
as H used for writing and certain kinds of formal speaking,
and a standard colloquial as L (as well as local L dialects)
used in ordinary conversation. There is a body of literature in
H going back many centuries which is highly regarded by Tamil
speakers today. H has prestige, L does not. H is always
superposed, L is learned naturally, whether as primary or as
a superposed standard colloquial. There are striking grammatical differences and some phonological differences between the
two varieties.[18] The situation is only slightly complicated by
the presence of Sanskrit and English for certain functions of H;
the same kind of complication exists in parts of the Arab world
where French, English, or a liturgical language such as Syriac
or Coptic has certain H-like functions.

Second, we may mention Latin and the emergent
Romance languages during a period of some centuries in various parts of Europe. The vernacular was used in ordinary
conversation but Latin for writing or certain kinds of formal

speech. Latin was the language of the Church and its literature,
Latin had the prestige, there were striking grammatical differences between the two varieties in each area, etc.

Third, Chinese should be cited because it probably
represents diglossia on the largest scale of any attested instance.[19] The wen-li corresponds to H, while Mandarin
colloquial is a standard L; there are also regional L varieties
so different as to deserve the label "separate languages" even
more than the Arabic dialects, and at least as much as the
emergent Romance languages in the Latin example. Chinese,
however, like modern Greek, seems to be developing away
from diglossia toward a standard-with-dialects in that the
standard L or a mixed variety is coming to be used in writing
for more and more purposes, i.e., it is becoming a true
standard.

Diglossia is likely to come into being when the following three conditions hold in a given speech community: (1)
There is a sizable body of literature in a language closely
related to (or even identical with) the natural language of the
community, and this literature embodies, whether as source
(e.g., divine revelation) or reinforcement, some of the fundamental values of the community. (2) Literacy in the community is limited to a small elite. (3) A suitable period of time,
on the order of several centuries, passes from the establishment of (1) and (2). It can probably be shown that this combination of circumstances has occurred hundreds of times in the
past and has generally resulted in diglossia. Dozens of examples exist today, and it is likely that examples will occur in
the future.

Diglossia seems to be accepted and not regarded as a
"problem" by the community in which it is in force, until certain trends appear in the community. These include trends
toward (1) more widespread literacy (whether for economic,

ideological or other reasons), (2) broader communication
among different regional and social segments of the community
(e.g., for economic, administrative, military, or ideological
reasons), (3) desire for a full-fledged standard "national" language as an attribute of autonomy or of sovereignty.

When these trends appear, leaders in the community
begin to call for unification of the language, and for that matter,
actual trends toward unification begin to take place. These
individuals tend to support the adoption either of H or of one
form of L as the standard, less often the adoption of a modified
H or L, a "mixed" variety of some kind. The arguments explicitly advanced seem remarkably the same from one instance of
diglossia to another.

The proponents of H argue that H must be adopted
because it connects the community with its glorious past or
with the world community and because it is a naturally unifying
factor as opposed to the divisive nature of the L dialects. In
addition to these two fundamentally sound arguments there are
usually pleas based on the beliefs of the community in the
superiority of H: that it is more beautiful, more expressive,
more logical, that it has divine sanction, or whatever their
specific beliefs may be. When these latter arguments are
examined objectively their validity is often quite limited, but
their importance is still very great because they reflect widely
held attitudes within the community.

The proponents of L argue that some variety of L must
be adopted because it is closer to the real thinking and feeling
of the people; it eases the educational problem since people
have already acquired a basic knowledge of it in early childhood;
and it is a more effective instrument of communication at all
levels. In addition to these fundamentally sound arguments
there is often great emphasis given to points of lesser impor-

tance such as the vividness of metaphor in the colloquial, the
fact that other "modern nations" write very much as they speak,
and so on.

The proponents of both sides or even of the mixed language seem to show the conviction—although this may not be
explicitly stated—that a standard language can simply be legislated into place in a community. Often the trends which will
be decisive in the development of a standard language are
already at work and have little to do with the argumentation
of the spokesmen for the various viewpoints.

A brief and superficial glance at the outcome of
diglossia in the past and a consideration of present trends suggests that there are only a few general kinds of development
likely to take place. First, we must remind ourselves that
the situation may remain stable for long periods of time. But
if the trends mentioned above do appear and become strong,
change may take place. Second, H can succeed in establishing
itself as a standard only if it is already serving as a standard
language in some other community and the diglossia community,
for reasons linguistic and non-linguistic, tends to merge with
the other community. Otherwise H fades away and becomes a
learned or liturgical language studied only by scholars or
specialists and not used actively in the community. Some form
of L or a mixed variety becomes standard.

Third, if there is a single communication center in
the whole speech community, or if there are several such
centers all in one dialect area, the L variety of the center(s)
will be the basis of the new standard, whether relatively pure
L or considerably mixed with H. If there are several such
centers in different dialect areas with no one center paramount,
then it is likely that several L varieties will become standard
as separate languages.

A tentative prognosis for the four defining languages over the next two centuries (i.e., to about A.D. 2150) may be hazarded:

Swiss German: Relative stability.
Arabic: Slow development toward several standard languages, each based on an L variety with heavy admixture of H vocabulary. Three seem likely: Maghrebi (based on Rabat or Tunis?), Egyptian (based on Cairo), Eastern (based on Baghdad?); unexpected politico-economic developments might add Syrian (based on Damascus?), Sudanese (based on Omdurman-Khartoum), or others.
Haitian Creole: Slow development toward unified standard based on L of Port-au-Prince.
Greek: Full development to unified standard based on L of Athens plus heavy admixture of H vocabulary.

This paper concludes with an appeal for further study of this phenomenon and related ones. Descriptive linguists in their understandable zeal to describe the internal structure of the language they are studying often fail to provide even the most elementary data about the socio-cultural setting in which the language functions. Also, descriptivists usually prefer detailed descriptions of "pure" dialects or standard languages rather than the careful study of the mixed, intermediate forms often in wider use. Study of such matters as diglossia is of clear value in understanding processes of linguistic change and presents interesting challenges to some of the assumptions of synchronic linguistics. Outside linguistics proper it promises material of great interest to social scientists in general, especially if a general frame of reference can be worked out for analysis of the use of one or more varieties of language within a speech community. Perhaps the collection of data

and more profound study will drastically modify the impressionistic remarks of this paper, but if this is so the paper will have
had the virtue of stimulating investigation and thought.

A preliminary version of this study, with the title
"Classical or Colloquial, One Standard or Two," was
prepared for presentation at the symposium on Urbanization and Standard Languages: Facts and Attitudes,
held at the meeting of the American Anthropological
Association in November, 1958, in Washington, D. C.
The preliminary version was read by a number of
people and various modifications were made on the
basis of comments by H. Blanc, J. J. Gumperz, B.
Halpern, M. Perlmann, R. L. Ward, and U. Weinreich.

NOTES

1. The terms 'language', 'dialect', and 'variety' are
used here without precise definition. It is hoped that they occur
sufficiently in accordance with established usage to be unambiguous for the present purpose. The term 'superposed
variety' is also used here without definition; it means that the
variety in question is not the primary, "native" variety for the
speakers in question but may be learned in addition to this.
Finally, no attempt is made in this paper to examine the analogous
situation where two distinct (related or unrelated) languages are
used side by side throughout a speech community, each with a
clearly defined role.

2. Cf. especially H. Kloss, Die Entwicklung neuer germanischer Kultursprachen von 1800 bis 1950 (Munich, 1952), with its valuable introduction on standardization in general.

3. The judgments of this paper are based primarily on the author's personal experience, but documentation for the four defining languages is available, and the following references may be consulted for further details. Most of the studies listed here take a strong stand in favor of greater use of the more colloquial variety since it is generally writers of this opinion who want to describe the facts. This bias can, however, be ignored by the reader who simply wants to discover the basic facts of the situation.

Modern Greek: H. Pernot, Grammaire grecque moderne (Paris, 1898), Introduction, pp. vii-xxxi; K. Krumbacher, Das Problem der modernen griechischen Schriftsprache (Munich, 1902); G.N. Hatzidakis, Die Sprachfrage in Griechenland (Athens, 1905); J. Psichari, "Un Pays qui ne veut pas sa langue," Mercure de France, October 1, 1928, 63-121; repr. in J. Psichari, Quelque travaux ..., I, pp. 1283-1337 (Paris, 1930); A. Steinmetz, "Schrift und Volksprache in Griechenland," Deutsche Akademie

(Munich), Mitteilungen: 1936, pp. 370-379.

Swiss German: O. von Greyerz, Sprache, Dichtung, Heimat (Berne, 1933): "Vom Wert and Wesen unserer Mundart," pp. 226-247; A. Senn, "Das Verhältnis von Mundart und Schriftsprache in der deutschen Schweiz," Journal of English and Germanic Philology XXXIV (1935), 42-58; K. Schmid, "Für unser Schweizerdeutsch," in Die Schweiz: ein nationales Jahrbuch 1936 (Basle, 1936), pp. 65-79; H. Kloss, Entwicklung (cf. fn. 2), pp. 126-138.

Arabic: W. Marcais, three articles in L'Enseignement public XCVII (1930), 401-409; CV (1931), 20-39, 120-133; J. Lecerf, Littérature dialectale et renaissance arabe moderne (Damascus, 1932-33), pp. 1-14; Majallat al-majmaᶜ al-ᶜilmī al-ᶜarabī (Dimashq), Vol. 32:1: ᶜAdad xạ̄ṣṣ bilmu' tamar al-'aww lilmajāmiᶜ al-lugawiyyah al-ᶜilmiyyah al-ᶜarabiyyah (Damascus, January, 1957); S. J. Al-Toma, "The Teaching of Classical Arabic to Speakers of the Colloquial in Iraq: A Study of the Problem of Linguistic Duality..." (Harvard Univ. D. Ed. thesis, 1957); A. Chejne, "The Role of Arabic in Present-Day Arab Society," The Islamic Literature X (1958), No. 4 (April), 15-54.

Haitian Creole: S. Comhaire-Sylvain, Le Créole haitien (Wetteren and Port-au-Prince, 1936); R. A. Hall, Jr., Haitian Creole (Menasha, Wisc., 1953).

4. Cf. H. O. McConnell and E. Swan, You Can Learn Creole (Port-au-Prince, 1945).

5. H. and R. Kahane and R. L. Ward, Spoken Greek (Washington, 1945).

6. E. Dieth, Schwyzertütschi Dialäktschrift (Zürich, 1938).

7. S. J. Al-Toma, op cit.

8. The situation in formal education is often more complicated than is indicated here. In the Arab world, for example, formal university lectures are given in H, but drills, explanation, and section meetings may be in large part conducted in L, especially in the natural sciences as opposed to the humanities. Although the teachers' use of L in secondary schools

is forbidden by law in some Arab ccuntries, often a considerable
part of the teacher's time is taken up with explaining in L the
meaning of material in H which has been presented in books or
lectures.

9.   Modern Greek does not quite fit this description.
Poetry in L is the major production and H verse is generally felt
to be artificial.

10.   Journal of the American Oriental Society LXXV
(1955), 124f.

11.   It has been very plausibly suggested that there are
psychological implications following from this linguistic duality.
This certainly deserves careful experimental investigation.
On this point, see the highly controversial article which seems
to me to contain some important kernels of truth along with much
which cannot be supported— E. Shouby, "The Influence of the
Arabic Language on the Psychology of the Arabs," Middle
East Journal (1951), 284-302.

12.   The exact nature of this borrowing process deserves
careful investigation, especially for the important "filter effect"
of the pronunciation and grammar of H occurring in those forms
of middle language which often serve as the connecting link by
which the loans are introduced into the "pure" L.

13.   Cf. J. H. Greenberg, "A Quantitative Approach
to the Morphological Typology of Language," in Methods
and Perspective in Anthropology (Minneapolis, 1954), pp. 192-
220.

14.   Not connected with French monde.

15. For details on certain aspects of this phonological interference in Arabic, cf. C. A. Ferguson, "Two Problems in Arabic Phonology," Word XIII (1957), 460-478.

16. Cf. Ferguson, op. cit.

17. All clearly documented instances known to me are in literate communities, but it seems at least possible that a somewhat similar situation could exist in a non-literate community where a body of oral literature could play the same role as the body of written literature in the examples cited.

18. There is apparently no good description available of the precise relations of the two varieties of Tamil; an account of some of the structural differences is given by Shanmugam Pillai, "Literary and Colloquial Tamil," to appear in Linguistic Diversity in South Asia (ed. C. A. Ferguson and J. J. Gumperz).* Incidentally, it may be noted that Tamil diglossia seems to go back many centuries, since the language of early literature contrasts sharply with the language of early inscriptions, which probably reflect the spoken language of the time.

19. An excellent, brief description of the complex Chinese situation is available in the introduction to Y. R. Chao, Cantonese Primer (Cambridge, 1947), pp. 1-17.

---

*IJAL 26:3: Part III (1960).

2 | Linguistic Diversity in South Asia

In Collaboration with John J. Gumperz

The diversity of languages in South Asia and some of its implications are often noted,[1] but relatively little attention is paid to the dialect diversity which exists within the individual languages in the area. All the major languages of India, Pakistan, and Ceylon have regional dialects as well as dialects which correlate with differences of social position, and they also have special literary forms of language which differ to a greater or lesser degree from the ordinary colloquial. Such variation in language is a widespread phenomenon in the world —it might almost be called the 'normal' state of languages— but the exact nature of the dialect diversity in South Asia is not well understood, and its relevance to non-linguistic aspects of South Asian society and culture has never been systematically explored. The studies in this volume constitute a first attempt to describe and interpret the facts of dialect diversity in several specific languages of this part of the world. No great effort is made to carry the interpretation far afield from linguistics, but each of the studies contains suggestive material for the approaches of other disciplines in the study of contemporary

South Asia. Since these studies are addressed both to linguists
and to non-linguists, the editors have felt it necessary to provide in this introduction a brief summary of the theoretical
framework which linguistic science currently offers for the
treatment of intra-language variability.

       1. First of all, one of the fundamental problems of
linguistics is the delimitation of languages as the 'natural'
units of linguistic analysis and classification. Put more directly,
one of the concerns of linguistics is to find a consistent, systematic way to answer such questions as: Are these two particular varieties of human speech one language or two? Questions
of this kind arise all over the world. Are British English and
American English one language or two? Do all the Arabic dialects constitute one language or several? Familiar examples
from South Asia include: Is Hindi one language or several?
Are Konkani and Marathi two languages or one? How many
Dravidian languages are there?[2] Questions like this cannot
be answered until some kind of definition of language is widely
accepted as valid, or possibly until the concept of language as
a unit is rejected and another formulation of the questions becomes accepted.

       Surprisingly little attention is paid to this problem,
however, and most definitions of language which are in vogue
among linguists today are more concerned either with setting
off speech behavior from other human activity or with setting
off linguistic systems from other semiotic systems than they
are with defining the limits of single languages. For example,
linguists frequently define language as "a system of arbitrary
vocal symbols by means of which a social group cooperates."[3]
This definition offers no clues whatever for the solution of the
problem since two social groups may use the same language or

the same social group may use two or more languages; and
in any case the definition fails to specify 'social group' either
in linguistic or non-linguistic terms. Accordingly, the best
that can be done here is to summarize in a relatively crude,
cover-all definition the uses of the term 'language' in this
sense by reputable linguists. [4]

In order to do this, one additional concept requires
definition, the minimal unit which serves as the 'normal' object
of linguistic description. A whole language is often too varied
to be readily analyzed by current descriptive techniques, and
descriptive linguists generally restrict their object of study
with considerable care. Harris[5] says, "The universe of discourse for a descriptive linguistic investigation is a single language or dialect." Bloch[6] uses the term 'idiolect,' the "totality
of the possible utterances of one speaker at one time in using
the language to interact with one speaker." These brief definitions, as the authors of them are fully aware, are not completely
satisfactory. The idiolect concept, for example, is a necessary
one, since in practice languages are always studied in terms
of the speech of single speakers. [7] As a unit of analysis, however,
an idiolect is defined by extra-linguistic criteria, and homoge-
neity of structure is not a necessary requirement. Thus the
speech of two individuals may be so very similar as to cause
no difficulty in description while two styles of speech of one
individual may be very different, and no one has shown how to
delimit styles rigorously in the speech of one person or of
many.

At the present state of linguistics it is probably wise
to sidestep the issues involved in devising a precise operational
definition and to settle for a suggestive description. There is
no term in regular use for this concept of the object of descrip-

tive linguistic analysis, but the word 'variety' has been used
by several authors in this sense and will be so used here. [8]
A <u>variety</u> is <u>any body of human speech patterns which is suffi-</u>
<u>ciently homogeneous to be analyzed by available techniques of</u>
<u>synchronic description and which has a sufficiently large reper-</u>
<u>tory of elements and their arrangements or processes with</u>
<u>broad enough semantic scope to function in all normal contexts</u>
<u>of communication.</u> With this concept clarified we may now
attempt to define a language.

     A first approximation to the definition may be in
terms of mutual intelligibility. Other considerations aside,
two varieties of human speech are said to be the same language
if each is readily intelligible to speakers of the other. The
difficulties of a definition of this kind are many, however, and
are reminiscent of the difficulties of the biologist's use of the
possibility of interbreeding as the primary criterion in the definition of the species.

     In the first place mutual intelligibility is difficult to
determine[9] (or even impossible, as with dead languages). Second, there seems to be little direct correlation between similarity of phonological or grammatical structure on the one hand
and mutual intelligibility on the other. This lack of correlation
is disturbing because linguists generally regard these structures
as fundamental in human speech and often prefer to describe
linguistic relationships in these 'internal' terms. Also, we
frequently find varieties of speech which do not show high mutual intelligibility but which on totally different grounds we wish
to regard as the same language, and vice versa. A well-known
example is found in the varieties at the extremes of the German-
speaking area which are quite different, with relatively low
mutual intelligibility. They are connected, however, by a

series of intervening varieties which provide a gradual transition, and linguists generally agree in regarding all as varieties
of one language.

On the other hand, certain varieties are regarded as
different languages in spite of their high degree of mutual intelligibility. For example, there is a gradual transition between
varieties of Dutch and German, but because of the existence of
two relatively stabilized, widely-used standard varieties,
Dutch (ABN) and German (Schriftdeutsch), two speech communities and hence two languages, are usually recognized; any transitional variety is assigned to the language whose standard form
is accepted in the community, regardless of the internal linguistic similarities.

Another commonly used criterion for differentiating
languages is that of difference in historical development. Two
sets of varieties are said to constitute different languages if
they differ significantly in their treatment of certain phonological and morphological features of a reconstructed parent variety.
In contrast to the problems encountered in the determination of
mutual intelligibility, historical relationship is relatively easy
to establish by the rigorous and generally accepted methods of
historical reconstruction. Grierson used this criterion in
classifying speech distribution in what is now called the Hindi
regional language area. He grouped the local varieties into
five groups, which he calls languages: Bihari, Eastern Hindi,
Western Hindi, Rajasthani, and Pahari. Each group is set off
from the others by peculiarities of grammar and pronunciation.
Modern Hindi-Urdu is part of the Western Hindi group, but its
historical relationship to the other local varieties is by no
means always very close. Bihari is more directly related to
Bengali, the regional language of Bengal; some forms of

Rajasthani are usually classed with Gujarati to the south and
the Pahari dialects are closest to Nepali, the language of
Nepal. [10]

Classifications of the above kind are essential in
historical linguistics, and they provide valuable information
for students of culture history. They do not, however, present
all the facts of language distribution. In spite of the diversity
of local speech forms and their relationship to neighboring
regional languages in Grierson's area, Hindi-Urdu is recognized as the language of literature and government throughout.
A large proportion of the modern urban population and of the
educated speaks it and in other ways regards itself as belonging to
a single Hindi-Urdu speech community. Many modern writers
thus disregard the historical relationships and refer to all
local speech forms as varieties of Hindi. [11] As in the case of
the German-Dutch area, the presence of a superposed variety,
such as a literary standard, is an important factor in the determination of language boundaries. This factor is irrelevant,
however, if the standard language in use in an area is extremely
divergent or obviously unrelated to the variety to be classified.
All this brings us to our working definition.

A language consists of all varieties (whether only a
single variety or an indefinitely large number of them) which
share a single superposed variety (such as a literary standard)
having substantial similarity in phonology and grammar with
the included varieties or which are either mutually intelligible
or are connected by a series of mutually intelligible varieties.

It is evident that, as with the term idiolect, purely
linguistic criteria are not currently accepted as sufficient for
the delimitation of a language. Rather, a given set of varieties
must meet certain minimum linguistic conditions (e.g. structu-

ral similarity within the set, structural difference from varieties outside the set) as well as certain sociological conditions
(e. g. use of standard, speakers' feeling of belonging to speech
community) in order to be regarded as a single language.

When the concepts of 'variety' and 'language' have
been explained it is feasible to define the linguistic notion of
'dialect,' which is crucial to the present studies. It must be
made clear at the outset that two conventional uses of this term
are to be disregarded. One is the use of 'dialect' to mean an
inferior language of some kind. This use of the term is still
widespread in such expressions as: "Mr. A speaks six languages and ten dialects. " "The inhabitant of that country
speaks dozens of languages and innumerable dialects. " Since
no linguistic criterion has ever been devised to differentiate
superior and inferior languages, linguists prefer to operate
without this distinction. [12] The other is the use of 'dialect' to
mean any non-standard variety of a language. This use is still
current in expressions such as: "He doesn't speak good German; he speaks only dialect. " "These children are learning
to speak the language without a trace of dialect. " "This is a
dialect word not preserved in the literary language. " Many
languages have one variety which is in certain respects dominant, the 'standard' variety, and it is often useful to distinguish
between the standard variety and non-standard varieties of a
given language, but linguists have found it more useful to leave
the word 'dialect' colorless and equally applicable to standard
and non-standard varieties. Thus linguists may refer to the
'standard dialect' of a given language, and even if they continue
to use the traditional expression 'standard language' they generally regard this as a dialect, often, of course, the most important from some points of view. [13]

In the terminology of linguistics a dialect is, roughly

speaking, something between a variety and a language. Sometimes in the analysis of a language an obvious classification of
varieties into dialects is clear to the linguist. More often a
number of alternative analyses are possible, and any particular
classification into dialects runs counter to at least some features
which could be used for classification. The elementary concept
of dialectology is the isogloss. Any boundary which constitutes
the limits of use of a particular linguistic feature is called an
isogloss. For example, the word frappé is regularly used in
the area around Boston to refer to a drink consisting of milk,
ice cream, and flavoring beaten together. In most of the United
States this drink is called a milk shake, a term which in the
Boston area refers to a similar drink made without ice cream.
The boundary which shows the limits of the use of frappé in
this sense, and which could be plotted on a map, is called an
isogloss. In addition to isoglosses concerned with the occurrence of words in certain meanings (lexical isoglosses), linguists also make use of phonological and grammatical isoglosses.

   In classifying dialects linguists generally prefer to
place emphasis on isoglosses (a) which cut boldly across large
areas as opposed to those which are relatively local, or (b)
which bundle together as opposed to those which are relatively
isolated, or (c) which correlate with non-linguistic criteria of
classification such as differences in material culture, religion,
political units, and the like.

   Since dialect classification is largely arbitrary it
might seem to be of relatively little value or even misleading,
but in fact the delimitation of dialects is of great importance,
both within linguistics proper and for extra-linguistic fields.
In linguistic theory, a dialect may be regarded as the beginning
of a linguistic split, as a step in linguistic differentiation. In
other words a dialect is a potential new language, and the

concept is comparable in validity and significance to that of the
'sub-species' or 'variety' of biology. For the extra-linguistic
importance of the dialect we need only note its obvious relevance to the units of other social sciences such as geographical
region, social class, or role.

A dialect is any set of one or more varieties of a
language which share at least one feature or combination of
features setting them apart from other varieties of the language,
and which may appropriately be treated as a unit on linguistic
or non-linguistic grounds. Because of the arbitrariness of this
concept, linguists using the term 'dialect' for a particular language generally feel under obligation to explain and justify the
criteria used for their classification in that language. [14]

2. Geographical dialects. The extent and nature of
dialect differentiation in a language may be described in terms
of two major correlates: density of communication and inter-
speaker attitudes. It cannot be maintained that these are the
only relevant factors since the significance of such matters as
the structure of the language (Sapir's 'drift'), [15] interference
of other languages, phonetic symbolism, or technological change
can be shown, but on the whole these two correlates provide a
satisfactory frame of reference for the analysis of dialect diversity.

The assumption with regard to density of communication may be phrased in general terms as follows: Other things
being equal, the more frequently speakers A and B of language
X communicate with each other by means of X, the more the
varieties of X spoken by them will tend to become identical. [16]
It follows from this that isoglosses will tend to coincide with
breaks or lines of weakness in communication. [17] Since such
breaks or lines of weakness will often correlate with natural
physical boundaries such as mountains or rivers, or with

political boundaries, or with economic limits (on the flow of goods and services), it is clear that a large proportion of dialect diversity will be subject to mapping. Possibly because of the effectiveness of cartographic representation of dialect differences, this has been one of the most highly developed fields of work in dialectology. Dialect atlases have been published for many languages, and many special techniques of mapping have been developed. Apart from limited special studies most books in dialectology are either dialect atlases or grammars of non-standard varieties.

In South Asia, surprisingly enough, there has been very little work of this kind. In the monumental Linguistic Survey of India Grierson offered sample texts and brief descriptions of many dialects and in some cases provided maps indicating what he believed to be the boundaries of major dialects, but he did not attempt dialect atlases.[18] Almost all the work in South Asian dialectology published since Grierson has been based on his work, with only a very meager amount of original investigation, and Grierson's volumes remain by far the most important source of data for the social scientist concerned with the distribution and dialect diversity of South Asian languages.[19]

None of the studies included in this volume is directed primarily to the analysis of mappable features of dialect difference although all of them assume a background of regional dialects. Accordingly, there is no need here for further discussion of the concepts of dialectology concerned with shape and distribution of regional isoglosses, such as 'relic area,' 'fan,' 'bundle,' 'transition zone,' 'focus.' The important thing is to note that all the techniques elaborated in the production of dialect atlases elsewhere in the world are available for use in the study of South Asian dialectology, and we may express the hope that significant studies in this field will be forthcoming in the next few years.

3. Social dialects. The assumption with regards
to inter-speaker attitudes may be stated in terms of two processes. First: any group of speakers of language X which regards
itself as a close social unit will tend to express its group solidarity by favoring those linguistic innovations which set it apart
from other speakers of X who are not part of the group. The
existence within a speech community of social distinctions such
as those of caste, class, professional guild therefore gives
rise to differential rates of linguistic change, favoring the
creation of new speech differences or the preservation of existing ones. On the other hand: other things being equal, if two
speakers A and B of language X communicate in language X and
if A regards B as having more prestige than himself and as-
pires to equal B's status, then the variety of X spoken by A will
tend towards identity with that spoken by B. It may seem that
this is a circular statement since one of the indications of the
attitude of prestige is linguistic imitation but it is assumed that
prestige relationships may be measured independently of language. As Leach puts it in describing a somewhat different
multi-lingual situation: "For a man to speak one language rather than another is a ritual act, it is a statement about one's
personal status: to speak the same language as one's neighbor
expresses solidarity with those neighbors, to speak a different
language from one's neighbors expresses social distance or
even hostility."[20]

The above two processes create a condition of equili-
brium:[21] as old speech differences vanish, new ones arise with
the addition of population elements from the outside or through
the formation of fresh social distinctions. The total range of
speech diversity within a speech community, i.e. the actual
language distance between all the varieties found there, is a
function of the density of intergroup communication. In societies like our modern American one where social class is fluid
and mass communication media are highly developed and shared

by most, we would expect the range of variation to be relatively small. Differences would most frequently appear on the level of phonetics or the lexicon but rarely affect the fundamental phonological or morphological structure of the language. In Asia, however, where intergroup communication is severely limited by ritual restrictions we would expect these differences to be much greater.

The parallels between speech variation and social stratification are manifold. This field of investigation has been worked very little by the dialectologist, however, whether because of the difficulty of presenting the data, or the problem of identification of social groupings, or simple historical accident in the development of the science. A handful of valuable studies in this field do exist for various languages and show great promise for the development of sociolinguistic analysis,[22] but until now very few such studies have appeared dealing with South Asian languages.[23]

Two of the papers in this volume have direct bearing on the problem of social dialects. Bright* describes the speech of a Brahmin and a non-Brahmin speaker of the Mysore dialect of Kannada. Both are members of the western educated class and have had college education; the linguistic gap between them is nevertheless considerable. Of particular interest is the difference in receptiveness to outside innovation. The non-Brahmin dialect has made a number of changes in the Old Kannada grammar and sound system but shows little influence from outside borrowings. The Brahmin dialect on the other hand, possibly because of the influence of the literary language, has been much slower to change the native Kannada patterns while it has been profoundly affected by borrowings from Sanskrit and

---

*William Bright. Linguistic change in some Indian caste dialects. IJAL 26:3:Part III. 19-26 (1960).

English. McCormack* in studying the Dharwar dialect of
Kannada finds three basic speech strata corresponding to the
division between Brahmin, touchable non-Brahmin and untouch-
able castes. He also discusses the function of dialect differences
as clues for the determination of a speaker's place in the caste
hierarchy, a problem which has received considerable attention
lately. [24]

The significance of the linguistic studies for broader
research is clear. For example the problem of quantifying
caste difference in terms of behavior and attitudes is a central
problem in the analysis of South Asian social structure. [25] The
limited amount of data we have already points to some interesting parallels. If we compare the dialect distribution described
by Bright and McCormack and before them by Bloch and Aiyar
with similar information on North India provided by Gumperz,
we find that the southern speech communities (or at least those
in the Kannada, Tamil and Tulu areas) show a fundamental gap
between Brahmin and non-Brahmin speech. In the North on the
other hand (or at least in the Western Hindi and Panjabi and probably also in the Bengal area) Brahmin dialects do not seem to
differ significantly from those spoken by other high caste touch-
ables. This bears out other recent independent anthropological
findings regarding the difference in status between northern and
southern Brahmins.

The analysis of linguistic behavior in the context of
social science offers a new dimension of measurement and one
that is particularly accessible and quantifiable compared to
many other aspects of behavior. There is every possibility that
more detailed and better planned sociolinguistic investigation of

---

*William McCormack. Social dialects in Dharwar
Kannada. IJAL 26:3:Part III. 79-91 (1960).

this kind in South Asia will lead the way into a whole new area of the analysis of society.

4. <u>Style and superposed varieties</u>. The third kind of variation to be described here is different in nature from the preceding two. Geographical or social dialects tend to be mutually exclusive in the sense that the normal individual is a native speaker of only one dialect, and if he speaks more than one this is a sign of geographical or social transition of some kind on his part. But there are also linguistic variations which regularly coexist in the speech of individuals, with their use reflecting some kind of situational or role differences.

It is part of the nature of language, or of human culture in general, that there should be individual differences in performance and differences in the performance of a given individual in various situations. For example, a speaker normally has 'favorite expressions' (e.g. words, phrases, constructions) which he uses more frequently than other speakers; and any adult speaker normally uses different kinds of speech talking to his young children, participating in a religious ceremony, chatting with old friends, and explaining something to a stranger. To take somewhat different examples, in English the two words <u>light</u> and <u>illumination</u> have roughly the same meaning, but <u>light</u> tends to be used in less formal, less pretentious situations. Or, again, the words <u>fore</u>, <u>aft</u>, <u>deck</u>, <u>companionway</u> have meanings very similar to those of <u>front</u>, <u>back</u>, <u>floor</u>, <u>stairway</u>, but the first set is generally used either in a maritime setting or to suggest it, or by people who regularly live and work in such a setting.

All languages seem to show variations of this kind. As is the case with social dialects, however, the exact range of these variations and the level of linguistic structure at which they appear vary significantly. In America we find only minor

differences in lexicon, syntax, stress and intonation, which
do not materially complicate the task of linguistic analysis.
Other parts of the world,however,shcw more fundamental variations. One of the most extreme situations of this type is that
described by Garvin and Riesenberg on Ponape, where different sets of bound morpheme alternants and lexical items
were used in social situations calling for honorific and non-
honorific speech. Whenever two styles have striking morphological variation (e. g. case endings vs. no case endings) or
extensive lexical pairing (e. g. pairs of different words for
common items such as 'head,' 'go,' 'now'), or when both
styles in question are regularly used under appropriate circumstances by a large segment of the speech community (e. g.
all educated speakers of the language), then special language
situations must be recognized which deserve study and which
clearly present theoretical and practical problems of quite a
different nature. The investigation of stylistic differences of
this kind is of interest to the linguist since they constitute a
fundamental mechanism of language and their analysis provides
an insight into more general aspects of speech dynamics. For
other social scientists correlation of style with social situation,
personality, and similar factors offers valuable clues to the
understanding of non-linguistic human behavior. [26]

Some styles of speech are sufficiently striking and
extensive to require study as more cr less autonomous marginal or partial systems within a language, [27] and often enough
the styles appropriate to certain occasions are full-fledged
varieties of the language existing over and above the primary
or 'natural' speech of individuals. There are many kinds of
these superposed varieties, the most important being the
various types of standard languages.

Very often one variety of a language, e. g. a certain
local dialect, becomes widely accepted as standard and is

learned by speakers of other varieties in addition to their
native variety. Among typical examples of this standard language vs. local dialect situation we may cite important languages of Europe and Asia (e.g. German, Italian, Persian)
where many speakers use a local dialect in familiar or 'home'
situations but use the standard language in more formal or
'outside' situations. In some speech communities there may
even be several layers of superposed varieties of this sort,
with national and regional standards in addition to local dialects. To complicate this picture there may also be regionally
standardized pronunciations of the national standard as well as
various mixed varieties appropriate to certain occasions or
used by individuals who have not fully mastered certain levels.[28]
This layer phenomenon is fairly frequent in South Asia and has
recently been described for Hindi.[29] Another kind of superposed variety is illustrated by the classical-colloquial dichotomy
of Arabic, modern Greek, or Swiss German where the standard
form of the language is used for written and formal spoken
purposes only, the other for ordinary conversation.[30] The
spread of a particular standard variety is determined by social
and political factors and often has little relation to the actual
language distance between the standard and the local dialects.
Thus, returning to our German example, we find High German
used as a standard by many speakers whose native dialects
are much closer to Dutch. Another interesting case in point
is that of Southern Nepal where native speakers of Maithili, a
dialect related to Bengali, are advocating the adoption of Hindi
as a standard language. Other Maithili speakers across the
border in Bihar are opposed to Hindi and favor the creation of
a new literary standard based on medieval literary Maithili.

Stylistic variation and superposition are important
factors throughout South Asian society and four studies in this
collection are explicitly concerned with this kind of variation:

Pillai's* study of Tamil deals with a situation which is quite
similar to the above mentioned cases of Arabic, modern Greek,
and Swiss German.   There are two distinct literary and colloquial styles, showing striking differences in phonology and
morphology.   The former serves as the sole medium of writing
and formal speech making, while the latter is used for conversation among the educated.   Dimock** deals with the two
standard varieties of Bengali, where conditions are somewhat
different.   Sadhu Bhasa, like literary Tamil, is employed for
writing and formal speeches.   Colit Bhasa, the conversational
medium of the educated, however, has become accepted as a
vehicle of literature in its own right during the last seventy-
five years.   It serves as the literary symbol of the newly
arising urban middle class, in contrast to traditional culture
represented by Sadhu Bhasa.   Chowdhury[+] describes the
relationship between the two standards and the regional dialects
of East Bengal and details the social situations in which they
are used.   He also points to the incipient development of a
third Eastern Bengali standard variety, resulting from political
conditions arising out of the partition of Bengal.   The Naim-
Gumperz[++] paper deals with the Hindi-Urdu area where two
literary varieties have developed from a single conversational
standard and have become symbols of the competing Hindu-
revivalist and Indo-Muslim cultural complexes.

---

* M. Shanmugam Pillai. Tamil — literary and
colloquial. pp. 27-42;
    ** Edward C. Dimock. Literary and colloquial
Bengali in modern Bengali prose. pp. 43-63;
    + Munier Chowdhury. The language problem in
East Pakistan. pp. 64-78;
    ++ John J. Gumperz and C. M. Naim. Formal
and informal standards in the Hindi regional language
area. pp. 92-118. IJAL 26:3: Part III (1960).

NOTES

[1]Cf. S. Harrison, The challenge to Indian nationalism,
Foreign Affairs 34.620-36 (1956); M. Windmiller, Linguistic
regionalism in India, Pacific Affairs 27.291-318 (1954); R.
Pieris, Bilingualism and cultural marginality, British Journal
of Sociology 2.328-39 (1951). The fullest factual account of
South Asian languages is still G. Grierson, Linguistic survey
of India (19 vols. Calcutta, 1903-28). A good summary is provided in S. K. Chatterji, Languages and the linguistic problem
(London, 1943). An extensive bibliography on politico-linguis-
tic problems of South Asia is found in S. Harrison, The dan-
gerous decades (New York, 1955). S. K. Chatterji, Indo-
Aryan and Hindi (Ahmedabad, 1942) is a valuable historical
treatment of one important area.

[2]For a discussion of the widely divergent statistics on
such questions in South Asia, see J.J.Gumperz, Some remarks
on regional and social language differences in India, in M.
Singer (ed.), Introducing India in liberal education (Chicago,
1957).

[3]Cf. B. Bloch and G. L. Trager, Outline of linguistic
analysis (Baltimore, 1942).

[4]For valuable recent discussions of the whole language-
dialect question, see A. Martinet, Dialect, Romance Philology
8.1 (1954) and C. F. Hockett, A course in modern linguistics
Chs. 38, 39 (New York, 1958). Perhaps the best discussion of
this problem in a broader sociological framework is that of H.
Kloss, Die Entwicklung neuer germanischer Kultursprachen
(Munich, 1952).

[5]Z. S. Harris, <u>Methods in structural linguistics</u>, p. 9 (Chicago, 1951).

[6]B. Bloch, A set of postulates for phonemic analysis, <u>Language</u> 24.7 (1948). Other authors define 'idiolect' differently. Cf. Hockett <u>op</u>. <u>cit</u>.

[7]Cf. Hockett, <u>op</u>. <u>cit</u>., 321.

[8]A. Kelkar in unpublished works has used for this the term 'synlect' based on the term 'lect' which is a key item in his comprehensive terminology for linguistics.

[9]Some first steps have been taken in this field, and as better testing techniques and more satisfying methods of quantification are developed, measures of mutual intelligibility may become increasingly useful for linguistic descriptions. Cf. C. F. Voegelin and Z. S. Harris, Methods for determining intelligibility among dialects of natural languages, <u>Proceedings of the American Philosophical Society</u> 95.322-9 (1951); J. E. Pierce, Dialect distance testing in Algonquian <u>IJAL</u> 18.203 -10 (1952).

[10]Grierson, <u>op</u>. <u>cit</u>., vol. I. The details of Grierson's classification are open to question on technical grounds but this does not invalidate the historical approach as such.

[11]See for example Dhirendra Varma, Hindi literature, in <u>Literatures in modern Indian languages</u> (Delhi, 1951). Much of the controversy regarding the linguistic affiliation of language units such as Maithili, Konkani, Bhili and others could be avoided if the distinction between language units defined by historical and superposed relationships were made clear.

[12]Non-linguistic criteria may of course be used to
rate languages, e. g. the use of writing, kind of religion, economic structure, etc. , but it seems wise not to use the term
'dialect' in this connection. Also, it may well turn out that
languages can be rated on certain purely linguistic scales,
such as regularity of morphophonemics, ability to form com-
pounds, or to transfer morphs from one word class to another,
etc. , but such classification has not yet been systematically
carried out and in any case will undoubtedly fail to provide a
linear scale of absolute rating for languages as wholes. Cf.
R. S. Wells, Archiving and language typology, IJAL 20.101-7
(1954).

[13]For discussions of the rise of standard varieties in
the languages of Europe, see J. Vendryes, Language; a linguistic introduction to history, tr. P. Radin 260-79 (London, 1931);
A. Meillet, Les langues dans l'Europe nouvelle, Chs. VIII-
XIV (2nd ed. Paris, 1928). H. Kloss, Entwicklung, attempts
an analysis of the process of standardization.

[14]Other definitions of dialect are, of course, used for
special purposes. For example, Bloch in the Postulates
defines a dialect for the purpose of that study as a set of idiolects sharing the same phonology.

[15]E. Sapir, Language 157-182 (New York, 1921).

[16]It must be noted that different kinds of communication
very probably have different strengths under this assumption
and that this whole area constitutes an important field for sociolinguistic investigation.

[17]Cf. L. Bloomfield, Language Chs. 3, 19 (New York,
1933).

[18]In noting that Grierson did little or no dialect atlas work, we have no intention of belittling his tremendous achievement. The LSI remains one of the world's major productions of linguistic scholarship, and Grierson himself was fully aware of the necessary limitations of his project.

[19]Important original work in South Asian dialectology has, however, been done in the detailed historical studies of particular languages or regional dialects. For example, S. K. Chatterji, Origin and development of the Bengali language (Calcutta, 1926); D. Varma, La langue Braj (Paris, 1935); B. Saksena, Evolution of Awadhi (Allahabad, 1938); S. M. Katre, Formation of Konkani (Bombay, 1942).

[20]E. R. Leach, Political systems of highland Burma 39 (London, 1954). Cf. also the following statement by Martin Joos, The medieval sibilants, Language 28.222-31 (1952), quoted in John L. Fischer, Social influences on the choice of a linguistic variant, Word 14.47-61: "The dialects and idiolects of higher prestige were more advanced in this direction and their speakers carried the drift further along so as to maintain the prestige-marking difference against their pursuers."

[21]Cf. also Fischer, op. cit., p. 52, footnote 7. Fischer states: "Joos seems to me to be unique in his recognition that the two processes (i. e. prestige imitation and the use of linguistic features to emphasize exclusiveness) combine to constitute a self perpetuating cycle."

[22]Two examples: R. McDavid, Post-vocalic /-r/ in South Carolina, a social analysis, American Speech 23.194-203 (1948); S. Sapon, A methodology for the study of socio-economic differentials in linguistic phenomena, SIL 11.57-68 (1953).

[23]Two excellent older studies exist: J. Bloch, Castes
et dialectes en tamoul, Mémoires de la Société de Linguistique
16.1 (1910-11); and L. V. Ramaswamy Aiyar, Tulu prose
texts in two dialects, Bulletin of the School of Oriental Studies,
6.897-931 (1932). One recent study is explicitly concerned
with this problem: J. J. Gumperz, Dialect differences and
social stratification in a North Indian village, American
Anthropologist 60.668-82 (1958).

[24]See G. N. Putnam and E. M. O'Hearn, The status
significance of an isolated urban dialect, Language 31, Supple-
ment, Language Dissertation No. 53 (1955) and the bibliography
given there.

[25]A recent issue of the Indian anthropological journal
Man in India was devoted almost entirely to this problem:
Man in India 39.2 (1959).

[26]Cf. Bloch, op. cit. ; Aiyar, op. cit. ; Gumperz, op.
cit. (1958) ; P. L. Garvin and S. H. Riesenberg, Respect
behavior on Ponape, American Anthropologist 54.201-220.
Most linguistic studies of style have been concerned with literary style, but increasing attention is being paid to the broader
aspects of style differences in language. For an interesting
modern discussion see John L. Fischer, op. cit. Cf. also the
Symposium on Casual and Non-Casual Language held at the
American Anthropological Association annual meeting, Chicago,
1957, papers from which were published in International Journal of American Linguistics 24.253-272; and see now especially T. A. Sebeok, ed. , Style in language (Cambridge, Mass.,
1960). A more traditional but interesting approach to
the subject is found in: P. L. Garvin, ed. , A Prague school
reader on esthetics, literary structure and style (Washington,
1955).

[27] For example, cf. C. A. Ferguson, Arabic baby talk, For Roman Jakobson 121-8 (The Hague, 1956).

[28] For this layer phenomenon in German, cf. W. Schönberger, Die sprachliche Verhältnisse der Tirol-Salzburg-Bayerischen Länderecke, Teuthonista 10. 62 (1934); H. Moser, Mundart und Hochsprache im neuzeitlichen Deutsch, Der Deutschunterricht 8. 36-61 (1956).

[29] J. J. Gumperz, Language problems in the rural development of North India, Journal of Asian Studies 16. 251-9 (1957).

[30] Cf. C. A. Ferguson, Diglossia, Word 15. 2 (1959), where this language situation is described in more detail.

3 | The Language Factor in National Development

Social scientists of various disciplines are concerned with the concept "national development", in particular, of course, economists and political scientists, but to a lesser extent scholars in other fields.[1] Structural linguistics, however, in spite of its concern with diachronic matters, has been resolutely opposed to any developmental or evolutionary approach in linguistic analysis. The purpose of this paper is on the one hand to suggest the relevance of "national development" for linguistic analysis and on the other hand to point to linguistic aspects of national development as it is studied by social scientists in other fields. The approach followed here has resulted from the work of the Survey of Second Language Learning in Asia, Africa, and Latin America which was carried out by the Center for Applied Linguistics in collaboration with outside specialists from the United States and other countries.[2]

1. Of the many scales which could be developed for measuring language "development" in a way which might cor-

relate usefully with nonlinguistic measures of development
two seem particularly promising: the degree of use of written
language and the nature and extent of standardization. Scales
suggested here represent a modification of the viewpoint of
Heinz Kloss.[3]

     1.1. The 3000 or more languages currently spoken
vary in the use of a written form of the language from cases
in which the language has never been written to languages with
an enormous and very varied use of written forms. It is difficult to arrange these cases in a simple, linear progression,
partly because of the complex variation and partly because of
the great range in the amount of use. As a first approximation
to a useful scale, we suggest the scheme
         W0. —not used for normal written purposes
         W1. —used for normal written purposes
         W2. —original research in physical sciences
             regularly published

     A convenient set of criteria for establishing "normal"
use of the written language is as follows. (a) The language is
used for ordinary interpersonal epistolary purposes. People
write letters in it. (b) The language is used in popular periodi-
cals. Newspapers appear in it. (c) The language is used in
books not translated from other languages. People write and
publish books in it.

     Languages with rating "O" include languages such
as Modern Aramaic for which no orthography has been suggested and which has no representative writing by members of
the speech community, as well as languages like Tuareg where
use of the writing system is limited to special and marginal
purposes, or Lugbara where an orthography has been suggested
which has been used in some dictionaries, grammars, text-

books, Bible translations and the like, but which has not yet
become widely used in the community. Most languages are
still at this level although there is a steady stream of languages moving up to level "1".

Examples of languages at level "1" include Amharic,
Thai, Slovenian. Many languages in category "1" have a substantial publication output. Languages with relatively small
output often have a considerable amount of poetry, folkloric
material and translations. Only a few languages fall in category "2". These are often also languages widely used for
intercommunication by other speech communities. The number of languages belonging in this category, however, is
steadily increasing and this suggests the need for a possible
additional level.

W3. —languages in which translations and resumés
of scientific work in other languages are regularly published.

1.2. The establishment of a scale of standardization
is much more difficult because there are at least two dimensions involved, one of which is itself quite complicated. One
such dimension is the degree of difference between the standard form or forms of a language and all other varieties of it.
This difference may be very small or very great independently
of the other dimension, which is the nature of the standardization and the degree to which a standard form is accepted as
such throughout the community. The simplest approach seems
to be to set up the end points of the scale at St^0. and St^2. Zero
refers to a language in which there is no important amount of
standardization. As an example, we may take Kurdish, where
there is a considerable dialect variation but where no form or
forms of the language has received wide acceptance as a norm
among people who do not speak it themselves.[4] At the other

end of the scale we have what may be regarded as the "ideal"
standardization. The term "ideal" is not inappropriate because individuals concerned with the development of their
nation who make proposals for change in the language situation
generally seem to make proposals aimed at achieving this
"ideal" standardization even though they rarely state the desired goal explicitly. Category "2." refers to a language
which has a single, widely accepted norm which is felt to be
appropriate with only minor modifications or variations for
all purposes for which the language is used. Differences
between regional variants, social levels, speaking and writing,
and so on, are quite small. An example of category "2." is
Swedish, where the difference between the written and spoken
standard is appreciable, but relatively minor and growing
less, and where none of the original dialects are too far removed from the standard.

Category "1." requires considerable sub-classifica-
tion to be of any use. Whatever scheme of classification is
developed, it will have to take account in the first instance of
whether the standardization is unimodal or bi- or multimodal,
and in the case of more than one norm, the nature of the norms
must be treated. Armenian may serve as an example of a
bimodal standardization where the standards are essentially
regional, East Armenian and West Armenian, both being used
for normal written purposes. Greek may be cited as an
example of a bimodal standardization based on a "vertical" or
role differentiation, one being used for ordinary conversation
and the other for most written and formal spoken purposes.
Serbo-Croatian has two norms based to a large extent on religio-cultural differences. Norwegian is an example of a bimodal standardization based on neither of these. As a single
example of a more complicated case of standardization, we
may mention the whole Hindi-Urdu complex with its regional
standards in addition to the religio-cultural split. [5]

2. Linguists have generally operated with the concept of speech community "a group of people who use the same system of speech-signals"[6] as the locus of linguistic behavior, although recently some attempts have been made to deal with multilingual communities.[7] Only rarely has the concept nation been utilized by linguists for this purpose, and then generally for describing certain features of language used in Europe.[8] From many points of view, however, it is desirable to use the nation as the basis for general sociolinguistic descriptions: communication networks, educational systems, and language "planning" are generally on a national basis and national boundaries play at least as important a role in the delimitation of linguistic areas as any other single social barrier. In the description of the language situation of a given nation two fundamental points must be treated, the number of languages and the relative dominance of languages.

2.1. In determining for taxonomic purposes the number of languages spoken in a country it seems advisable to distinguish between major and minor languages. A definition of major language which has proved useful in the work of the Survey is: a major language of a nation is a language spoken by at least ten million people or one-tenth of the population. The number of major languages in a nation may vary from one to a dozen or more. It seems likely, however, that the important categories are: one major language (e.g. Thailand, Costa Rica, Holland), two major languages (e.g. Canada, Belgium, Paraguay), and three or more major languages (e.g. Switzerland, Nigeria, India).

2.2. In a nation with more than one major language, it is often true that one is clearly dominant over the others or, in some cases, several languages are dominant over the others. One indication of dominance is numerical superiority:

one language is dominant over others it is is spoken by more
than half the population of the country.   Another important
indicator of dominance is the extent to which a given language
is learned by native speakers of other languages in the country.
For example, Persian and Pashto are spoken by about the
same number of people in Afghanistan, but Persian is often
learned as a second language by speakers of Pashto and other
languages in the country, while Pashto, in spite of official
government support and formal classes, is rarely learned well
by speakers of other languages in the country.   A third indicator of language dominance is the use of one of the languages
of the nation for such clearly national uses as publication of
official texts of laws or decrees, medium of instruction in
government schools, normal channel of military communication.

Full agreement among these three indicators provides
the "normal" form of national language dominance.   Cases
where these indicators are not in agreement seem generally to
have serious social tensions connected with language problems.

2.3.   In many nations, especially in Asia and Africa,
languages of wider communication (LWC) such as English and
French, play an important role in the national language situation and this must be separately assessed.   For one thing, the
LWC may be the language used for the clearly national purposes
listed under the third indicator of dominance.   In addition it
may be an LWC rather than one of the local languages which is
used as the means of access to scientific and technological
knowledge or to communicate with other nations in the expanding network of international communication.

3.   With the fairly simple machinery outlined in the

previous two sections, it is possible to draw up for a nation a profile which will be of value for comparison with other non-linguistic indices of development. The great drawback here is not the theoretical complexity or even the practical man-hours of work involved. It is the lack of reliable data for most nations.

The preparation of a national sociolinguistic profile in the sense described here calls for putting down on paper about a given nation the following information: how many major languages are spoken; what is the pattern of language dominance; are there national uses of an LWC; for each major language spoken in the country, what is the extent of written uses of the language (W0. -W2.) and what is the extent of standardization (St0. -St2.) and its nature (multimodal? range of variation from the norm?).

Even with the preliminary profiles which can be put on paper on the basis of currently available data, it is evident first that there is a wide range of variability although certain types are quite common, especially the one nation—one major dominant language W1. St2. It is also evident that certain types of profile occur only in underdeveloped countries, espe-cially the one with no dominant language and an LWC used for national purposes as well as for access to science and interna-tional communication. Before any useful theorizing can be done, it is necessary to collect the data and prepare reliable national profiles. The possibility of significant conclusions arising from such study seems very promising.

NOTES

[1]As examples of recent works concerned with the theory of national development we may cite W. W. Rostow, The Process of Economic Growth (New York, 1952); G. A. Almond and J. S. Coleman (eds.), The Politics of the Developing Areas (Princeton, 1960). One work which emphasizes the role of communication in the concept of nationhood is K. W. Deutsch, Nationalism and Social Communication (New York, 1953).

[2]For an account of the Survey and some of its results, see Second Language Learning. . .in Asia, Africa, and Latin America (Washington: Center for Applied Linguistics, 1961).

[3]Cf. H. Kloss, Die Entwicklung neuer germanischer Kultursprachen (Munich, 1952), in particular pp. 24-31, "Stufenfolge des Ausbaus eines Idioms zur Kultursprache."

[4]Kurdish may not be a fully satisfactory example since the dialect of Suleimaniya is beginning to be accepted as a norm by a considerable segment of the Kurdish speech community. Cf. E. N. McCarus, A Kurdish Grammar (New York, 1958) p. 1; D. N. Mackenzie, Kurdish Dialect Studies I (London, 1961) p. xviii.

[5]Cf. J. Gumperz and C. M. Naim, "Formal and Informal Standards in the Hindi Regional Language Area," in C. A. Ferguson and J. Gumperz (eds.), Linguistic Diversity in South Asia (Indiana University, RCPAFL 13, 1960).

[6]L. Bloomfield, Language (New York, 1933) p. 29.

[7] Cf. U. Weinreich, <u>Languages in Contact</u> (New York, 1953) pp. 83–110.

[8] See, for example: L. Dominian, <u>The Frontiers of Language and Nationality in Europe</u> (New York, 1917); A. Meillet, <u>Les langues dans l'Europe nouvelle</u> (Paris, 1928); S. Rundle, <u>Language as a Social and Political Factor in Europe</u> (London, 1946).

4 | Background to Second Language Problems

To understand the problems involved in the large-scale teaching of languages of wider communication such as English and French in the developing countries it is necessary to become familiar with the very different kinds of language situations which exist in these countries. In a previous study of the Center (Information Series 1 1961) an outline was given of the major language characteristics of Asia, Africa and Latin America. The present study will take up some of the points made there and enlarge upon them, attempting to provide a somewhat more sophisticated theoretical background and much more detailed information on certain sample areas.

Perhaps the most obvious point to deal with in describing the language situation of a country is its linguistic diversity, i. e. the number of different languages spoken and the incidence of multilingualism among the inhabitants. Strangely enough, apart from one article by the anthropological linguist Joseph Greenberg (Greenberg 1956), there has been no attempt on the part of social scientists to devise a numerical index of linguistic diversity which could be used to give a simple characterization of a locality or country, or larger area which

could readily be used for comparative purposes. Certainly
the planner or administrator in the language education field
would welcome an index of this sort which would measure the
level of linguistic diversity in one region as compared with
that of another.

Greenberg in his article suggested several possible
indices of this kind and calculated two of them for parts of
Mexico and a few other areas. His simplest index, method A,
the "monolingual nonweighted method", measures the probability that two members of the population chosen at random
would not speak the same language. The scale runs from 0 to
1, calculated by the formula,

$$A = 1 - \Sigma_i(\, i^2)$$

where i is the proportion of speakers of each language to the
total population. If in a population, to use his example, 1/8
speak language M, 3/8 speak N, and 1/2 speak O then the
index figure of linguistic diversity (method A) is .5938. Using
this index, a country like Costa Rica where almost 100% of the
population speak one language (Spanish), the figure would be
very close to zero, while for an area like the Plateau Province
of Northern Nigeria, an area noted for its linguistic diversity,
the figure is .9539, very close to 1.

This index A does not take into consideration the
degree of similarity among the languages in question or the
possibility of multilingualism on the part of the inhabitants,
and Greenberg suggested several other means of calculating
indices (B C D E F G) which take these questions into account.
Perhaps his most interesting index, method H, the "index of
communication", measures the probability that two members
of the population chosen at random would have at least one
language in common.

Although Greenberg's indices are promising, they can be of very little immediate help to the planner or administrator, first because accurate information on which to calculate them is not available for most countries and second because they do not take into account the very different importance and range of use of the various languages spoken in a given country. Let us hope, however, that in the next few years more work is done in the development of one or more satisfactory indices of linguistic diversity which could serve as useful tools both for setting a base line in language planning and for measuring achievement of a second language learning policy in a country.

Closely connected with the notion of linguistic diversity is the question of how the various languages in a community are used. To say, for example, that a country has two languages spoken by such-and-such percentages of the population says very little about the language situation, and even a fully quantified specification of this which would reflect the number of speakers of each, the number of bilinguals in the population, the degree of mastery of the second language achieved by various segments of the population, and data on the similarity between the two languages would still leave out the fundamental matter of when and under what circumstances each language is used and what the attitudes of the people are toward the two languages.

For example, France is a country of two languages, where about 97% of the population speak French and about 2% speak Breton; almost all of the Breton speakers are able to speak French to some extent and many are completely bilingual. The Malagasy Republic also is a country of two languages; about 97% of the people speak Malagasy in one form or another and about 2% of the people speak French; the overwhelming majority of the French speakers also speak Malagasy. In simple quantitative terms these two language situations are similar, but the differences in usage of the respective languages and the attitudes toward them are enormous. In France the minority language is used as a home language in one part of the country while the majority language is used throughout the entire range of national life, including government, education, literature. In the Malagasy Republic, on the other hand, the majority language is the home language of the population and the minority language is used for many facets of national life including most education and many government activities.

A language in a multilingual situation may serve as the identifying language of an ethnic group or it may be the language used only for certain ritualistic purposes in the religion or it may be the means of communication between the different speech communities. General studies of multilingualism have attempted to list the variables involved (cf. Lewis 1962) and a number of linguists have commented on the "uses" of language and the existence of "restricted" languages used for limited purposes (cf. Firth 1960) but no satisfactory classification has yet been worked out which can be used to characterize either a language or a language situation from a sociolinguistic point of view. One very tentative proposal was made in a paper on languages and national development (Ferguson 1961, reprinted in this volume) and another, somewhat fuller attempt is made in Stewart's paper on typology in Rice (1962)[*]. This is a field of considerable importance for the understanding of societies which has been neglected almost completely by sociologists and linguists.

If a typology of languages or language uses were worked out this could be transferred to a typology of nations or other sociopolitical units in language terms. Such a typology was mentioned under the name "national profiles" in the

Ferguson paper just cited and is to some extent implicit in the
charts by Miss Roberts included in Rice (1962)[*]
    The discussion up to this point has been chiefly in
terms of the existence of separate languages in a country and
the nature and extent of the differences between them. Another
question which must be touched upon is the amount of dialect
variation within a single language. Some languages are relatively homogeneous, i. e. all speakers talk about the same way,
while other languages may show dialect cleavages so great as to
offer serious obstances to communication within the speech
community. Distinct varieties of speech within a language are
called dialects.

    It must, of course, be emphasized here that the terms
"language" and "dialect" as used by linguists are technical
terms without evaluative or emotional character. A dialect in
this sense is neither a substandard variety of a language nor a
second-class language. A language in this classificatory sense
refers to the homogeneous speech form of a whole linguistic
community or to a group of such speech forms which are mutually intelligible or constitute a chain of mutual intelligibility.
This use of "language", although as basic to linguistic science
as the concept "species" is to biology, involved external non-
linguistic factors. Mutual intelligibility is difficult and sometimes impossible to test, and it alone does not serve to delimit
satisfactorily the units of analysis referred to as languages,
since the dialects of some languages are further apart in structure and mutual intelligibility than whole languages are from
each other in other cases (Voegelin and Harris 1951, Pierce

_____
    [*]Rice, Frank A., ed. 1962. Study of the role of second
languages in Asia, Africa and Latin America.
Washington, D. C.: Center for Applied Linguistics, 1962.

1952). It is necessary to include such notions as the existence
of a unifying standard form or the attitudes of the speakers
toward their language in order to arrive at a fully satisfactory
definition of a language. A recent discussion of this question
examines the possible kinds of variation and the appropriate
definitions, with examples chiefly from South Asia (Ferguson
and Gumperz 1960).

It is tacitly assumed by many that one of the features
of ideal nationhood is the possession of a standardized national
language. The absolute ideal would apparently be a language
which has a community of native speakers coterminous with
the national boundaries and which has a single accepted norm
of pronunciation, spelling, grammar, and vocabulary, used
for all levels of speaking and writing, including both a unique
national literature and work in modern science.

The actual language situation in a given nation is often
far from this ideal, and the selection of a national language and
the means of standardizing the language are often among the
problems of developing countries. In some nations the selection of a national language has in effect been made by the demographic fact of the country's having one language used by the
overwhelming mass of the population (e. g. Thailand—Thai,
Somalia—Somali). In some multilingual countries the choice
of a national language is simple because of the clearcut dominance of one language in the country (e. g. Iran—Persian,
Burma—Burmese, Ethiopia—Amharic). In a few cases (e. g.
Indonesia—Malay/Bahasa Indonesia) a minority language has
become accepted as the national language. In many countries
of Asia and Africa the question of a national language is still
troublesome, with no clear solution in sight.

The standardization of a language, i. e. the development of a norm widely accepted throughout the speech commu-

nity, takes place in various ways. Standardization as a sociolinguistic process is not well understood. There are accounts
of the standardization of a number of European languages (cf.
Vendryes 1931 pp. 260-279; Meillet 1928) which show quite
different sets of historical events in the standardization process of different languages, but there are not enough detailed
studies of standardization in various parts of the world and
under various circumstances to yield useful generalizations.
It is clear that there are limits to what can be legislated or
decreed in linguistic change and that certain kinds of change
can take place more rapidly than others, but this is far from
an adequate understanding of the process. Ray's study in Rice
(1962) is devoted to a number of aspects of this problem of
standardization, expecially insofar as it can be a conscious,
deliberate operation.

Against these background notions of linguistic diversity, national languages, and language standardization, what
is meant by the term "second language" in Asia, Africa, and
Latin America? If we assume that it is normal for each
human being to learn one language in a "natural" way from his
communication partners at an early age (one to five years),
this question may be rephrased: When and why does an individual learn another dialect of his language or another language
altogether? The answer is twofold. Either the speech community into which he is born uses different dialects or different languages in functionally different ways so that full communication within the community requires a second language,
or the individual for one reason or another desires or needs
communication with another speech community. In the remainder of this discussion the term "language" will be used to mean
either dialect or language.

The existence of marginal, overlapping, or anomalous cases does not invalidate this general formulation: an

individual normally learns the primary language of his speech community at an early age and adds to it (a) additional languages required for full communication within the community and (b) additional languages needed for communication outside the community. Insofar as additional languages learned as (a) or (b) are regional or national languages or are required for access to modern science and technology or are needed for international communication they are directly relevant to the social, economic, and educational development of the nation.

Second language learning takes place either by relatively informal, unplanned imitation and use in actual communication situations or by formal study in a system of education. The impression of specialists in the language field is that languages learned by the informal "using" method are learned faster, more completely, and with greater retention than languages learned as subjects in school or special educational situations.

If this is so, then experimentation should be undertaken to find out the basic facts here. The problem for the educator is how to make the acquisition of languages through formal education—which must be the chief agency—either as much like the more natural learning as possible or else to discover and use methods of language learning different from the natural ones but superior in results.

REFERENCES

Ferguson, C. A. 1962. "The Language Factor in National Development" Anthropological Linguistics 4:1. 23-28. In this volume, pp. 51-59.

Ferguson, C. A. and Gumperz, J. J. 1960. "Introduction" in
    Linguistic Diversity in South Asia. Bloomington:
    Indiana University. Pp. 1-18. In this volume, pp. 27-49.

Firth, J. R. 1960. "The Teaching of English Overseas in
    Relation to Uses" [London] Multilithed. 7 pp.

Greenberg, J. H. 1956. "The Measurement of Linguistic
    Diversity" Language 32. 109-115.

Information Series 1. 1961. Second Language Learning as a
    Factor in National Development in Asia, Africa and
    Latin America. Washington: Center for Applied
    Linguistics. v, 18 pp.

Lewis, E. G. 1962. "Conditions Affecting the 'Reception' of
    an 'Official' (second/ foreign) Language." London:
    CCTA/ CSA. Mimeog. 27 pp.

Meillet, A. 1928. Les langues dans l'Europe nouvelle.
    2nd ed. Paris.

Pierce, J. E. 1952. "Dialect Distance Testing." International
    Journal of American Linguistics 18. 203-210

Vendryes, J. 1931. Language: A Linguistic Introduction to
    History. Tr. P. Radin. London.

Voegelin, C. F. and Z. A. Harris. 1951. "Methods for
    Determining Intelligibility Among Dialects of
    National Languages" Proceedings of the American
    Philosophical Society 95. 322-9.

5 | Problems of Teaching Languages with Diglossia

In this discussion, I should like to outline the special problems involved in the teaching of languages with diglossia, as distinct from the general problems involved in all language teaching. The discussion will be limited to the kind of teaching which has as its aim enabling native Americans to understand, speak, read, and write a modern language in a manner approximating that of the educated native speaker of the language. The approach to language teaching which will be assumed for the discusssion is roughly the so-called audio-lingual approach, which is currently accepted by many specialists as one of the best approaches to language teaching in terms of current educational aims and resources in this country. It may be worthwhile to summarize first some of the general assumptions of this approach. It is assumed that, other things being equal, the learning of a modern foreign language is more effectively accomplished if:

1. the learner concentrates first on understanding and speaking and later on reading and writing;

   2. the learner has as a model a native or near-native
speaker of the language he is studying;

   3. the basic phonology and grammatical patterns of
the language are learned to a great extent through extensive,
carefully-planned drills intended to develop automatic responses similar to those of the native speaker;

   4. the instruction is planned and supervised by someone with sound orientation in linguistics and is carried out with
the use of materials prepared on the basis of sound linguistic
analysis;

   5. the learning is on an intensive basis, that is, involves at least ten contact hours a week with a model to be
imitated;

   6. audio-visual materials are employed to the extent
feasible as an integral part of the course work, whether in the
classroom or outside.

   The acceptance of these assumptions eliminates or
radically simplifies the discussion of many problems of procedure and content in a course of instruction in a modern language with diglossia. Some of the problems which remain,
however, are serious and deserve careful examination.

1. Learning two languages in one

   One point must be made at the outset. The problem
of teaching a language with two major forms cannot be solved
by teaching only one of the forms. I realize that there are
teachers of these languages who feel that the only satisfactory
solution is just this, and limit the aims of their courses to the

mastery of just the H variety or just the L variety.*   It is no
doubt possible that this solution is adequate for certain individuals who are studying the languages for certain limited purposes, but it is clear that this solution will not meet the needs
of someone who wants to learn to understand, speak, read,
and write these languages in a manner approximating that of
the educated native speaker.   The teacher and student alike
must face the fact that there is more to be learned than one
language; perhaps it is not as much as two full languages, but
it is certainly more than is generally attempted in a single
language course.   All apart from considerations of the content
and procedure of courses, it seems clear that more time will
be required to achieve results comparable to those obtained in
other language courses.   An American college student or
government official who undertakes a program of study of
Arabic or modern Greek must be prepared to learn double sets
of forms and vocabulary items for most of the language, as
well as a whole set of skills involved in selection of the appropriate variety for a given context.

      Three problems are immediately apparent for the one
who is planning the language curriculum:

      What is the relative emphasis to be accorded the two
      major varieties of the language?

      In what order should the two varieties be studied?

      How can skill in one variety be maintained when
      the learning is concentrated on the other variety?

      Since about 1940, modern Arabic and modern Greek
have been taught intensively along the lines of the audio-lingual
approach at a considerable number of universities, government

---
*H = High variety. L = Low variety.

agencies, and private organizations in the United States.
Haitian Creole has been taught very rarely in this way and to
my knowledge there has been no intensive teaching of Swiss
German in the United States. During these two decades of
teaching, many shades of relative emphasis have been tried
for the two varieties. It is probably correct to say that the
trend in intensive Arabic teaching has been from courses
where the emphasis was over 75% on the L variety, towards
courses with exactly the opposite emphasis. In the teaching
of Greek, the trend is less apparent, but it seems, if anything,
to be mildly towards increased emphasis on the L variety.

In view of the heavy emphasis at early stages on understanding and speaking, it was only natural that most intensive
courses in the 40's and 50's began with colloquial Arabic.
Recently, some intensive or semi-intensive courses have
attempted to begin with the H variety, making such oral use of
H as the ability and inclination of the instructor would permit.
One factor in the choice of order is the highly debated question
of whether the transition and carryover of knowledge is easier
H to L or L to H.

Whether one begins with H or L, there is a serious
problem in maintaining the skill acquired during the first part
of the course while concentrating on a different set of skills in
the second part. Students who have learned to converse fluently
in some variety of spoken Arabic and have gone on to study the
classical, often in a year's time lose their ability to converse.
On the other hand, as people who have started with Classical
Arabic acquire proficiency in the spoken language, they develop a tendency towards errors in the written language. No
Arabic program with which I am familiar has solved this problem satisfactorily and only a very few of them have attempted
any systematic solution.

It would be premature at this point to suggest promising ways of coping with these three problems, but at least
one observation can be made. The nature of the problems is
different in instances of diglossia such as Swiss German and
Haitian Creole, where H is a standard language used as a
medium of ordinary conversation in another speech community,
and the instances of diglossia such as Arabic or Greek where
this is not the case.

2. Dialect problems

Strictly speaking, the question of which dialect or
dialects should be chosen for instruction in L is not a problem
directly connected with diglossia. If there is a single standard
variety of L (as in Haitian Creole and Greek), this is obviously
the one to be chosen, but if there is no standard L the situation
is parallel to a language without diglossia which has no standard
form. In this case the one who is planning the course must
decide on the variety of spoken language to be taught.

Often in the past the decision has been taken on the
basis of which dialect has the best instructional materials or
has native speakers most readily available for models or best
prepares a student for work in a particular region or country.
While these are all valid considerations, they probably should
not be decisive in any general curriculum planning for language
instruction. Additional criteria which may be suggested for
dialect choice are: relative number of speakers; degree of
intelligibility throughout the entire speech community; ease of
transition to H. As an example of a possible solution to this
problem for Arabic, I would like to repeat a suggestion originally made in 1951.

The solution suggested here for most American students of Arabic is to concentrate on learning well the ordinary conversational Arabic of educated people of any of the important urban centers of the Arabic-speaking world. The four such dialects which are to be recommended because of the number of speakers, probable future importance, and availability of teaching materials and native speakers, are:

Cairo ("Egyptian Arabic"), Baghdad ("Iraqi"), Damascus-Beirut-Jerusalem ("Syrian"), Rabat-Salé-Fes-Meknes ("North Moroccan"). Specific recommendations would be:

a. For a particular company, project, or government agency: Where possible teach the most appropriate local dialect.

b. For universities, institutes, etc. offering a program of Middle East studies: choose Egyptian, Iraqi or Syrian Arabic and teach it regularly or, if facilities permit, alternate years among the three.

c. For universities, institutes, etc. offering a program of North African studies: teach North Moroccan.

One question not mentioned in the suggestion just quoted is the need for facilitating the student's adaptation to a local dialect when he goes to a part of the Arab world where the people do not speak the kind of Arabic he has studied. This problem exists, of course, for native speakers of Arabic, but for them it is much less serious because of the far greater language resources at their command. It would seem that any responsible course of Arabic instruction at the college or university level should offer sufficient information on the nature

and range of dialect variation, in particular lexical differences, to enable the student to make an adequate adjustment
to a new dialect area within a matter of weeks, assuming that
he has a solid basis in one particular variety of L.

3. Intermediate forms of language

Up to this point, we have not mentioned the existence
of mixed forms of language intermediate between H and L
which are used in certain kinds of situations. These actually
constitute the most interesting problem from the point of view
of those concerned with the theory of language learning and
with general principles of methodology.

Most language teaching is based on the assumption of
a single set of relatively stable forms and lexical items in the
language being learned. Every language probably has alternative forms or constructions as well as synonyms when the
choice depends on style, context, speed of utterance, and the
like. But these alternates generally constitute a very small
part of the whole language. The mixed varieties in a case of
diglossia, on the other hand, involve exactly this kind of choice
on a large scale. The native speakers mix elements from H
and L in a highly variable way. In a semi-formal discussion a
speaker may use the H word for "man" in one sentence and the
L word in the next; he may use an H stem with an L grammatical ending (e.g. ra?éto "I saw him" = ra?aytuhu crossed
with šufto). How does one teach a student to produce such
mixed utterances? At a meeting on the teaching of modern
standard Arabic (H) held at Harvard in the summer of 1958, it
was agreed that the first step in answering this question would
be the gathering of reliable data on intermediate varieties
One such study has appeared, but this is not yet enough on
which to base the new materials and techniques required. The

descriptive work is a job for the linguists, the subsequent
work really would include the cooperation of linguists, language teachers, and psychologists.

4. Suggested experimental programs

It is very difficult to use experimental methods to
determine the most effective procedures for teaching one of
the "neglected" languages in the U.S. Not only does the experi-
menter have the usual problem of numerous complexly inter-
related variables which make the construction of satisfactory
experimental designs almost impossible in the language field,
he also has such small populations of subjects to deal with that
"pure" controlled experimentation is out of the question. What
can be tried, however, is a careful clinical approach limited to
several major plans. What I am suggesting is that specialists
should try to work out programs of study which seem very
likely to produce desirable results, although with major differences in content and procedure. Then as these programs are
put into effect in a number of institutions, those concerned with
the planning and with the actual teaching should meet from time
to time to talk over points which emerge in the courses. By
the end of a four or five year period of such limited experimentation, it ought to be possible to agree on a fair number of
matters which are currently judged by guesswork and bias.

Plan No. 1

One such plan would be to begin with H, using the
kinds of procedures and materials which are appropriate to the
audio-lingual approach. In the case of Haitian Creole and Swiss
German this is relatively easy since material produced for
regular instruction in French and German could be used with

only minor supplementation.   For Arabic and Greek there are
no materials available for such a course.   It would take at
least two years of collaborative work to produce a core of
instruction in H which would emphasize learning the oral use
of the language insofar as this can be done given the limitations
on the spoken use of H.   This first stage of the plan would constitute the first year's work at a college course of 8-10 hours
per week.

The second stage of the plan would be directed primarily to L, but with a continued heavy dose of H.   Something
like one-fourth of the student's time and effort should continue
to be focused on H, with the material concentrating now on the
reading and writing and integrated as much as possible with the
L material being presented for oral skills.   This might constitute the second year of a college program.

The third and last stage of elementary instruction in
this plan would consist of a course about two-thirds of which is
devoted to reading in H with accompanying oral and written
drills and about one-third to L, this time being taken up largely
with planned conversation and discussion designed to review the
oral material of the second year and to give conversational skill
on certain topics met primarily in the reading.

At the end of such a course one would hope that the
student would be able to make extensive use of the language for
documentary research, travel to the country, listening to the
radio, and so on.   He would be ready to begin the serious study
of literature in the language.

Plan No. 2

Another plan would be to begin with L and shift to H.

Since this plan has been tried in a number of places, some
instructional materials exist which could be used. Programs
of this kind have in the past generally suffered from one or the
other of two defects—either the study of L was dropped too
soon, before the student had really acquired the basic structure, or no systematic attempt was made to maintain competence in L after the shift. Some courses suffered from both
these defects.

Here again it must be assumed that three years of
college courses will constitute the minimum elementary program of instruction before the student is expected to make great
use of the language or is encouraged to proceed to a study of
literature or to advanced linguistic studies.

Plan No. 3

Of all the programs in Arabic instruction reported on
in the U.S., only the Army Language School program has tried
to present H and L simultaneously, or nearly so, with textbooks and recorded materials designed accordingly. This plan
is well worth attention and its planners and teachers should
participate in the discussion of the followers of the other plans.
In this connection it must be pointed out that discussions and
reports on courses are not sufficient—the instructors and
planners must visit each other's programs often enough to get
an adequate understanding of the problems and the results.

An Experiment

One final proposal: a group of specialists should
design one or more experiments to throw light on the psychological and linguistic   problems involved in teaching mixed

varieties of languages when the variation is embarrassingly random and current methods of teaching are clearly inappropriate.

DISCUSSION

PAUL GARVIN: It seems to be very useful to differentiate rather clearly in all these situations between function and structure. On the one hand, there seems to be a scale of stylistic functions, and we might say perhaps the end points are more or less universal; that is, in most cultures you would have as one end point 'intimate' and as the other end point 'frozen' or 'superformal' with as many subdivisions as can be observed, perhaps with a finite limit. This is one critical dimension. The other critical dimension is that of structure, that is, the particular different languages or different dialects that are used jointly by the speech community in question. And then you get into the problem of the relation between the two, and it seems to me, that apparently the same functional differentiation can be carried by structures which are linguistically more different as in the case of French Creole, or not very different from each other, as in the case of American English. Perhaps this would be one way of easing the burden of description.

MR. FERGUSON: I think that it would be fair to comment that the original definition of diglossia was based almost completely on factors outside pure linguistics. That is, they were social factors, or factors of function rather than structure. And I would stand by this approach to the problem. As soon as we try to define socio-linguistic situations in terms of linguistic structure, we find, just as Mr. Garvin said, that the same kind of structure can be used for different purposes

in different speech communities, and vice versa. This gives
me a chance to comment on some of the observations that were
made before. First, whether diglossia is not really about the
same as the standard language with dialect situation, which is
found in many parts of the world. In my article, I specifically
tried to show the difference between these two situations. It
was this difference that really led me to discuss it at all. In
communities with diglossia, as described here, the H language,
(the 'standard' or 'higher' language) is not the normal conversational language of the speech community. In a standard language
with dialect situation, such as Persian or Italian or Bengali,
there may be speakers of dialect who then learn to speak standard language in addition, and do so on certain occasions, and
sometimes the functions may be quite parallel to those described
here for diglossia. But in each of those speech communities I
just mentioned, that is, in the Persian speaking world, the
Italian speaking world, the Bengali speaking world, there are
substantial numbers of people who carry on ordinary every day
conversations in the standard language. On the other hand, no
one speaks classical Arabic in ordinary conversation; and Swiss
German speakers don't speak standard German in ordinary conversation. This is a major difference. As to the question
whether diglossia could be parallel to bilingualism, or whether
we should shift over in that direction, I explicitly mentioned in a
footnote in my article, that this situation does occur with bilingualism. That is, where the two varieties that are being described
are generally recognized as two different languages, better yet,
two unrelated languages, there is no question where to draw the
boundary line. The functional description is the same. Here the
language structural difference enters, and I have the feeling that
when someone some day works out a general typology of sociolinguistic situations, the linguistic structure will play a relatively
unimportant role, and that those kinds of bilingualism as distin-
guished from other kinds would fit together with these diglossia
situations. But I felt it was best to start from one fairly small

group of situations which, as you can see, have much in common. And I would still insist that the four defining languages, or rather their speech communities, do share all the factors which were mentioned in the rather lengthy definition of diglossia with which we started this panel, even though each case has certain unique characteristics.

PAUL PIMSLEUR: It seems to me that the introduction here of Joos' notion of level of discourse is an extremely important one that serves as a very useful instrument for clarifying many things that linguists find difficult to talk about. I would like to propose, as an operational way of distinguishing between diglossia and bilingualism, that bilingualism exists in those situations in which the two languages in question both have relatively complete levels of discourse, whereas diglossia exists in the situation in which the burden is shared by certain levels in the one, and different levels in the other.

MR. FERGUSON: This has been suggested before, but it runs into several difficulties. One is the use of two different varieties outside this speech community, in some other speech community where they may have the full range of language available, although they do not in the speech community under discussion; another is that this would include in diglossia large numbers of language situations which are quite different in other respects, like for example, speakers of Syriac in Baghdad who do not have a complete language, that is, they have one that is restricted to certain limited situations, because in a sense it is a dying language which is used for ever more limited purposes in the society. However, the occasions in which it is used, and the limitations, are startlingly different from the ones that we have described for languages discussed today, so that this would then have diglossia include a much larger number of sociolinguistic situations. It might well be, however, that this is still a valid classification to suggest.

MR. PIMSLEUR: If I may comment on the preceding statement just very briefly, I think that the term bilingualism, since it has the word 'language' in it, should only be applied to those cases in which the language is a language, that is, in which a sufficient number of levels of discourse exists so that it is still functioning as a language and evolving as a language. And I would suggest that what is needed is the lower end of the scale. If the lower end of the scale does not exist, then in fact it is not functioning as a language and therefore should not be used under the term bilingualism.

MR. FERGUSON: This raises a difficulty. What do we call 'Syriac' then? If it is not a language, or a dialect, or anything else, we have to invent another term to describe a language with limited use, or which is on its way out, or something similar.

ERIC HAMP: On the matter of bilingualism, it seems to me too, that we have to recognize that the natural world provides every conceivable gradation and sometimes we are going to have to clarify what we really mean by differences on this scale. In my own experience, for example, in Albanian enclaves in the south of Italy, we have people in the diglossia situation. We have separate things, which have, I suspect, the same transformational syntaxes, but with different phonologies, as between Italian and Albanian, and to a great extent different morphophonemics and nuclear morphologies. In the Balkans, in my experience, it is very widespread to find what appear to be the same transformational syntaxes spoken with identical phonologies, and in some cases almost a total carryover of morphophonemics. Thus it becomes a little difficult to say where you have different morphologies or where you have merely just different shapes occupying the same syntactical slots, and everything else the same. Finally, I have found that same situation between Vannetais Breton and the local French that they speak there. In many cases, what has been conventionally called bilingual situations from the structural point of view, quite apart from function, may very well turn out to be somewhat varying situations of part-systems.

CHARLES BIDWELL: To return to the pedagogical, I think perhaps one factor which might help in making a choice between your first or your second plan, namely whether to start with L or the H, would be: is one form of the diglossic language derivable from the other in great part by the application of rules for sound change, what we might call phonological transformations? It would be true, for example, of Slovenian that the colloquial spoken language could be derivable in large part, though not totally, from the written standard by the application of rules of sound change. But the reverse would not be true, because many phonemes are lost through these sound changes.

EINAR HAUGEN: I think this discussion has clarified a number of things and I was particularly glad to have it clearly brought out that the term diglossia was not strictly a linguistic, but a sociolinguistic term. This is very important, because otherwise we get involved with the whole problem of what is language, what is dialect, and how we distinguish different varieties within that infinite scale that Prof. Garvin mentioned. Perhaps one could define diglossia as those linguistic situations which create difficulties for teaching. It does not seem to me that the situation in Switzerland is entirely parallel, though it has points in common with the others. We have been accustomed to call such peoples bilingual, but we should distinguish between bilingual and bidialectal. I thought at first that perhaps the term 'diglossia' could be equated with bidialectal, but I see now that it cannot, because in some situations it would be impossible to refer to these idioms as dialects. In the case of French and Creole, some say that they are two dialects and some that they are two languages. The Greek situation may be susceptible to an interpretation by which one could say that there is one Greek language written in two different ways. When I say "Greek

language" I mean it in the same sense as I might say there is
a German language, that is, apart from the writing, one which
is used among educated people who associate with one another
and have no very marked local characteristics in their speech.
As I understand it, katharevusa words can be used in cultivated
speech, and so can demotic words. So perhaps we really have a
one to two relation rather than the diglossic relation suggested.

As for the teaching problem, this is one that I have had
to face too —what kind of Norwegian to teach. The situation in
Norwegian is clearly diglossic, though I would worry about
applying the terms 'high' and 'low'. In the case of two accepted
standard languages, which is 'high' and which is 'low'? The
people who use either one would resent the use of these terms.
There is a difference also between teaching for production and
teaching for reception. I think we should expose the student to
all possible varieties, but not ask him to produce anything but
one norm. This is where the intermediate form in Arabic might
some day become the real norm. This would be the result of a
development in the Arabic community and something that no one
can impose on the Arabs. They have to work it out for themselves, as they no doubt will some day, with more communication.
This point is one I was trying to make in my discussion of linguistic norm, that the norm of the foreign language is a useful
thing to teach Americans who go abroad in order that they may
sound like educated people. The situation when the Spoken Series
was created was, to my mind, a totally anomalous one in this
respect, because the manuals stated specifically that any native
speaker could be used as a guide for this series, and that it did
not matter who or what he was. No attempt was made to suggest
that some native models would permit you to be accepted in the
circles you would like to be accepted in, while others that you
might learn from would not.

6 | Assumptions about Nasals: A Sample Study in Phonological Universals

Although linguists hesitate to make statements of universal (panchronic, cross-language) validity about the details of phonological structures, they often operate either in their own field work or in their evaluation of others' descriptions as though they held certain assumptions of this kind. Certain common features of the sound systems of human languages are so fundamental, of course, that linguists would exclude from the label "language" a signaling system that lacked them. Such universals may be regarded as definitional; that is, they are implicit in the linguist's concept of language, whether included in his formal definitions or not. For example, the linguist would find it inconceivable that a language should operate without phonemic contrasts, without a small set of distinctive features (or phonetic and distributional classes) in terms of which phonological elements of a segmental sort could be identified, or without differences in frequency of occurrence of such phonological elements.

1. Value of Nondefinitional Assumptions

The present paper is an attempt to formulate several nondefinitional assumptions which the author holds in one section of phonology. Most of them are probably shared with many other linguists; some may be of little validity. No attempt will be made to provide a theoretical framework for the assumptions, but the formulation of a set of statements like this may prove of value in at least three ways.

First of all there is the advantage gained in any field of science from making unspoken assumptions explicit. This process may reveal mistaken or mutually inconsistent assumptions, or may give new insights into the theory of the particular science.

Second, there is the value which universal, nondefinitional statements have for linguistic typology. For example, it is a widely held assumption that a language never has a greater number of phonemic contrasts in the vowels of unstressed syllables than it has in stressed syllables.[1] Any attempt to formulate this assumption carefully and to investigate its validity empirically soon shows that this point classifies languages with distinctive stress into three main types: (1) Languages, typified by Spanish, in which stress has no important effect on the quality of vowels. In languages of this kind, apart from accidental gaps in distribution, there is only one system of vowels appearing in both stressed and unstressed syllables. (2) Languages, like English and Russian, in which stress has the effect of lengthening a vowel and enhancing its characteristic coloration. In such languages the stressed vowels are clearer, and there are in effect two vowel systems, one for stressed syllables and one of fewer contrasts for unstressed syllables, always with some slight tendency for analogical formations to create unstressed vowels from the stressed system (e.g., Russian /e/) or to transfer a neutral vowel of the unstressed system to the stressed system (e.g., English / ɨ/). (3) Languages, like certain Tajik dialects[2] and certain varieties of Syrian Arabic, in which stress has a leveling effect on vowels. In such languages the stressed

vowels are not greatly lengthened and are less clear than the
unstressed vowels. These languages usually have a greater
number of vowel contrasts in unstressed position.[3]

The third value of the formulation of phonological universals lies in the materials it provides for extralinguistic
treatment. A nondefinitional universal in linguistics may serve
either as an exemplification of principles of some other field of
knowledge or as a suggestion toward reformulation of such principles. For example, it is commonly assumed that extensive
voiced-voiceless neutralization in a language takes place most
commonly in final position and never intervocalically.[4] Or
again, in diachronic studies it is generally assumed that a phoneme of [s] type may change to one of [h] type but not vice versa,
or of the [k] type to [t] but not vice versa, and so on. Linguistic
statements like these suggest interpretation in physiological or
psychological terms.

An experienced linguist working in the field of phonology
probably operates with many assumptions which could be identified and formulated. This may be shown by the ease with which
one can construct an artificial phonemic system which would
seem to be perfectly adequate for communication purposes but
which the practicing linguist would regard as implausible.[5]

2. Phonological Assumptions—Nasal Phenomena

A full list of phonological assumptions could run well
over a hundred. The list of fifteen statements that follows (identified by Roman numerals) is limited to nasal phenomena and is
offered as a sample.[6] Three of the statements are diachronic,
two are synchronic frequency statements, and the remainder are
synchronic existence statements. The statements are generally

explained in all-or-none terms, although most are probably only
statistically valid; that is, the probability of "exceptions" is
very low, and a language showing an exception may be regarded
in some sense as abnormal or pathological.

Nasal phonemes are of four general types, which are
called here primary nasal consonants, secondary nasal consonants, nasal vowels, and nasal syllabics. These types will be
defined, and universal statements will be listed where most
appropriate under each type. Two kinds of nasal phenomena
have been excluded from the listing: (1) nasal or nasalized allophones or phonemes the most characteristic allophones of which
are nonnasal, and (2) prosodic features of nasality. The first
are felt to be outside the system of nasal phonemes and not
covered by the kinds of universal statements given here. The
second are usually analyzable alternatively in terms of segmental phonemes, and in that case the universal statements made
here are held to be valid.

2.1. Primary nasal consonants (PNC)

Definition: A PNC is a phoneme of which the most
characteristic allophone is a voiced nasal stop, that is, a sound
produced by a complete oral stoppage (e.g., apical, labial),
velic opening, and vibration of the vocal cords.

When, in a given language, there are no nasal phonemes
of other types with ranges of phonetic values which might conflict
with the PNC's, a PNC may have allophones without full oral
stoppage, with incomplete velic closure, or without voicing.
Even in such a language, however, a PNC in phonological positions or communication situations calling for maximum clarity
will have the normal voiced nasal quality. In some languages the

PNC's function is in part like that of the vowel phonemes of the language; for example, it may constitute syllable peaks or bear accents, but this is always in addition to consonantal function.

I.   Every language has at least one PNC in its inventory. (Complete absence of nasals is reported for three Salishan languages[7] where the PNC 's assumed for an earlier period are said to have become voiced stops.)

II.   If in a given language there is only one PNC, it is /n/, that is, its most characteristic allophone is apical. When there is no other nasal phoneme in the language with a range of phonetic values which might conflict with the /n/ , the /n/ may have labial, velar, or other allophones, but in positions or situations of maximum clarity it has the normal apical value. In the rare instances where a language has only /m/ , there seems always to be an apical [n] as an allophone of something else. (In Hockett's analysis of Winnebago [n] is /r/ plus nasality;[8] in Ladefoged's analysis of Yoruba [n] is /l/ next to nasal vowels.[9] Examples of languages with /n/ as the only PNC are chiefly in the Western Hemisphere, for example, Tlingit, a number of Iroquoian languages, Arapaho.

III.   If in a given language there are only two PNC's, the other one is /m/ , that is, its most characteristic allophone is labial. Languages with /m n/ are extremely common, including examples from Indo-European, Semitic, American Indian (various families), Altaic, Caucasic.

IV.   In a given language, the number of PNC's is never greater than the number of series of obstruents. For example, if the language has stops and affricates in four positions (e.g., /p t č k/) the number of PNC's will be four or fewer (e.g., /m n ñ ŋ/ , /m n ŋ/ , /m n ñ/ , or /m n/), never five or more.

A number of different arrangements are possible, for example:

Bengali	p t t̬ č k	Nuer	p t̬ t c k
	m n ŋ		m n̥ n n

French	p t k	Fiji	t k
	m n ñ		β ð
			m n ŋ

V. When in a given language there is extensive neutralization among the PNC's, this occurs in prejunctural and/or pre-
consonantal positions. (Examples include Spanish, Classical
Greek; Trubetzkoy cites a number of others.[10])

2.2. Secondary nasal consonants (SNC)

Definition: An SNC is a nasal consonant phoneme the
most characteristic allophone of which is not a simple voiced nasal.
In many cases a phone type which may be analyzed as an SNC
may alternatively be analyzed as a cluster (e.g., /hn/ , /mb/).
The statements made here refer to languages where the mono-
phonematic analysis is required either because of contrast with
clusters or because of striking parallels of distribution. At
least six subtypes occur:

voiceless nasals	(e.g., Kuanyama[11])
aspirated nasals	(e.g., Marathi[12])
glottalized nasals	(e.g., Chontal [Oaxaca][13])
palatalized nasals	(e.g., Russian)
"emphatic" nasals	(e.g., Syrian Arabic[14])
prenasalized (voiced) stops	(e.g., Fiji[15])
"nasalized clicks"	(e.g., Zulu[16])

VI. No language has SNC's unless it also has one or more PNC's. (Corollary to I.)

VII. In a given language the number of SNC's is never greater than the number of PNC's.

VIII. In a given language the frequency of occurrence of SNC's is always less than that of PNC's.

IX. SNC's are, apart from borrowing and analogical formations, always the result of diachronic developments from clusters. (This assumption is based on the very few cases when the history of SNC's is well known. It is quite probable that other sources exist; in particular, it seems likely that prenasalized stops have developed from voiced stops in certain languages).

2.3. Nasal vowels (NV)

Definition: An NV is a phoneme the most characteristic allophone of which has oral and velic opening and vibration of the vocal cords. When in a given language there are no phonemes with conflicting phonetic values, an NV may have allophones with oral closure, velic closure, or lack of voicing, but clarity positions and situations have normal nasal vowels. (Sample languages: French, Bengali, Taos.)

X. No language has NV's unless it also has one or more PNC's. (Corollary to I.)

XI. In a given language the number of NV's is never greater than the number of nonnasal vowel phonemes.

XII. In a given language the frequency of occurrence of NV's is always less than that of nonnasal vowels. (Reliable frequency counts of phonemes exist for very few languages with nasal vowels. One small count for Bengali[17] shows an oral-nasal vowel ratio of 50:1.)

XIII. When in a given language there is extensive neutralization of NV's with oral vowels, this occurs next to nasal consonants. (Two well-documented examples of this kind of neutralization are Bengali[18] and Yoruba.[19])

XIV. NV's, apart from borrowing and analogical formations, always result from loss of a PNC. (This assumption is based on a small number of languages where the history of the NV's is known. These are chiefly Indo-European—[Indic, Slavic, Romance]—and it is possible that this assumption will have to be modified when more is found out about the history of NV's in other families. One case where an NV may be of quite different origin is in Iroquoian, where one of the NV's posited for the protolanguage seems, on considerations of internal reconstruction, to have derived from earlier /a/ + /i/ or sequences like /awa/ .)

2.4. Nasal syllabics

Definition: A nasal syllabic is a nasal phoneme which patterns like a syllable rather than like a consonant or vowel in the language (e.g., Japanese /ñ/ ,[20] Ewe, Xhosa /m/ [21]).

XV. A nasal syllabic phoneme, apart from borrowings and analogical formations, always results from loss of a vowel.

NOTES

1. Cf. Trubetzkoy, Principes de phonologie, 255-256 (Paris, 1949).

2. Cf. Sokolova, Fonetika tadžikskogo jazyka, 19 (Moscow, 1949).

3. It is interesting to note that in the Lebanese Arabic spoken in Marjayoun, where the i-u contrast which has disappeared in stressed position in much of Lebanese Arabic is still present, the phonetic distance between /i/ and /u/ is less than it is for the i-u contrast in unstressed syllables.

4. A fully satisfactory formulation of this would be considerably more complicated and would have to take into account the very rare instances of initial neutralization (as asserted by Trubetzkoy for one variety of Mordvinian) and initial-and-final neutralization (asserted for Kirghiz). Cf. Trubetzkoy, op. cit., 254-255.

5. The author has on a number of occasions reported to fellow linguists a system summarized in the following list of phoneme symbols: č k kᵂ v s ž ð m' n' ñ' ŋ' l λ yˀ ü ü· æ æ· Λ Λ. ĩ õ ũ. The reaction runs from mild surprise to disbelief.

6. Two brief treatments of nasal universals are known to the author, Trubetzkoy, op. cit., 189-196, and Hockett, Manual of Phonology, 119-120 (Baltimore, 1955).

7. Cf. Hockett, op. cit., 119.

8. Cf. ibid., 80-81. Even in the absence of further evidence

Hockett's analysis seems less convincing than a more
traditional one of /n/ and /r/ as separate phonemes;
other treatments of Winnebago recognize /m/ , /n/ ,
and /r/ , with either an additional /n$_2$/ or certain
morphophonemic interchange between /n/ and /r/ .

9. Cf. Ladefoged, A Phonetic Study of West African Languages,
     23-24 (Cambridge, 1964).

10. Cf. Trubetzkoy, op. cit. , 193.

11. Cf. Westermann and Ward, Practical Phonetics, 65
     (London, 1957).

12. Cf. Lambert, Introduction to the Devanagari Script (London,
     1953).

13. Cf. IJAL 16:35 (1950).

14. Cf. Language 30:566-567 (1954).

15. Cf. Hockett, op. cit. , 124.

16. Cf. Doke, The Phonetics of the Zulu Language (Witwaters-
     rand, 1926).

17. Cf. Language 36:51 (1960).

18. Cf. Language 36:44 (1960).

19. Cf. Ward, An Introduction to the Yoruba Language, 13
     (Cambridge, 1952).

20. Cf. Language 26: 112 (1950).

21. Cf. Doke, The Southern Bantu Languages, 92 (London, 1954).

7 | Linguistic Theory and Language Learning

Scholars whose chief intellectual interest has been in the development of linguistic theory have generally looked on the problems of language learning either as of little concern to them or as an appropriate field for the application of linguistics. In this discussion today I should like to present the view that language learning is of great interest to the linguist and that the application can work the other way: the study of language learning has value for the construction of linguistic theory.

The first great advance in modern linguistics came in the nineteenth century with the historical and comparative study of Indo-European and other language families. The languages were studied chiefly from written documents and the principal procedures were the comparative method and internal reconstruction. Important notions such as genetic relationship and regularity of linguistic change entered the body of linguistic theory.

The second great spurt came in the 20's, 30's and 40's of this century in descriptive studies of dozens of languages all over the world. The languages were studied chiefly from spoken material elicited from informants, and the principal techniques were segmentation, matching, substitution and the other familiar "discovery procedures" of linguistic books and articles. Important concepts such as contrast, constituent and allo- became part of linguistic theory.

Continuing this oversimplified view of the history of linguistics, I want to hazard the guess that in the last few years a great new third period of development in our science has begun. I am not referring to the intensive work on grammatical analysis typified by the approaches of Pike, Chomsky, Trager-Smith and others, important and fruitful though this is. I am referring to the increasing concern with a new kind of diachrony, and new techniques to deal with it.

In what we may perhaps call now the "classical" kind of descriptive, synchronic linguistics, the analyst was concerned with the description of relatively homogeneous bodies of data, and the structuralist approach was most immediately concerned with single dialects and styles, often even idiolects or parts of idiolects. In spite of the application of structural principles to historical problems and the fitful development of techniques of dialectology and "over-all analysis," the successes of the past decades were most spectacular in the treatment of limited corpora of homogeneous data.

I have noted elsewhere[1] that this kind of language material represents only the exceptional situation, the special case, and that an adequate theory of linguistics—or even merely better sets of discovery procedures or "protocol sentences"—must be able to cope with the complex reality of interpenetrating styles, dialects and languages extending out both in social space and in time. Here, I want to refer to structural variation along the time axis.

Most work in diachronic linguistics has been concerned in one way or another with the change of one total structure to another, such as Old English to Modern English, or a proto-language to its daughter languages. The kind of diachrony I am now referring to is that which goes from zero structure towards full structure.

As the first example, let me take the child learning his first language, his "mother tongue." At the beginning, the child has no language and at age six, let us say, he controls close to the full structure of the language. The linguist's problem of dia-chronic description is to account for the development step-by-step, stage-by-stage, from the beginning to the chosen stopping point. Here the linguist cannot work with written records, as in 19th century diachronic work, and he cannot elicit spoken material with the same degree of assurance and verifiability he is accus-tomed to enjoying in his normal synchronic analysis. He must turn increasingly to new methods of observation, techniques of experimentation with complex control of variables, new uses of statistics.

But what has this to do with the linguist's understanding of the nature and function of language ? What has this to do with linguistics, the theory of language ? A great deal. If Roman Jakobson, for example, maintains that human beings speak and hear speech in terms of distinctive features, that these are in some sense universal and that they are arranged in a hierarchical order of some kind, [2] then he must maintain and, in fact, he has maintained that the child's learning to speak his own language must progress in terms of distinctive features and in accordance with the hierarchy he posits. Actual work with children has shown that Jakobson is in part right and in part wrong: for example, voicing and palatalization are often mastered as distinctive fea-tures and applied to a whole series of consonants almost simul-taneously, then remaining available for use in new consonants

learned subsequently, while on the other hand some other distinctive features are not learned this way. Or if he says that
an [š]-type phoneme is learned before a [č]-type phoneme, he
can be shown many counter instances of /č/ acquired before
/š/ which will force modification of this hypothesis.

Without pushing this point any further, it seems clear
at least that any comprehensive theory of phonology must include definitions and postulates accounting for the way children
learn sounds and that such a general theory then becomes testable at least in part by actual observation and analysis of the
changing structure of the child language.

Yesterday, Henry Lee Smith offered us as evidence of
the universality of his "true word" that children begin their
speech behavior with items closely similar to the "words" the
linguist posits for the adult language. This little piece of theory
given us in passing was not of course phrased in such a rigorous
fashion that it could be tested, but surely it is worth rephrasing
with care so that it may become susceptible of controlled experimentation of the kind familiar to us from many other sciences.
If it cannot be so phrased, then the material on child language
can hardly be adduced as "evidence."

At several places in the work of Chomsky, there is the
hint that he feels his kind of grammar writing reflects more
closely the way a child learns his language. And it would be
easy for us to go beyond this hint. For example, if transforma-
tion rules have any real validity in linguistic description it should
in some sense be true that children learn in terms of them and
in terms of the ordering of rules to which generative gram-
marians attach such great importance. Again, I would say: if
there is to be a comprehensive theory of grammatical structure
it must account for the way in which children learn the grammar

of their language, and if this is so, one of the most pressing tasks of grammatical theorists is to phrase their theories in such a way that they are testable by accepted methods of controlled experiment. If it should turn out that such a phrasing or such experimentation is impossible—or for that matter trivial or uninteresting—then even the hints that one kind of grammar writing or another is more powerful in this respect should be eliminated.

So far we have been talking about the testing with child language learning of theory arrived at in other ways. There is another approach, the direct study of child language learning for its own sake and for the development of linguistic theory from that. This is, in fact, already beginning to happen. This is not the occasion to report on these developments and, indeed, there are others much better qualified to do so than I, but I would like to refer to two instances of interest to me.

Three recent studies[3] carried out independently have agreed in giving this picture. When the child moves from the stage of one-word sentences to two-word sentences, it soon appears that the two-word combinations he uses have a grammatical structure consisting of a "pivot word," or "operator" and an "X-word," or "content word." The pivot word is one of a small number of high-frequency items, some of which do not occur as single word sentences, and the X-word is one of a larger class of less frequent words, all of which occur as single-word sentences. This is a remarkable indication of the importance at some level of the nucleus and satellite kind of phrase structure. It will be fascinating to see how future observations follow this and detail the expansion and change of structure. It will be most instructive to see the kinds of grammatical analysis which the investigators will be led to adopt to portray most effectively this changing structure.

The other instance is in the functions of language. In her recently published book Language in the Crib ('s-Gravenhage, 1963), Ruth Weir shows us the incredible extent to which at least one child played with his language in a purposeful and creative way. Her child in his tape-recorded evening monologs drilled paradigm systematically and created rhymed and rhythmic sequences which show that what Jakobson and others have called the metalingual and poetic functions of language can be surprisingly well developed at age two and a half. Even for the child, language is not just communication; it is grammatical analysis and artistry. Our theories of linguistics must cope with this.

In this paper we are discussing the linguistic analysis of change from zero towards full structure. Our first example was the child learning his language. Let us take a very different example: the creation of a pidgin language. Linguists have been acquainted for over a century with the kind of language called a pidgin, which, instead of continuing in the usual genetic way the language of a certain speech community, comes into being as a means of communication among speakers of different languages by a process which seems to take over the grammatical structure of one language or set of languages involved and the lexicon of the other language or languages involved.

Linguists have become accustomed to brushing this phenomenon aside as something rare and isolated, the product of an unusual social situation, but it is becoming increasingly clear now that this process takes place fairly frequently in the world, in a variety of social situations, and that it deserves deeper study as an important type of human language behavior. From our point of view here today, there are two aspects of this I would like to note in particular.

One is the notion of simplification. Observers, including competent linguists, generally have the impression that a
pidgin language is in some way "simpler" than its source languages. And it also seems true that there are remarkable
structural similarities among pidgins no matter what their
sources and uses. Even if it should turn out that the very close
similarity of a number of French-, English- and Spanish-based
creoles is really understandable by virtue of the apparently wild
theory that they had a common origin in a Portuguese-based
creole of the Cape Verde Islands subsequently relexicalized, I
say even if this is true, the important point of simplification
remains. If some features of language are to be regarded as
simpler, hence presumably more basic and fundamental than
others, this is an important matter for the linguist, and surely
the intensive study of pidginization in various places, at various
times, and from various source languages, should prove extremely
instructive. Linguists could develop some very powerful pieces
of theory if they had solid empirically-based notions of simplicity
of structure.

The other point of relevance of pidgins to linguistic
theory which I wanted to mention is in the realm of historical
linguistics as traditionally practiced. Many months ago,
Graham Stuart in a conversation put forward the hypothesis that
many of the languages of Southeast Asia were originally pidgin
languages. I do not know the evidence on which he bases this
view, nor do I know how one could test its correctness with present techniques, but if there is any truth to the proposition that
many apparently "normal" languages are in reality the descen-
dants of creoles, then it should be very unsettling for linguists
who are concerned with comparative linguistic work. It would
seem that we could hardly rest until we had determined by careful sociolinguistic study the conditions under which a pidgin and
then a creole is produced, or until we had determined by purely

linguistic study the telltale marks of the pidgin origin of a
language. If we cannot succeed in either of these efforts then
we must reconcile ourselves to a degree of uncertainty in historical reconstruction much greater than we have hitherto been
forced to do.

The obvious place to start is with the description of a
pidgin language in the process of formation, beginning with no
structure and progressing towards the full structure of a creole.
This process is known to be taking place in such areas as parts
of the Congo, and I hope linguists are beginning to work on it.

Let us turn now to a final example of diachrony of the
zero-toward-full type, the learning of a foreign language in the
classroom. A good deal of attention has been focussed on this
situation in the last few years, but it has been almost completely
in terms of the effectiveness of the language teaching, i.e., how
to achieve optimum results in the learning process, or it has
been in terms of discovering the basic principles of human language learning from the psychologist's point of view. These
interests of the language teacher and the psychologist are both
quite legitimate, but I find it a little surprising that the numerous
linguists who have participated in studies along these lines have
shown no interest from the purely linguistic point of view. With
all the concern there has been for the teaching of French, for
example, to speakers of English, I do not know of a single study
which describes the linguistic structure of the French being
learned by an English speaker. Starting from zero, how does
this acquired structure grow step-by-step, stage-by-stage,
towards full mastery?

No doubt the major variable in accounting for this diachronic progression will be the order in which the material of
the target language is presented, and other variables will include
the methods of instruction. Also no doubt it will be difficult to
elicit valid material by the normal informant elicitation technique

But these particular aspects of the linguist's problem here do not detract from the general interest. People all over the world study languages in classrooms, and the careful linguistic study of this process should tell us something about the structure of the learner's language, and the structure of the target language, something about how language structures can change through time and perhaps some fundamental things about human language in general. And we need not be frightened of the variables mentioned and the difficulties of elicitation. These are in some ways an advantage: the presentation can be controlled for experimental purposes in this situation much more easily than in the natural child language-learning situation, and the problem of elicitation is, after all, only another way of looking at the important question of proficiency testing in a foreign language which teachers, psychologists and even linguists have been concerned with from other points of view.

More immediately productive, however, in this situation is the increasingly fashionable procedure of making contrastive studies between two languages to account for the learner's difficulties with his new language. Interestingly enough, we see these studies slowly changing their orientation. They are still concerned chiefly with analyzing and predicting the kind of interference which takes place in bilingual situations, including the classroom language-learning situation, but we are beginning to see concern with general typology of language structures, i.e., with linguistic theory.

As I have pointed out on several previous occasions, contrastive analysis presents the descriptivist with his basic dilemma in its sharpest form. He maintains, on the one hand, that every language must be described and its structure identified in the terms of the language itself, not by an imposition of categories from outside. He maintains, on the other hand, that comparison of two language structures will yield useful predictions on interference in bilingual situations. In order to contrast

two language structures, however, the linguist must have some
frame of reference into which both structures fit. One cannot
compare, for example, the noun system of language A with the
noun system of language B without making it clear why the term
noun has been given to two classes differently defined and having
different relationships within each language. The linguist is
being called to create a new universal grammar, in other words,
a comprehensive theory of linguistics. Some who are working
on contrastive studies have taken the first halting steps towards
this. Comparisons of demonstrative systems, of accentual
systems, of relative clause types, for example, have suggested
general typologies for further elaboration and verification.

       To illustrate briefly what I mean, comparison of a few
structurally divergent languages has yielded the following set
of hypotheses about relative constructions, stated here quite
unrigorously and without the necessary background of general
theory and relevant definitions.

       1. Every language has a construction in some
       grammatico-semantic sense equivalent to the
       English relative clause.

       2. Either this construction involves a subordinate
       clause with connective morphemic matter, or it is
       an attributive phrase without such connective mate-
       rial. As examples of the latter type, one may cite
       the normal relative equivalents in Japanese and
       Turkish, such as Mr. Komai's example about the
       trout eater in Tokyo mentioned yesterday.

       3. If the construction involves a clause with con-
       nective, the connective material may lie outside
       the main and subordinate clauses, and in this
       case there is generally a resumptive pronoun

when the connective corresponds to what
would be the object of the subordinate clause
in English. Arabic is a good example of this
type.

4. If the connective lies within the clause, it
may be either in the subordinate clause, as in
English or most modern European languages,
or in the main clause as in Bengali, most modern Indo-Aryan languages and possibly proto-
Indo-European. In this latter case the relative
connective normally precedes what is traditionally called the antecedent and is resumed by a
demonstrative elsewhere in the main clause.

Along with such hypotheses, we may note interesting
correlations such as the further hypothesis that if a language is
of the type which has no relative clause but rather an attributive
phrase, it generally has verb-final word order.

Typological hypotheses of this kind are stateable in
forms which can be tested against further empirical data. Thus
the process of contrastive analysis which has grown out of the
problems of language learning leads towards the development of
general theories of language.

This paper has suggested that the study of the acquisition of language from a purely linguistic point of view will help
the linguist to a better understanding of the nature and function
of human language and will contribute to the development of
better procedures in the analysis and presentation of the structure and history of specific languages. Three examples were
used as illustration: the child's learning of his first language,
the formation of a pidgin language and the learning of a second
language in the classroom. But it is the author's feeling that

the purely linguistic study of almost any phenomenon of this
general type can have the kind of value suggested, and further,
that here is the growing edge of linguistic theory and methods
of analysis where much of the effort of institutions and individuals should now be directed.

NOTES

[1]Word, XIII, 3 (1957), 479; IJAL, XXVI, 3 (Publication 13 of the Indiana University Research Center in Anthropology,
Folklore and Linguistics, 1960).

[2]Roman Jakobson and Morris Halle, Fundamentals of
Language ('s-Gravenhage, 1956), pp. 32-36.

[3]W. Miller and S. Ervin, "The development of grammar
in child language," pp. 9-34; R.W. Brown and C. Fraser, "The
acquisition of syntax," pp. 43-79. The Acquisition of Language,
ed. by U. Bellugi and R. Brown. Chicago, Illinois: Society for
Research in Child Development, 1964. M.D. Braine, "The
ontogeny of English phrase structure: the first phase," Language
XXXIX, 1 (1963), 1-13.

DISCUSSION

J. C. THOMPSON: My comment is not as a linguist, but as a polygot with various degrees of proficiency in English, Chinese and Chinese pidgin English. Hall, in his article on pidgin English in the <u>Britannica</u>,[1] points out that the idea of a pidgin as the grammar of one language clothed in the speech of another is not accurate; the grammar comes from both languages. The point that I would like to make is that the pidgin language can also pick up structures of its own, independent of both of the other languages.[2]

FERGUSON: This is perfectly possible. I tried to phrase my statements carefully so as not to take sides in any of the views put forth about the structure of pidgin languages. Certainly I would recognize many cases where a pidgin language has some features of grammar not found in the language on which it is said to be based. It is more questionable that one could find a pidgin language with grammatical features occurring in none of the languages which serve as its sources, but I would see no reason why such innovations could not develop in actual fact.

REV. FRANCIS P. DINNEEN: In the interest of unity of the Round Table Meeting, I would like your comments on a point raised in two of the other papers. Professor Stuart suggests that a natural language can be examined as a kind of natural logic. Professor Chafe suggests that there is a certain percentage of items that we cannot correlate definitely with any class of experience type. This suggests to me that the natural logic of a natural language is really the logic of "common sense" which lives quite happily with contradictions and that the need for an explicit or formal logic is derived from this situation. As a consequence, I wonder about the necessity of not putting any psychological correlates on things that we establish by linguistic methods.

FERGUSON: I would prefer to sidestep most of the questions that were raised by that comment. There is one point, though, that I do want to make. I said that I would like to see linguists of all persuasions tackle with the same kind of intellectual vigor not only whole language structures, which are relatively homogeneous, but partial structures of all kinds and changing structures as well. I recommend this with the full expectation that any of the approaches that we now have would become modified in the course of confrontation with the other kind of data.

DONALD TUTTLE: I would like to ask a question about the assumption that children go from one-word sentences to two-word sentences. My most recent grand-child went from one- to three-word sentences, and I think that this is a more normal English pattern. His first sentence was: "I said: no!"

FERGUSON: The way children learn language varies very much from one child to another, from one language to another and from one set of circumstances to another. The particular frame of reference that I was discussing dealt with a total of about 30 children—all within a certain age range and all speakers of American English. Although the progression took place in a different way for each child, in certain cases in a strikingly different way, it made sense to talk at one stage in the children's development of having only one-word sentences and at a subsequent stage of having principally single-word and two-word sentences. There were a few marginal cases which did not fit.

CHARLES FRIES: I am very glad that there is taken the view of one-word and two-word sentences. The idea that the child learns words and then sentences is hardly tenable. The one-word utterance would have, of course, its intonation. It would fit the situation of a sentence rather than that of just a word.

NOTES ON DISCUSSION

[1]Vol. 17 (1962 edition), 905-7.

[2]Mr. Thompson submitted the following as a postscript to his remark: "I had in mind a structure from Chinese-Pidgin English such as, That man yesterday come Round Table, he belong my friend. The he comes neither from English, which would say: The man who came to the Round Table yesterday is my friend, nor from Chinese, Dzwotyan lai Ywanjwo de neige ren shr wode pengyou. A morpheme-by-morpheme translation of the Chinese would be: 'Last-day come Round Table (particle indicating that what precedes modifies what follows) that-one person is I (possessive particle) pair-friend'."

8 | Baby Talk in Six Languages

Occasionally linguists have turned their attention to the description of marginal systems within languages, such as animal calls, hesitation forms, or baby talk. Such phenomena have sometimes been studied because of purely linguistic interest in synchronic description: they often have elements of sound or form which do not occur in the "normal" central system of the language or have unusual arrangements or frequencies of occurrence of elements which do occur in the central system. This kind of study is of particular relevance to the question of the monosystemic nature of languages versus polytypical analyses of "coexistent" systems. These marginal phenomena have also sometimes been studied from a psychological point of view, in relation to questions of language acquisition or language function.

The present paper approaches the analysis of baby talk from a rather general taxonomic, linguistic interest. The intention is to initiate cross-language studies of marginal phenomena of this kind which will lead to a general characterization of them and to a framework for the characterization of single-language marginal phenomena in such a way that synchronic classification and historical explanation become possible.

By the term baby talk is meant here any special form of a language which is regarded by a speech community as being primarily appropriate for talking to young children and which is generally regarded as not the normal adult use of language. English examples would include choo-choo for adult train, or itty-bitty for little. In most cases the baby-talk item can also be used in some other situation with special value; in some cases (e.g., peek-a-boo) the item has no counterpart in normal language since it refers to an activity or object appropriate chiefly for children.

The method used here will be the comparison of baby-talk phenomena in six languages, selected for variety of linguistic structure and sociolinguistic setting within the limits of available material: (Syrian) Arabic, Marathi, Comanche, Gilyak, (American) English, Spanish. The first two are major languages of Asia with millions of speakers and strong literary traditions; the second two are of small nonliterate communities, one New World, one Old World; the last two are major European languages. The primary source materials for the first four languages are the articles of Ferguson (1956), Kelkar (1964), Casagrande (1948), and Austerlitz (1956); the material on English and Spanish was compiled from informants for this study. [1]

ASSUMPTIONS

Before proceeding to examination of the material, certain assumptions of this study should be made explicit since they are not in agreement with general views of baby talk. Here it is assumed that baby talk is a relatively stable, conventionalized

part of a language, transmitted by "natural" means of language
transmission much like the rest of the language; it is, in general, not a universal, instinctive creation of children everywhere, nor an ephemeral form of speech arising out of adults'
imitation of child speech. Like other marginal systems such
as animal calls, however, baby talk tends to show somewhat
different patterns of diffusion from the normal language: for
example, particular baby-talk items are often present in conti-
guous but genetically unrelated languages.

 The assumption of relative stability as opposed to ad
hoc creation is suggested by such cases of historical documentation as in Arabic where there is a record of Arabic baby talk
used at the beginning of the nineteenth century which is very
much like Arabic baby talk today. [2] An even more impressive
case is the persistence of baby talk words for food, drink, and
sleep for some two thousand years in the Mediterranean area.
The Roman grammarian Varro (116-27 B. C.)[3] cites Latin bua
and pāpa or pappa as baby talk for 'drink' and 'food' respectively,
and the use of Latin naenia 'dirge, lament' in the baby-talk
meaning of 'lullaby' is attested.

 At the present time the general Arabic baby talk for
'drink' is mbu or mbuwa. The baby-talk word for 'food' is
papa throughout the Spanish-speaking world; this is regarded
by some speakers of Spanish as a special use of the adult word
for potatoes, but it is attested in Spanish before the introduction
of potatoes. The modern Moroccan Arabic baby-talk word for
'bread' is ḫappa (or babba, or pappa). A common Arabic baby-
talk word for 'sleep' or 'lullaby' is ninnī or ninnē, which occurs
also in Italian. The details of diffusion are quite unclear, but
there can be little doubt of a historical connection between the
Latin words and the contemporary Arabic, Spanish, and Italian
ones.

The assumption that baby-talk items are conventionalized and culturally transmitted, not universal, can be appreciated from a glance at Table I, below. There are similarities in the structure of these items, which will be commented on below, but any simple notion of universality is refuted by such contrasts as the Syrian Arabic and Spanish baby-talk items for 'father' (bāba : tata), 'baby' (bubbu : nene), 'food' (mamm : papa), 'little' (nūnu : tiquitito). [4]

The assumption that most baby talk is taught as such by adults to children can be validated in an impressionistic way by simple observation. Adults inform the baby that a train is a choo-choo and a dog a bow-wow and in effect drill the child in such items until he produces his version of them. The alternative explanation, that millions of children independently create items like choo-choo and bow-wow instead of the hundreds of equally satisfactory onomatopoeias that could be imagined, is clearly unsatisfactory. It is, of course, true that adults sometimes do imitate an item of child speech and it gets accepted in a family; it is also true that there are resemblances between features of child speech and features of baby talk and tha adults often feel that baby-talk items are imitations of child speech, but the general assumption seems safe that adults usually initiate baby talk, using the material familiar to them as appropriate for this. There are instances of baby-talk words becoming incorporated in normal language, e.g. English tummy, several Gilyak items (Austerlitz 1956: 271-2), Spanish pininos.

MATERIAL

Baby talk includes at least three kinds of material: (1) intonational and paralinguistic phenomena which occur with normal language as well as with other baby-talk material;

(2) morphemes, words, and constructions modified from the normal language; and (3) a set of lexical items peculiar to baby talk.

Intonational features have been noticed by many authors, and even casual observers may notice the higher overall pitch, preference for certain contours, and special features such as labialization which occur in baby talk in a number of languages. Much of this is subsumed under the term Ammenton. Very little systematic description of this kind of baby-talk material has as yet been attempted[5] and it will not be discussed further here.

The baby-talk material derived from normal language shows considerable variability in the six languages, but a number of patterns of modification, phonological or grammatical, are sufficiently common to be of interest.

MODIFICATIONS OF NORMAL LANGUAGES

Phonology[6]

Simplification of consonant clusters (e.g., English tummy for stomach) is attested for all except Arabic and may well occur there too. There is an interesting variation in this: Gilyak has many final clusters and, even though it simplifies them, its final clusters in baby talk are more complex than those of baby talk in the other languages.

Replacement of r by another consonant (e.g. English wabbit for rabbit), either by a liquid l, y or w or by an apical stop t or d, occurs in all six languages. The replacement by l in several languages is surprising since some linguists feel that trills are more "basic" than laterals in that there are many languages with trills and no laterals but few the reverse.

TABLE I

	Arabic	Marathi	Comanche	Gilyak	English	Spanish
KIN						
1. mother	māma	(m)ai	—	yma	mommy	mama
2. father	bāba	baba	ʔapíˑʔ	da(j), dyj	daddy	tata
3. baby	bubbu	baḷ	nɨní·ʔ	(nena)	ba-by	nene
BODY						
4. food	mamm	məmməm	tatáˑʔ	mama, ñaña	—	papa
5. drink, water	mbŭ (wa)	papa	papáˑ/	—	dink	(a)guita
6. sleep	ninni, ninnē	nini, ʒ°ʒ°, gai (gai)	—	qoq	sleepy-bye, night-night	tuto, meme
7. urination	ʔaḥḥ	mumu, šu	—	hisa, cisa	wee-wee, pee-pee	pipí; pichí, chichi
8. defecation	kaʕʕo	(i)ši	ʔaʔh, ʔasíˑ	[aʔa]	poop(oo)	popó, kakú
9. bath	ğullu ğullu	toto	—	ypyp	—	—
10. hurt	wāwa	bau	naná·; naná·ʔ	ykyk	ow, booboo	yaya, coco
11. walk, foot	dāde	calcal	—	ŋonk, amqamq, myñy	footsie	patita, pininos
12. breast, milk	zēze, zizz	pipi	cicíˑʔ	myñk, myñy	—	—
13. penis	—	nuni, nunu	wíʔasI	coc(k)	-·	—
14. vagina		čimi	táˑʔsI	bew, peḷŋa		—

TABLE I (*Continued*)

	Arabic	Marathi	Comanche	Gilyak	English	Spanish
QUALITIES						
15. nice	dahh	čhan čhan	ʔumːáʔ	ulak	p(r)it-tie	nino
16. bad, don't!	didde, (hu)mm	hǎ(ʔ)	ʔaʔháːʔ	—	(ʔæʔɑ)	*alveolar click*
17. dirty	kixx, kaʕʕ	yakk, isiʔ	ʔáx	alqalq	[yix]	fuchi, chocho
18. hot	ʔuhh	hay	ʔitíʔ	—	burnie	ssss
19. cold	hü	gar gar	ʔicíʔ	—	—	fío
20. nothing left	bahh	koko	—	ap(k)a	a(ll) gone	cabó
21. little	nünu	pitukla	—	—	teenie (-weenie), itty-bitty	tiquitito
ANIMALS & GAMES						
22. dog	ʕaw ʕaw	bhʊbhʊ	ɲa/ŋóʔ	gvck, gvcv	doggie, bow-wow	guau guáu, gua guá
23. cat	nawnaw, biss	mau, mini	waʔóʔ	—	pussy(-cat), kitty(-cat)	cuchito, michi, bicho
24. bird	küku	čiu	kakáʔ	bic-(ŋ)aq	birdie	pipi
25. goblin	buʕbuʕ	bagul-bua	mukíʔ	humk	boogeyman	cuco, coco
26. going out	tišš	bhur	—	—	bye-bye	mamoch calle
27. peek-a-boo	naww, baʔʕéno	kukk, bua	—	—	peek-a-boo	onetá
28. carry on back	haʔha?	kokru ho-	mamáʔ	aci, (b)apu	piggy-back	upa
29. noise, ear	kurr	kurr	—	—	—	—
30. goodies, candy	nahh	khau	kokóʔ	—	—	uches

(*Continued on next page*)

Notes to Table I

1. Marathi and English have many baby-talk words for 'mother' and 'father.' Marathi *mai*, *ǰiǰi, ai* (regular adult word), *məmi* (English loan), 'mother'; *baba, əṇṇa, dada, tatya, tata, əppa, nana, aba, bhau*; *pəpa, ɖæɖi* (English loans), 'father.' English *mom, ma, momma, mommie; dad, daddy, dada, pop*. Casagrande says "There is no special baby word [for mother] in common use," the regular adult *piá* being used (1948: 12); *mamá·ʔ* is included in the alphabetized listing, however, identified as English. Spanish baby talk *mama* (also *mami*) is stressed on the first syllable,; *mamá* with final stress is a somewhat informal adult word.

2. Comanche *ʔapi·ʔ* also means 'father's brother' and 'father's friend'; baby talk *tokó·ʔ, totó·ʔ* 'grandfather' (adult counterpart 'mother's father') is sometimes used for 'father.' Spanish *tata* may also be used for 'grandfather.'

3. Arabic *bubbu* and Comanche *niñiʔ* are also used for 'doll.' Marathi *baḷ* is also an adult word, but is usually in baby talk with a special intonation, and other adult words for 'baby' are not used in baby talk. The Gilyak *nena* is glossed only 'doll.' A feminine *nena* occurs in Spanish, although in Chile *nene* may be used for both sexes.

4. English apparently has no common baby-talk word for 'food'; *yum-yum* 'delicious' is sometimes used.

5. Marathi *papa* also means 'kiss.'

6. Arabic has variants such as *ʔaʔʔā ninnī (-ē)*, *ʔoʔʔō ninnī (-ē)*. Spanish *hacer tuto* is attested for Chile, *hacer meme* (or *mimi*) for Mexico.

7. Spanish *pichi, chichi* are not attested for Mexico.

8. Chile: *popó* is 'anus,' sometimes 'vagina,' never 'defecation' or 'feces'; *kaká* is not attested for Mexico.

9. Arabic *ǧullu ǧullu* is from McCarus.

10. Spanish *tener una yaya* (or *yayita*) is attested for Chile, *hacerse coco* for Mexico.

11. Gilyak *amqamq* is 'walk'; *yonk* (variants *yon, yonyon, yono*) is 'legs and feet.' Spanish *patita* 'foot' is attested for Mexico and Chile; in the sense of 'walking, taking steps' Chile has *andando patita*, Mexico *hacer pininos*.

15. Marathi *čhan čhan* is a reduplicated form of adult *čhan*. Spanish *nino* (adult *lindo*) is attested only for Chile.

16. Arabic *didde* means 'don't or I'll slap you, spank you'; *(hu)mm* means 'don't touch.'

17. Spanish *chucho* is a baby talk form of *sucio* 'dirty'; possibly *fuchi* is also related to this.

18. Spanish *ssss* is accompanied by a gesture of shaking the fingers loosely as though just burnt.

19. Marathi *gar gar* is a reduplicated form of adult *gar*.

22. Chile *guau guáu*, Mexico *gua guá*.

24. Marathi *čiu* is glossed 'house sparrow.' Comanche *kaka·ʔ* is also 'headlouse.'

25. Comanche has several words for frightening children; the *muki·ʔ* is some kind of giant owl, the *mumú·ʔ* is darkness or thunder, the *ʔïnï·ʔ* is a noxious insect or small animal like a snake or scorpion. Chilean Spanish sometimes has *cuca*, feminine of *cuco*.

27. English *peek-a-boo* is chiefly American; the usual British form is *bo-peep*.

28. Marathi *kokru ho-* means 'play lamb,' i.e., be carried piggy-back. Comanche *mamá·ʔ* is glossed "horse; said by a child when he wants to be carried on someone's back."

Replacement of velars by apicals (e.g., English <u>tum</u> <u>on</u> for <u>come on</u>) is attested for all except Arabic and Gilyak, and considering the frequency of velars in the Arabic and Gilyak baby talk it seems likely that this replacement does not occur in these.

Some kind of interchange among sibilants, affricates, and stops (e.g., English <u>soos</u> for <u>shoes</u>) occurs in all but Comanche and Gilyak, but is of three different types: (a) hushing sibilants replaced by hissing sibilants (Arabic, Marathi, English); (b) sibilants replaced by [č] (Marathi, Spanish); (c) affricates replaced by stops (Marathi). The most interesting of these is probably the replacement of [s] by [č] (e.g., Spanich <u>becho</u> for <u>beso</u>) since the latter is felt by some linguists to be a less "basic" sound and this replacement seems very unnatural for English speakers. In Spanish baby talk the use of [č] for [s] is widespread and in fact is an identifying feature of baby talk; of the languages discussed here it occurs also in Marathi, and it is attested for Japanese baby talk as well.

Distant nasal assimilation is attested for Marathi, Gilyak, and Spanish (e.g., Spanish <u>mamoch</u> for <u>vamos</u>), and may also occur in the others.

Examples of loss of unstressed syllables occur in English and Spanish (e.g., Spanish <u>tines</u> for <u>calcetines</u>).[7]

Grammar

At least one diminutive or hypocoristic affix is of frequent occurrence in each language. This may be a regular diminutive form (as Spanish –<u>ito</u>, –<u>ita</u> or Comanche –<u>ci</u>) or a form used chiefly in baby talk and only infrequently in normal language (e.g., Gilyak <u>k</u>/<u>q</u>, Marathi –[<u>k</u>]<u>ula</u>/–<u>ukla</u>, Arabic –<u>o</u>, English –<u>ie</u>).

Greater use of nouns rather than pronouns and verbs is general: equational clauses without verbs replace normal construction with copula or verb (e.g., English <u>dollie pretty</u> for <u>the doll is pretty)</u>, and third person constructions replace first and second person ones (e.g., English <u>daddy wants</u> for <u>I want</u>).

In two of the languages, Arabic and Marathi, a shift in gender is used as a mark of endearment; i.e., a feminine noun, pronoun, adjective, or verb form is used in reference to a boy or vice versa. For example, in Arabic <u>wēn ruħti yā binti</u>? 'Where did you go (fem.), little girl?' said to a boy; <u>inta žu‘ān</u>? 'Are you (m.) hungry (m.)?' said to a girl.[8] In Marathi the examples are with the use of a feminine ending on a boy's name and vice versa.

LEXICON

The number of lexical items given in the references varies from about 25 to over 60. The commonest topics reported are: kin names, nicknames and the like; body parts and bodily functions; basic qualities like "good," "bad," "little," "dirty,"; and the names of animals and nursery games. About 30 such items common to most of the six languages are listed below, classified under four headings; in several cases attested items modified from adult words are entered when there is no special word.

CHARACTERISTICS

Baby-talk words either as modifications of normal words or as special lexical items show certain general characteristics. In the first place, baby-talk items consist of simple, more basic kinds of consonant, stops and nasals in particular, and only a very small selection of vowels. One would expect that the rarer, more peculiar consonants or the consonants which tend to be learned later would not be found in baby talk, and generally this is true but there are some exceptions. Gilyak, for example, uses four phonemically distinct nasals in baby talk, and a variety of velars as mentioned above. Arabic has many baby-talk items with pharyngeal spirants although these are often assumed to be learned late in Arabic. The best example is the fact that labial emphatics exist in Arabic baby talk and may well be the first emphatics learned by Arabic children even though they are marginal in the adult language.

A second phonological characteristic is the predominance of reduplication, both of parts of words and of whole words, in the baby talk of all six languages. For several of these languages reduplication plays a grammatical role of some sort in the adult language, but the reduplication in baby talk is generally separate and unrelated to the use in the normal language. Reduplication can probably be regarded as a feature of baby talk throughout the world.

Each of the six languages has a typical ("canonical") form of baby-talk items. There is variation, dependent at least in part on the canonical forms of morphemes in the corresponding adult language, but the commonest form is CVC, i.e. a monosyllable beginning and ending with a consonant, with CVCV as next most common. Many items have CVCCV with a double consonant in the middle even if this is not common in the adult language. As an example of the variation conditioned by normal canonical forms we may cite Spanish: in adult Spanish, monosyllabic words of the shape CVC are extremely rare, and this form seems not to occur in Spanish baby talk, where CVCV is the commonest form.

On the grammatical side, apart from the reduplication and canonical forms already mentioned among phonological characteristics, the most striking features are the absence
of any inflectional affixes, the presence of a special baby-talk
affix and the use of words in different grammatical functions.
The semantic fields showing a special baby-talk vocabulary
most commonly represented include kin, food, body parts, and
animals.

It must be noted that the features listed here as
characteristic of baby-talk items are in general characteristic
of the one-vocable utterances ("monoremes") used by children
at the stage of linguistic development between the stage of call-
sounds and other prerepresentational items and the stage of
two-vocable utterances where words and sentences emerge. [9]
Common characteristics include reduplication; primitive
affixes; food, animals, toys, etc., as referents.

In view of this similarity one is tempted to make the
hypothesis that every language community provides a stock of
baby-talk items which can serve as appropriate material for
babies to imitate in creating their monoremes but which do not
interfere with the normal words of the language and can gradually be discarded as real words emerge in the children's
speech. The child may, and often does, create his monoremes
from other sources such as sound imitation or fragments of
adult utterances, but the baby-talk items tend to be one of the
principal sources. The baby-talk lexicon of a language community may thus play a special role in the linguistic development of its children: the facilitation of each child's acquisition of a set of monoremes from which he can go on to the
beginnings of real grammar. Experimental confirmation of
this hypothesis would be difficult; perhaps the most relevant
data would come from societies with radically different attitudes
toward child language learning. (Cf. Voegelin and Robinett
1954.)

FUNCTION

Under what circumstances and with what intentions is baby talk used? The published material is very limited on this point. There are, however, several situations or purposes mentioned in the articles or by informants, and these may be considered.

Perhaps the primary purpose is felt to be teaching a child to talk; that is, people asked why or when they use baby talk will say that they use it when talking to young children to make it easier for them to learn to talk. If asked in more detail they may explain that what they are saying in baby talk is easier for the child to learn and that it is clearer, i.e., easier for the child to hear; also, especially in the Marathi material, whenever there is a choice between two ways of saying something, baby talk uses the more colorful, more "marked" in the linguistic sense. This feeling is obviously incorrect in details (is pussy so much easier than cat?) and too vague in formulation, but it seems to reflect in a folk-wisdom way the function hypothesized above. A moment's consideration, however, shows this is not the only time baby talk is used. It is used for one thing in talking to infants who are not yet learning to talk, and it is apparently used in talking to pets in every one of these six language communities. Obviously one is not teaching the infant or the pet to talk.

Secondary uses of baby talk generally seem to reflect a desire on the part of the user to evoke some aspect of the nurturant-baby situation in which the primary use of baby talk occurs. This evocation may be from the side of the baby. For example, a child who has just gotten past the use of baby talk by his parents may then revert to baby talk—in fact, even use baby talk that he has not used before—in order to get attention or to be treated in some way as a baby. Also, adults use baby

talk in reporting children's speech; in several language communities (e.g. Marathi, Norwegian) baby talk is often used to
represent child speech in written literature such as novels and
stories.

The evocation of the nurturant–baby situation may
also be from the side of the nurturant. For example, the use
of baby talk to pets or small infants seems to show the kind of
protectiveness and affection characteristic of the nurturant's
relation with the baby. The Marathi author notes that the
speaker gets a sense of pleasure from doing this.

In Marathi, English, and Spanish, lovers' use of
baby talk is attested, and in this case it may not always be
clear whether it is the protectiveness of the nurturant or the
dependence of the baby that is evoked. It is worth noting that
Kelkar reports, on the basis of observation in multilingual
situations, that adults who are using baby talk with other adults
do not use baby talk in anything but their own language. It
seems very likely, however, that this varies depending on a
number of factors; it is in any case related to the important
general issue of relationship-signaling styles in a second language.

Finally, it is clearly documented for several languages
that baby talk is used in certain kinds of songs, riddles, and
word-play on the part of adults which bear little direct relationship to the uses with children (Austerlitz 1956:272-3).

VARIABILITY AND DIFFUSION

The fact of variability in baby talk was mentioned
above; it requires further comment here. First, there is
great family variation: an item gets used in a certain family

and becomes well entrenched there but does not spread beyond
that.   There are also examples of items spreading from one
family to another but not becoming general.

Second, there is the areal diffusion previously referred to.   Baby-talk items often diffuse within an area rather
than according to the lines of genetic relationship followed by
the great mass of linguistic phenomena.   A good example is
the baby-talk word [kix] meaning 'dirty, don't touch' and the
like.   This word, with slightly different forms depending on
the phonological systems of the respective languages, occurs
in almost every language of the Middle East.   It is attested
(McCarus 1963) for Arabic, Kurdish Persian, and Syriac
although these languages represent two different language
families, Semitic and Indo-European (Iranian branch).   The
word [kix] is not attested for Turkish, which has no phoneme
of the [x] type.   Another good example is the use of a word like
wāwa, uwwa, or vava in the meaning 'hurt, sore, injury'
throughout the Middle East (Arabic, Syriac, Turkish, Persian,
Armenian, Greek), with a [v] in languages like Persian and
Greek that have no regular phoneme of the [w] type.

The explanation for this kind of diffusion might lie in
the fact that the baby-talk items are not well integrated into
the grammatical system of the language even though they are
fairly well integrated into the phonological system.   Because
of this lack of integration it is clearly easier to borrow these
terms from one language to another but presumably social
factors in addition to this linguistic factor should be sought as
explanation.

This kind of variability, being relatively independent
of genetic relationship, offers a chance for the study of distribution of baby-talk items on a statistical basis throughout
the world and the kind of analysis of statistical

universals of one sort or another that Jakobson has tried
(Jakobson 1962), at least with <u>mama</u> and <u>papa</u>, suggesting
certain reasons for their occurrence with far more than
chance frequency in languages of the world. It is a rare
pleasure for the linguist to have a language phenomenon which
can be studied all across the world without need for corrections
from the genetic relationships that are involved.

Another way in which baby talk can vary from one language to another is the size of the lexicon or the range of variation of a particular part of the lexicon. Actually one of the
surprising features of the present study is the similarity of
baby-talk phenomena in the six languages considered, when one
might have assumed that there would be serious cultural differences in the kinds of items that would appear in baby talk
and the situations in which they would be used. Further study
along this line, however, would be useful.

One other point of variability should be mentioned, the
differences in attitude toward public use of baby talk. In our
society baby talk is mentioned with an air of apology by adults
talking seriously, and one feels a good bit of embarrassment
in citing examples of baby talk. Also in our society it is quite
widely believed that the use of baby talk inhibits learning of the
language. That is, people feel that if they use too much baby
talk at home, the child is not going to learn the normal language
properly. This belief is presented explicitly in books on child
development, although there seem to be no experimental data
which would substantiate it.[10] In the Arab world, however, there
seem to be no such feelings. Adults may discuss baby talk perfectly easily, and they use it freely if it is appropriate. There
seems to be no trace of the notion that use of baby talk may in-
hibit the acquisition of the adult language. Among both American
and Arabs, however, it seems to be felt that baby talk is more
appropriate for women to use than men.

SUMMARY

Baby talk is a linguistic subsystem regarded by a speech community as being primarily appropriate for talking to young children; it consists of intonational features, patterned modifications of normal language, and a special set of lexical items. The special lexical items typically number between 25 and 60 and cover kin names and appellations, bodily functions, certain simple qualities (e.g., dirty, pretty, hot, cold), and vocabulary concerning animals, nursery games, and related items. Baby-talk words typically contain stops, nasals, and a limited selection of vowels, have the structure CVC or CVC(C)V, are frequently reduplicated, and often have a diminutive suffix characteristic of baby talk in that language.

Baby-talk works are not universal, but are transmitted much like other language phenomena in the community. Baby talk seems to serve in each language community as a special source for children's pregrammatical vocables, enabling them to create items at that stage which they can discard as they acquire true words and grammar. Baby talk in addition to this primary use is also used to talk to infants and pets and between adults in situations with "baby" aspects. Baby-talk items are fairly well integrated into the phonological system of the language, but are so unrelated grammatically to the normal that on the one hand they show considerable variability within a speech community and on the other hand tend to diffuse readily across language boundaries regardless of genetic relationships. A given baby-talk system may be characterized in terms of internal structure by the size of the special lexicon and the range of variability. Externally it may be characterized by the extent of its secondary uses and the attitude toward its public use.

NOTES

[1]As an additional source for Syrian Arabic,
McCarus' notes were used; they also provided information on
baby-talk items in Iraqi Arabic, Turkish, Kurdish, Persian,
Syriac, and Alexandrian Greek.   Further checking of Arabic
was done with Mr. and Mrs. Moukhtar Ani of Damascus.
Kelkar provided some additional Marathi information in a
personal communication.   Chief informants for the Spanish
were Mrs. Raquel Saporta of Chile and Miss Yolanda Lastra
of Mexico; English items came from the author and his colleagues.   Susan Ervin-Tripp read the manuscript and made
valuable suggestions.

[2]Sabbagh's sketch (Sabbagh 1886) of colloquial Syrian
and Egyptian Arabic, written in 1812, has five baby-talk words
(voweling uncertain): bahh 'all gone,' dahh 'shiny, nice,' uhh
'hot,' nčiġġ 'goo,' said to elicit smile and first word, mnahh
'sweet, goodies.' All these are in use in Syrian Arabic today
(modern form for the last two nkiġġ, nahh).

[3]Varr. ap. Non. 81.2 cum cibum ac potionem buas ac
pappas vocent et matrem mammam patrem tatam (Heraeus
1904, repr.: 170-172).

[4]This notion of universality is found even in such
careful works as Lewis (1957:80):"In fact, baby language is
an international language. If we make a short list of the
earliest words actually spoken by children, with their meanings, we have a vocabulary that every one will recognize."

[5]Kelkar pays considerable attention to intonation in
his study 3.2.

[6]The careful account of the phonological characteristics
of Norwegian baby talk in Haugen (1942: viii-x) includes most of
the characteristics listed here.

[7]Surprisingly enough, Spanish baby talk shows distinctive use of stress, e. g. pipi 'bird': pipí 'urination.' Also,
several baby-talk items differ from other adult words only in
stress; for example, baby talk mama 'mother' and papa 'food'
differ from informal adult mamá, papá 'mother,' 'father,' and
baby talk guá gua differs from adult Caribbean Spanish guágua
'bus' and Bolivian guá gua 'child.' Spanish baby talk has both
CVCV (= CV́CV) and CVCV́ as canonical forms.

[8]Arabic examples are from McCarus (1963).

[9]Some monoremes persist as vocables in more complex utterances, but the notion of a monoreme stage in language
development seems valid. A convenient recent account of the
characteristics of monoremes is in Werner and Kaplan (1963:
134-137). Full recognition of the similarity between baby talk
and actual items of child language is found in Jakobson (1962:
539): "Nursery coinages are accepted for wider circulation in
the child-adult intercourse only if they meet the infant's linguistic requirements .... "

[10]This notion appears even in careful reviews such as
McCarthy (1954: 536): ". . . baby-talk used by adults in the
child's environment often makes for preservation of infantile
speech habits." A more balanced statement on this point appears
in Lewis (1957: 89): "But a mother who, because of a theory that
baby-language is too 'babyish'—not 'correct language'—refuses
to speak it to her child may be doing him harm, retarding his
language development. On the other hand, if baby language is
spoken to a child for too long in his life he may be retarded in
another way—his speech may remain childish at a time when he
should have grown out of this. "

REFERENCES

Austerlitz, Robert. 1956. Gilyak nursery words. Word 12: 260–279.

Casagrande, Joseph B. 1948. Comanche baby language. International Journal of American Linguistics 14:11–14.

Ferguson, Charles A. 1956. Arabic baby talk. In For Roman Jakobson, Morris Halle et al., eds. The Hague, Mouton.

Haugen, Einar. 1942. Norwegian word studies, Vol. I, Part III (Baby talk, pp. vi–x). Mimeographed, on deposit Library of Congress.

Heraeus, Wilhelm. 1904. Die Sprache der römischen Kinderstube. Archiv für lateinische Lexikographie 13: 149–172. Repr. in Kleine Schriften von Wilhelm Heraeus. J. B. Hoffmann, ed. Heidelberg, Carl Winter's 1937, pp. 158–180.

Jakobson, Roman. 1962. Why "mama" and "papa"? In Selected writings. Vol. I. The Hague, Mouton.

Kelkar, Ashok. 1964. Marathi baby talk. Word 20:40–54.

Lewis, M. M. 1957. How children learn to speak. London, George G. Harrap.

McCarthy, Dorothea. 1954. Language development in children. In Manual of child psychology, Leonard Carmichael, ed. New York, John Wiley.

McCarus, Ernest. 1963. Near Eastern baby talk. Unpub-
    lished notes.

Sabbagh, Mikha'il. 1886. Mîhâ'îl Ṣabbâġ's Grammatik der
    arabischen Umgangssprache in Syrien und Aegypten,
    H. Thorbecke, ed. Strassburg, K. J. Trübner.

Voegelin, C. F. and Florence M. Robinett. 1954. 'Mother
    language' in Hidatsa. International Journal of Ameri-
    can Linguistics 20: 65-70.

Werner, Heina and Bernard Kaplan. 1963. Symbol formation.
    New York, John Wiley.

9 | Applied Linguistics

The term "applied linguistics" has become more popular in recent years, as courses with this title have multiplied and centers and schools of applied linguistics, professional journals, and even an international association for applied linguistics have come into being. Naturally enough the meaning of the term varies a great deal depending on the user and the context, ranging from synonymy with "mathematical linguistics" to being used as the name of an approach to language teaching. In this presentation we shall use the term to mean simply the application of any of the insights, methods, or findings of linguistic science to practical language problems, in particular—because of the interests of this conference—to the problems of the acquisition of language in our educational institutions.

There are still some respected linguists who maintain the view that so little is known about human language that linguists should spend their time learning more rather than trying to apply the little they already know or think they know. There are also some language specialists today who assert that linguistics offers solutions to the problems of language teachers and that the education of language teachers should include a heavy component of

linguistics, which would largely provide the methodology side
of their training. The point of view taken here is between such
extremes. We can agree that linguists are just at the threshold
of understanding human language behavior, and at the same time
insist that the small body of linguistic theory and related attitudes and techniques contains much that is of relevance to language teaching. Also, we can acknowledge that linguistics has
very little to say directly to the questions of language pedagogy
and yet firmly maintain that it should have a special place in the
education of language teachers beyond the important place that
it deserves, along with the study of foreign languages and litera-
tures, at the very core of any liberal education.

If we accept this understanding of applied linguistics
and its role in language teaching, it will be reflected in our view
of what constitutes research in applied linguistics. Apart from
what might be called "developmental research" such as the preparation of teaching materials, language texts, and the like,
there is a small but growing body of experimental research which
takes data and hypotheses from linguistics and experiments with
them in language learning situations. In the strictest interpretation of our topic we might well limit our discussion to this kind
of research. It seems preferable, however, to take a broader
view, and after giving only two examples of it we shall move on
to larger questions of more general interest in applied linguistics.

Linguists have long felt that a contrastive study of the
structure of two languages is of value in predicting the problems
the speaker of one will have in learning the other, and in fact the
production of contrastive studies for possible pedagogical application has become one of the standard examples of applied linguistics.
Until very recently, however, no theoretical rationale for this
has been attempted, and experimentation has been of the grossest
kind. At the present time a number of linguists and language
specialists are trying to formulate principles of contrastive

analysis that will yield fairly precise predictions which can then
be systematically tested under laboratory conditions in language
learning situations. The principles should predict, for example,
relative ease of perception and production of various sound differences under various sets of circumstances, and it is good to
report that such experimentation is being carried out. As with
all such experimentation in human behavior we may safely expect
that a whole range of external variables will interfere with the
validation of the principles and that the principles themselves
will often turn out to be inadequately formulated. Beyond this,
however, we have reason to hope that new and improved formulations of the principles will emerge, with solid experimental evidence to back them up, and that the study of such principles and
experimentation will become a normal part of university work in
linguistics and the methodology of language teaching.

  Similarly, language teachers have long felt that the
grading of material in terms of syntactic complexity is important
in achieving maximum effectiveness in language teaching, and the
current interest in programmed language learning is a new example of the traditional pedagogical concern with the question of what
presupposes what in the language material to be learned. However,
most grading of grammatical structures, even when done by competent and experienced linguists, has been based on impressionistic judgements and vaguely conceived theoretical principles or
none at all. Recently, transformational generative grammar has
suggested some measures of syntactical complexity which have
appealed to experimenters. The current versions of transformational generative grammar make no strong claims for the "psychological reality" of their ordered rules or even, for example, the
division between deep grammar and surface grammar, but the
suggestion of such a simple linguistic measure of complexity as
the number of transformations between an underlying kernel
string or strings and a given sentence to be taught offers the
researcher in applied linguistics a promising field for experimenta-

tion. The assumption of some kind of relationship—other things being equal—between complexity of syntax and ease of learning can provide predictions as to the language learner's perception, comprehension, production, and memory of particular sentences or sentence types, and these predictions can be tested. There are obvious pitfalls here: the measures of complexity may change with the changes in transformational generative grammar and its analysis of English, or the relationship between grammatical complexity and ease of learning may turn out to be so complex or indirect that it is of little use in pedagogy. But this represents a line of research in applied linguistics which will probably slowly become a recognized field, possibly under the label of psycholinguistics.

These two examples of research in applied linguistics point up a characteristic of the field. They are both intended to give help to language teachers, but they both have implications for the linguistic theoretician, and the feedback from them into the realm of "pure" linguistics may have a considerable effect. The contrastive research may, for example, alter considerably our notions of phonological structure, while the research on syntactic complexity may help push linguistics itself toward a more experimental approach in which its theories are phrased in ways subject to experimental study for confirmation or disconfirmation.

From these simple examples of research let us shift to more general considerations. When linguists and linguistics began to move significantly into the field of language teaching in the United States in the nineteen forties, certain aspects of the linguists' knowledge about language and their attitude toward it came to be regarded as basic principles in any application of linguistics to language teaching, and it may be worthwhile now, some twenty years later, to examine several of those principles, to see what has happened to them. First, let us mention the implicit assumption of all linguistics, Principle (1): Language is patterned human behavior subject to systematic, objective analysis.

Although this principle sounds dispassionate and coldly "scientific" it is actually a way of stating the linguist's tremendous reverence for language. The linguist acts under the strongly, almost passionately, held assumption that if you observe genuine language phenomena carefully enough you will find all kinds of complex patterning and regularities in design of which the user is largely unaware. It was this "reverence for language" which made the linguist insist on native speakers and recordings of native speakers as models in language teaching. It was this same reverence for language which made the linguist reject many of the prescriptive rules of the teacher which were based not on the facts of language but on someone's idea of how the language should be. It was even this same reverence for language which made the honest linguist admit he did not know the answer to a student's question and set him to work trying to discover it from actual utterances or written passages in the language.

This principle, with its insistence on the possibility of objective analysis, has made the linguist devote time to the description of varieties of language the teacher regards as inappropriate for classroom instruction. It has also caused the linguist to put aside traditional attitudes on the relative beauty, logic, and expressiveness of different languages or varieties of the same language, not because such attitudes are unimportant but because they may interfere with the kind of analyses which the linguist finds rewarding for his own purposes.

This first principle, that language behavior can be studied systematically to discover its structure, is more than simply the linguist's reverence for language, since it has led

to a number of discoveries about universal characteristics of
language. Linguists speak with some confidence about the
nature of phonological systems and the universal phenomena of
phonemic contrast, distinctive and non-distinctive sound features,
and regular phonetic change. They expect every language to
have a limited number of major clause types and grammatical
processes and they note certain statistical patterns of lexical
occurrence.

Some of the implications of this principle have become
widely accepted among language teachers in the past two decades.
For example, the importance of accurate models of the language
to be learned is recognized in the higher demands on the teacher's
competence in using the language and in the spread of language
laboratories with their possibilities of genuine, native language
material on tapes. The importance of the unconscious, automatic nature of much language behavior has been recognized in the
development of drills and pattern practice and the willingness to
use mimicry and memorization as the basis for certain kinds of
learning. The importance of objectivity in language analysis
has been reflected in the decreased insistence on the acquisition
of features of pronunciation, grammar, and lexicon which are
traditionally held to be "correct" but are not actually used by
educated speakers of the language.

On the other hand, this principle has given rise to some
misunderstandings, and its implications have been wrongly read
by some teachers and administrators. Perhaps the most serious
misunderstanding, which seems now happily to be disappearing,
has been the feeling that the setting aside of value judgments
for linguistic analysis meant the scrapping of standards in grammar. One of the ironies of the application of linguistics to language teaching has been the spread of the idea that linguists are
in favor of "abolishing grammar" and abandoning the identification and description of grammatical phenomena. In fact, the

linguist has always been deeply concerned with questions of
grammar and spends most of his professional life dealing with
them. He is interested in describing grammatical systems, i.e.,
in constructing sets of statements which will account for the ob-
servable grammatical phenomena of human languages.

Linguistics, of course, has nothing directly to say
about how grammatical systems should be taught, but a number
of linguists who have been interested in language teaching or
have taught languages themselves have noticed the apparent in-
effectiveness of explicit teaching of grammatical rules under
certain conditions and have called attention to the fundamental
difference between being able to talk about the grammar of a
language and being able to use the grammar in actual comprehension and production of utterances in the language. It is probably this idea, along with the linguist's rejection of false pres-
criptivism, which have led to the misunderstanding.

In spite of the progress made toward incorporating the
linguist's attitude toward language structure—both his "reverence for language" and his discoveries about its nature—into the
thinking and action of language teachers, there is a long way to
go before the full implications of a scientific view toward language analysis are understood and acted upon. It is for this reason that many of us urge the inclusion of regular study of "pure"
linguistics in the education of teachers as one of the most important aspects of applied linguistics, even though the results may
be indirect and long delayed in appearance.

A second principle, which developed a little later in
linguistics but was central to much linguistic work for several
decades is Principle (2): Every language presents a unique
structure which must be analyzed on its own terms. This principle makes explicit the linguist's conviction that within the
framework of the universal characteristics of human language

there is such an enormous amount of variation among languages
that an elegant and convincing characterization of any particular
language may be inadequate or misleading if applied to another.
For example, a grammatical terminology suited to Classical
Greek may be very unsatisfactory for Classical Chinese or
Modern French. This principle suggests that another contribution of the linguist might be the description and presentation of
the facts of particular languages being taught.

It was obvious in the forties that the linguist could provide information about some of the Asian and African languages
being taught for the first time in America which was fuller and
more reliable than that to be found in the poor teaching manuals
available. It was less obvious, and much more disruptive, when
linguists sometimes claimed to have better information about
well-known European languages and were openly scornful of
grammatical statements in respected textbooks. It might be
better to pass quickly over this battle, but unfortunately the
issue is still with us. Today's linguists are sometimes less
arrogant and the teachers less defensive, but the misunderstanding and poor communication here are serious, since accurate
description of the facts of particular languages remains one of
the most important contributions linguists can make to language
teaching.

In the last several years, for example, new information
about the use of negatives in English (e.g., the use of too and
either after negative clauses) has been discovered, new generalizations about the use of the instrumental case in Russian have
been formulated, and new descriptions of noun phrases in French
have been made. The new descriptive material being published
in linguistic journals and monographs throughout the world ranges
from detailed specifications of pronunciation to studies of the
relative frequency of synonymous grammatical constructions.
All of this material should be digested and transmitted to the

language teacher or course developer, but it is not easy to see
how this can be done when linguists themselves find it hard to
keep up with the flow of information.

Linguists who publish descriptive studies of particular
languages generally do not have in mind the problems of language
learning. They are interested in showing a parallel with a previously described language, explaining some historical developments, demonstrating the superiority of a particular theory of
grammar writing or simply taking pleasure in a craftsmanlike
job of linguistic description. None of these aims are of much
relevance for the language teacher, and ways must be found of
insuring the gathering and dissemination of this kind of material
in forms which make it accessible to language teachers. It may
be out of place to emphasize this question here, but it is my personal expectation that the provision of reliable language data and
descriptions will be the most important single contribution of linguistics to language teaching for some time to come.

A special case of this is the publication and use of contrastive studies, especially those between English and another
language. One partial bibliography in this field has jumped from
about 200 items in 1961 to almost 500 in 1965. The output is considerable, and although the studies vary greatly in quality and in
usefulness for application to language teaching, this material also
needs organization and transmission to the language profession
in general.

The third aspect of linguistics which has served as a
principle in applied linguistics is the emphasis on oral language,
which may be phrased as Principle (3): Speech has primacy over
writing.

For most linguists the primacy of speech is so clear as
to require no demonstration. Human beings spoke languages for

thousands of years before writing was invented. Most languages of the world today are not normally used for written purposes. Most human beings today are not able to read and write the languages they speak. And even the highly literate adult first learned to speak in early childhood and only later learned to read. Since, however, the established folk belief in our own speech community, as in most highly literate societies, is that the real language is the written language and the spoken language in only a corruption of it or at best a poor approximation, it is easy to see that the linguists would clash with many language teachers on this issue.

The linguist's view of the primacy of speech coincided with a national need for competence in the oral use of foreign languages, and this consideration led to heavy emphasis on spoken language and ultimately to audiolingual methods of language teaching which were felt to have the blessing of linguistics. It was widely asserted that even the acquisition of a reading knowledge was improved and accelerated by concentration on oral competence first. In spite of the fact that linguistics has nothing directly to say on the question of how to teach oral and written competence, the term "applied linguistics" is sometimes used to refer to the audiolingual methodology. The blessing of linguistics on this particular approach—if indeed it may be called blessing—derives from the rather commonsense observation that if one's goal in foreign language teaching includes oral competence and if the linguist's notion of primacy of speech over writing has even limited validity, then there probably should be a heavy component of oral work in the early stages of language learning.

In fact, of course, linguists have always been involved also with written language. It is not only that linguists admit the existence of such phenomena as spelling pronunciation or the use of constructions in writing which do not occur in speech, but the linguist's own professional work has been largely concerned with the analysis of written texts and the devising and manipulation of elaborate systems of transcription. Linguists without paper and pencil or blackboard and chalk find themselves severely handicapped in the most elementary linguistic discussions, and even phonetic textbooks have rarely been provided with accompanying recordings. Most interesting of all in this question of speech versus writing has been the strange insistence on the part of many American linguists that the word "language" should only be applied to speech, not to writing—this from the very group of scholars most convinced of the arbitrary nature of word meanings and the futility of language legislation.

The last several years have seen an increased professional interest by linguists in the phenomena of written language and the interrelationship of speech and writing. A handful of linguists are working on the analysis of writing systems; a number are studying in great detail the relation between orthography and pronunciation and between orthography and morphophonemics and dialect variation; some are even turning directly to the problems of the relationship between written styles and spoken styles. The emphasis on oral competence has been a healthy corrective in the teaching of foreign languages in the United States, and the linguistic primacy of speech over writing must still be asserted. We can now hope, however, that vigorous analyses of writing systems and more sophisticated hypotheses about the relation of speech and writing systems will generate a whole new subfield of applied linguistics in which linguistics will be able to contribute substantially to improvement in language teaching.

The fourth and final principle which we shall examine is somewhat different from the other three in that it places in a broader perspective the language phenomena so important to the linguist. Principle (4): Language behavior is part of a communi-

cation process and takes place within social and situational contexts. Most American linguists regard themselves as social
scientists and very naturally recognize language as a part of
human behavior to be analyzed in socio-cultural terms, but they
have tended not to see the implications of this view in applying
linguistics to language teaching problems.

It has, however, been linguists who have pointed to the
importance of other channels of communication than speech and
have in a series of conferences and special studies attempted to
stimulate or themselves undertake investigations into such "semiotic" phenomena as gestures and bodily movement and so-
called "paralinguistic" behavior, including voice quality and
other non-linguistic vocal signalling. The application of the research results to actual language teaching has been only spora-
dic or amateurish up to the present, but it seems reasonable to
hope that there will be much more research in this field and that
much more thoroughgoing attempts to apply the new knowledge
and insights will be made in connection with foreign language
teaching.

The other half of this principle has also been neglected
far too much by linguistic investigators, and many of its most
obvious implications for language teaching have been disregarded.
Linguists have long recognized the importance of social dialects
and the existence of different levels of style and different modes
of use of language depending on the situation and the role of the
individuals taking part in the communication process, but they
have devoted relatively little research to phenomena of this kind.

It is encouraging that since 1957 a series of conferences
on sociolinguistics have taken place and a number of articles and
volumes of readings in the field have appeared. Linguists are
now actively investigating the linguistic correlates of social stratification, the use of appropriate "registers" in different situatior

and a whole range of problems connected with the functions of language within a given society. The relevance of such research to language learning is clear. The more explicitly the sociolinguistic phenomena are described and analyzed, the better they can be treated in textbooks and classrooms. Examples which come to mind range from teaching the appropriate use of intimate and polite personal pronouns to the teaching of languages with diglossia where two drastically different varieties of the language are used for different purposes. Contrastive studies of pronoun usage and comparable matters such as the use of first names and other marks of informality or intimacy are just beginning, but already a wealth of fascinating information has been brought to light, some of which seems relevant even to early stages of language study.

Here is certainly an area in which linguists, other social scientists, language teachers, and scholars in humanistic studies can join in the investigation of the incredibly complex phenomena of human language and can translate their findings in many cases into improvements in language teaching.

The four principles which we have examined and the two examples of research problems in applied linguistics by no means cover the field or give a full indication of the range of applied linguistics, but they offer some clues as to the trends of the past two decades and possible trends of the years to come. At the present time the application of linguistics to questions of orthographies for unwritten languages, translation of technical documents, and government language policies in multilingual countries probably employ more man-hours of linguists than application in the area of foreign language teaching, but the contributions of linguistics to language teaching problems in the United States in the past twenty years offer assurance that linguistics will continue to play an important role in language teaching and that applied linguistics even in this limited sense will become a professional field in its own right.

10 | On Sociolinguistically Oriented Language Surveys

Many countries in Asia, Africa, and Latin America, as a matter of national development or even of national existence, must answer a set of language questions. The policy decisions which these answers constitute then require implementation, often on a large scale and over long periods of time.

Some of these questions are of <u>language</u> <u>choice</u>: What language(s) shall be the official language(s) of the government, used in laws, administration, and the armed forces? What language(s) shall be used as medium of instruction at the various levels of the educational system? What languages will be accepted for use on the radio, in publishing, in telegrams, and as school subjects?

Other questions involve <u>language</u> <u>"engineering."</u> Once a language has been chosen for certain purposes in a country it may be necessary to take steps to assure its adequacy for these purposes. The questions to be answered generally refer to standardization and modernization: What variety of the language

should be selected or created as the standard form for written
and spoken purposes? What means shall be used to provide
modern terminology and the needed literary and scientific forms
of discourse?

Finding suitable answers to language questions like
these in most of the developing countries is of crucial importance in their economic, political, and social development.
Development of the educational system and development of
communication networks in a country are increasingly recognized as critical elements in national development as a whole,
and both of these are dependent on language policies. Decisions
must be taken on language questions in terms of at least three
important goals: national unity and national identity, access
to modern science and technology, and international communication.

Language policies are rarely set quickly and decisively.
Like many national policies, they often develop gradually,
vacillate, and are modified again even after they are thought to
be final. Occasionally, however, a single decision, e.g. the
choice of Bahasa Indonesia in Indonesia, may have enormous
consequences for the country. Whether the language policies of
a country grow gradually or by jumps, it seems likely that the
decisions involved will be better, i.e. will achieve the desired
results more efficiently, the better the information is on which
the decisions are based.

It must be recognized, of course, that language
policies—again like many other national policies—are not
determined simply on the lines of rational analysis. In fact,
decisions on language questions are notoriously influenced by
emotional issues such as tribal, regional and religious
identification, national rivalries, preservation of elites, and
so on. They may even go directly against all evidence of

feasibility. The fact remains that the availability of accurate,
reliable information on the language situation of a country can
be influential in making policy decisions and is of tremendous
value in planning and carrying out the implementation of the
policies.

Strangely enough, very few countries or regions have
attempted systematic surveys of the language situation. The
most famous such survey was the monumental Linguistic Survey
of India carried out by Sir George Grierson at the turn of the
century, and even today when Indian officials need information
on which to base decisions they have no better source to turn
to. The existence of the LSI does not guarantee sensible decisions, and the LSI is now outdated in its methods and much of
its information, but the availability of such information as is
contained in it has been important.

One of the most important recent attempts to survey
the language situation in a country or region is the West
African Languages Survey carried out since 1960 under the
direction of Professor Joseph Greenberg with the aid of grants
from the Ford Foundation. This survey has concentrated on
the more narrowly linguistic problems of language description,
and most of the publications coming out of it are technical
articles and monographs of more direct interest to professional
linguists than to government officials or language teachers. As
a byproduct of this survey, however, the linguist-investigators
have accumulated a considerable store of information on the
language situation in West African countries, although there
are as yet no definite plans for publication of the material.

Since previous language surveys have generally been
motivated chiefly by interest in the collection of linguistic
data, especially on languages little known or not known at
all to the world of scholarship, it may be useful to describe
the purposes and procedures of a survey not characterized by

this "anthropological purism," as it has been called, but by concern with the language problem of government and, in particular, education.

1. Basic data on major languages. The first task of a country language survey is to determine which are the major languages of the country and to assemble the basic sociolinguistic information about them. Sometimes the determination of major languages is relatively simple, sometimes it is difficult; often the criteria must be worked out for the specific country. For example, Madagascar has two major languages: Malagasy, spoken by 90 per cent of the population; and French, the language of government and education. Bolivia has three: Spanish, Quechua, and Aymara, the native languages of roughly equal thirds of the population. Kenya probably has ten major languages: eight languages spoken by more than 200,000 each; Swahili, a widespread lingua franca; and English, the principal language of government and education.

It is presumably only from these major languages that candidates can be considered for a national language, official language(s) of government, and language(s) as mediums of instruction. In order to make decisions of this kind and—even more important—to undertake the necessary programs of language teaching, materials preparation, teacher training, publication, and so on, further information must be collected about each major language.

Who speaks the language as a first language, where and under what circumstances? To take a simple example, if a given country chooses English as its national language and language of education, and finds it necessary or desirable to have special English teaching materials for speakers of different major languages, the ministry of education must know the geographical extent of each of these languages, the amount of its use in linguistically heterogeneous urban centers, and the social limitations on its use in order to plan distribution of materials and teacher training.

How much dialect variation is there in the language? For example, a given language may be spoken by a third of the population of a country and the government may wish to choose it as a language for literacy training, limited publication, and use as a medium of instruction at the primary level. If, however, the language in question has no standard form, but shows several major dialect areas with strong feelings of dialect identification by the speakers, the government policy may not be feasible.

To what extent is the language used as a second language or lingua franca by others, and to what extent do native speakers of the language use other languages? Two languages may have roughly equal numbers of native speakers, but there is a long tradition of speakers of the one language learning the other in addition, while members of the second speech community do not reciprocate. In such a situation, the government can probably settle for the use of only one of the languages in education.

To what extent is the language used in education? It might be expected that this information would be easy to obtain since the use of a language as the medium of instruction is presumably set by government policy. It often happens, however, that a given language is in fact used in the first two grades of school or as a preliminary step in adult literacy training when government policy either has not required this or has even forbidden it.

2. Language attitudes. In many ways the effectiveness of language policies in education is determined more by the

attitudes of the people on language use than it is by the simple
demographic facts of language distribution and use.   Discovering language attitudes is more difficult than finding the basic
data and also may raise political issues which threaten the
successful carrying out of a language survey, but it is of fundamental importance.

What do the speakers of a language believe or feel
about its esthetic, religious, and "logical" values ?   About the
appropriateness of its use for literature, education, and
"national" purposes ?

What do the speakers of a language believe or feel
about other languages in the country ?   Are they better or
inferior to their own language in general or for specific purposes ?

As an example, speakers of Berber languages generally feel that Arabic is superior to Berber for all purposes
except intimate, domestic conversation.   Speakers of Kurdish
generally feel that Arabic is better than Kurdish for statements
of religious truth and as a lingua franca with Arabs and Muslim
speakers of other languages, but that Kurdish is more expressive and generally better than Arabic for other purposes.
Obviously, educational policies in Arab countries with Berber
or Kurdish minorities are related to this difference of attitude.

3.   Survey techniques.   Linguistic research uses
principally techniques of elicitation, recording, and analysis.
Such techniques are, however, only marginally relevant to a
sociolinguistically oriented survey.   The four techniques most
likely to prove effective are: the culling of information from
published sources, consultation with experts and persons
knowledgeable about specific areas or problems, the use of
questionnaires, and field observation and interviews.   There
is almost no published guidance on these survey techniques;

the best discussion is apparently William Reyburn's "Problems and Procedures in Ethnolinguistic Surveys," reproduced for the American Bible Society in 1956.

In many developing countries a considerable amount of sociolinguistic information can be found in articles, books, monographs, and reports on the area published in the languages of European scholarship, including former colonial languages. The material is generally scattered and difficult of access, and one element of a language survey would be the rather demanding library work of exploring this material for the relevant information.

The most fruitful source of sociolinguistic information in many countries will be consultation with language teachers, missionaries, archeologists, government officials, and other informants. Much can often be done in the capital of a nation, but some consultation must be in the provinces.

Questionnaires can be effective means of collecting sociolinguistic information from special subpopulations, in particular, school and university students. In the case of a country like Ethiopia there is a special resource for this kind of mass data collection: the university students in various parts of the country under a national service scheme.

The critical technique remains the personal on-the-spot investigation of a country survey worker. Collection of data by the other techniques will show gaps and inconsistencies which can only be corrected by observation of classrooms and local life and interviews of selected individuals and groups.

A sociolinguistically oriented language survey of a developing country should be closely associated with whatever linguistic research and teaching is taking place in the country. This usually would mean that the survey would be based at a

university department of languages or linguistics, though in
some cases the survey might be based at a research or language
teaching institution other than a university, if the institution is
clearly the center of linguistic research and training in the
country. In either case the presence of survey personnel and
activities can strengthen the existing work in linguistics and
lead to further development of the university or other institution.

A language survey in a developing country can also
serve as a means of bringing together people who are working
on related problems but who are not normally in touch with
one another. In many countries this means three kinds of
people: scholars in traditional fields of linguistic and philologi-
cal study of Classical and modern literary languages; anthro-
pologically-minded linguists doing field work on local languages;
and foreign language teachers, especially of English and French.
In some cases a further group, literacy specialists, are to be
included.

The most effective means of bringing these different
kinds of people together on a regional basis is the holding of
recurrent international conferences. The International Sym-
posia held every eighteen months under the sponsorship of the
Inter-American Program in Linguistics and Language Teaching,
financed in large part by grants from the Ford Foundation,
have been successful in this, as has the Annual Congress of
the West African Languages Survey. In many developing countries there is very little contact between groups within the
country itself, let alone throughout the region of which it is a
part. International conferences for reading of papers and discussion of specific problems in linguistics and language teaching are not only valuable for the exchange of information, but
also for the strong stimulating effect they have on language
research and the development of teaching materials.

11 | National Sociolinguistic Profile Formulas

Can a condensed, algebraic formula present the socio-linguistic profile of a nation adequately for comparative purposes? It is assumed here that a full-scale description of the language situation in a given country constitutes a useful and important body of data for social scientists of various interests. The question that is raised is whether it is feasible to summarize such a description in a quasi-mathematical way which will make it more convenient in characterizing a nation and more helpful for cross-national comparisons.

The term "language situation" as used here refers to the total configuration of language use at a given time and place, including such data as how many and what kinds of languages are spoken in the area by how many people, under what circumstances, and what the attitudes and beliefs about languages held by the members of the community are. A "sociolinguistic profile" is a special summary description of the language situation based in part on a series of indices and classifications.

A number of sociolinguistic indices and taxonomies have been suggested in the last few years. Greenberg (1956) proposed

eight indices of "linguistic diversity" which would provide, in a
simple numerical form, information about the variety of languages in use in a given area. Ferguson (1962) suggested crude
scales of rating languages by degree of standardization and the
extent of written use, based in large part on Kloss' views (1952,
24-31) of language development. Stewart (1962) devised a sociolinguistic "typology" of languages which classifies languages
according to type and function in a given political unit. Rustow
in the prepublication version of a book on developing countries
(1963) presented a sociolinguistic classification of "linguistic
constellations" in emerging countries. None of these indices
and classifications have yet become widely used, although several of them are now being tried out in sociolinguistic research
projects. [1]

     In the present paper a kind of profile formula is offered
as an answer to the question asked in the first sentence. It is
based, not on a comprehensive theoretical frame of reference,
but on the simple need to summarize and compare mentioned
above, and was developed in class discussions which concerned
the preparation of students' papers describing language situations
in various countries. [2]

     First of all, it seemed clear that in a summary presen-
tation some languages should simply be disregarded as not of
sufficient significance in the total sociolinguistic picture, important and interesting though they might be from some other
points of view. Of the languages to be included in the statements,
some seemed to be clearly of major importance in the process
of national communication, others of less importance, and still
others of little direct communicative importance, but with special statuses which gave them suficient importance to be included. These three kinds of languages may conveniently and trans-

parently be called major language (Lmaj), minor languages (Lmin), and languages of special status (Lspec).

While it was generally clear which languages belonged in which category, in any given country for which we had a substantial amount of information, it was not easy to formalize the criteria which had determined the assignment. Discussion and experimentation led eventually to the following definitions:

A MAJOR LANGUAGE of a given country is a language which has one or more of the following characteristics:

(a) It is spoken as a native language by more than 25% of the population or by more than 1,000,000 people. Example: Quechua in Boliva, where roughly a third of the population speaks Quechua, but Spanish is the only official language and the language of education.

(b) It is an official language of the nation. Example: Irish in Eire, where only 3% of the population speak Irish natively, but it is an official language.

(c) It is the language of education of over 50% of the secondary school graduates of the nation. Example: English in Ethiopia, where only a negligible percentage of the population speaks English natively and Amharic is the official language, but English is the medium of instruction in most of the secondary schools and higher education in the country.

A MINOR LANGUAGE of a given country is a language which has one or more of the following characteristics:

(a) It is spoken as a native language by no more than 25% of

the population and by either more than 5% or more than
100,000 people. Example: Basque in Spain.

(b) It is used as a medium of instruction above the first years
of primary school, having textbooks other than primers published in it. Example: Dagbane in Ghana.

A LANGUAGE OF SPECIAL STATUS in a given country
is one which does not fall in the two preceding categories, but
is used in one of the following ways:

(a) It is widely used for religious purposes. Example: Pali in
Ceylon, where it is the language of the Buddhist scriptures
and is widely studied by monks and scholars.

(b) It is widely used for literary purposes. Example: "Classical" Chinese in Taiwan, used for some forms of modern literature and studied for the classics of older Chinese literature.

(c) It is widely taught as a subject in secondary schools. Example: French in Spain, where most secondary school students
study French as a foreign language.

(d) It is used by a substantial number of people as a lingua franca
within the country. Example: Pidgin English in Liberia,
used for inter-tribal communication along main transporta-
tion routes.

(e) It functions as a major language for an age-sector of the
population. Example: Japanese in Taiwan, where most educated people in the age-group 35-55 were educated in Japanese and still use it for a variety of purposes.

A simple formula based on this threefold classification
of languages within a nation offers basic information on the num-

ber of languages used in a nation. For example, in Spain there
are two major languages: Spanish, which is the official language
and the language of education and wider communication throughout the country; and Catalan, which is the native language of
5,000,000 people in the northeastern part of the country and has
been used fairly extensively for literary purposes. There is one
minor language,[3] Basque, which is the native language of 800,000
in the north and northwest part of the country. There are two
languages of special status: Latin, which is widely used for religious purposes in the Catholic Church, and French, which is
studied by most students in secondary schools. Some of these
facts are summarized in the simple formula:

(1) $$5L = 2Lmaj + 1Lmin + 2Lspec$$

A formula of this kind, however, hardly offers enough information to be of real value for comparative purposes, since so little
information is given about the type and function of the respective
languages. This additional information can be specified simply
and directly by using Stewart's typology. Stewart classified languages into seven types—two of which, his artificial and marginal languages, can be disregarded here. The five basic types
are:

Vernacular (V):	The unstandardized native language of a speech community.
Standard (S):	A Vernacular which has been standardized.
Classical (C):	A Standard which has died out as a native language.
Pidgin (P):	A hybrid language which combines the lexical stock of one language with the grammatical structure of another language or group of languages.
Creole (K):	A Pidgin which has become the native language of a speech community.

It is generally a simple matter to classify a particular
language as one of these types, although the line between V and
S is sometimes difficult to draw. For our purposes a language
will be regarded as S rather than V only if it has reached the
"normal" levels of standardization and use for written purposes
labelled St 1 and W 1 by Ferguson (1962). The formula for
Spain, incorporating the notation of language types, now reads:

(2) $5L = 2Lmaj(2S) + 1Lmin(V) + 2Lspec(C,S).$

The added information about the "types" is less important, however, than information about the functions of the respective languages in the life of the nation. Of the seven functions suggested
by Stewart and represented by lower-case letters, five have
proved with slight modification to be useful in the kind of sociolinguistic analysis attempted here, and two additional functions
have been added. The revised list is as follows:

g: Used primarily for communication within a particular
     speech community, marking it as an identifiable group
     in the nation.
o: Used for official purposes: either designated by law
     as official or used for general governmental, educa-
     tional, and military purposes at the national level.
w: Used as a lingua franca or language of wider commu-
     nication within the nation (Stewart did not distinguish
     between national lingua francas and languages used
     for international communication; see i below.)
e: Used for educational purposes above the first years
     of primary school, having subject matter textbooks
     published in it. (More careful specification of e than
     Stewart indicated proved desirable. Cf. the definition
     of "minor" languages above.)

r: Widely used for religious purposes.

i: Used "internationally" as a language of wider communi-
nication with other nations.

s: Widely studied as a subject in schools.

The expanded formula for Spain now reads:

(3) $5L = 2Lmaj(So, Sg) + 1Lmin(Vg) + 2Lspec(Cr, Ss)$

The Stewart typology makes provision for one additional bit of
information. If a language exists in two varieties in the kind of
functional complementation called diglossia (Ferguson 1959),
this is shown by a colon with C or S on the left and V or K on the
right. Thus, for example, in Morocco Arabic is represented by
C:Vorw, where the lower case "function" letters refer in part to
the C variety and in part to the V variety, in accordance with
the characteristics of diglossia.

Probably one of the most important indicators of language problems in a nation is the number of major languages it
has: the more there are, the more difficult national communication would seem to be. Probably an even more important indicator, however, is the presence or absence of a nationally dominant language. In the sample formulas here the symbol for a
major language will be in boldface if the language represented
is spoken as first or second language by over three-quarters of
the population. Of the fourteen sample national formulas in this
paper, four show a dominant language in this sense: Finland,
Spain, Morocco, and Mexico; Taiwan belongs in this category
if Mandarin Chinese is spoken as a second language by enough
Amoy Chinese speakers there.

In developing profile formulas for certain countries,
the problem arose of how to represent the fact that the total num-

ber of speakers of a group of languages might be quite high even though the speakers of any one of them might be well below the minimum for minor languages. In Ethiopia, for example, such languages as Bilen, Awiya, Afar-Saho, and Harari have numbers of speakers ranging from a few thousand to as many as 50,000, but the total of all may be nearly a million and constitutes a bloc which should be included in the formula. Such substantial blocs of small language communities are regarded as a single language element for the purpose of the profile formulas; they are designated by a raised plus after a number and, in the parenthetical enumerations, by a capital letter enclosed in braces, e.g. $\{V\}$. The letter is usually V, but may be S or unspecified L when appropriate. Thus the formula for Ethiopia includes the component 5^+Lmin(Sei, 4Vg,$\{V\}$). If the total number of speakers in the bloc should reach the minimum figure for a major language, this element would be included in that part of the formula; such would possibly be the case in a country like the Cameroun Republic.

The formulas as presented here fail to show several kinds of information important in the analysis of a language situation, but it proved difficult to devise a symbolization which would not make the formulas too complicated to be readily usable. One kind of information omitted is the extent of dialect diversity within a language, another is the amount of bilingualism or multilingualism among the inhabitants of the country. Also omitted is the difference, which seems of importance in a number of countries, between indigenous and immigrant languages. Finally, no information is offered on the nature of the writing systems used, or on the degree of literacy of the population.

The fourteen countries whose formulas are listed below were chosen chiefly on the basis of availability of data, but some effort was made to have representative coverage of areas and kinds of sociolinguistic profiles. None of the sociolinguistic "giants" (China, India, Indonesia, USSR) were included, but in principle it would be possible to devise formulas for them in spite of their complexity.

[See Table on page 166.]

In an appendix, sample summary descriptions of the language situations in each of four countries are provided in order to explain and justify the formulas. In some respects the summaries themselves are more directly informative and even perhaps more usefully comparable from country to country, which would suggest the need to review or replace the kind of formula used here. It seems profitable, however, to use this kind of formula as a starting point in giving a fully satisfactory answer to the question posed at the beginning of the paper.

APPENDIX

BELGIUM, a country of Western Europe situated on the Atlantic coast and bounded by Netherlands, Germany, Luxembourg, and France, has an area of about 12,000 square miles and a population of about nine million. There are two major languages: Flemish, spoken natively by about 53% of the population, and French, 42%. About a third of the Flemish speakers are bilingual in French, and French has a dominant though declining position in national life. German is the native language of about 2% of the population and has a legal status in certain parts of the country. Flemish and French are both official languages: government administration, military communication,

	Total	Lmaj	Lmin	Lspec
EUROPE				
Belgium	5 =	2(Sowi, So)	+1(Sgs)	+2(Crs, Ss)
Finland	4 =	2(So, Soi)	+0	+2(2Ss)
Hungary	5 =	1(So)	+2(Sg, Sgsi)	+2(Crs, Ssi)
Spain	5 =	2(So, Sg)	+1(Vg)	+2(Crs, Ss)
AFRICA				
Ethiopia	10^+ =	4(Sow, Sg, Vg, Sei)	$+4^+$(4Vg, {V})	+2(2Cr)
Ghana	9^+ =	2(Sowi, Sge)	$+6^+$(2Sge, 3Vg, Ve, {V})	+1(Crs)
Morocco	5 =	3(Corw: V, Sei, Vg)	+2(2Vg)	+0
ASIA				
Ceylon	5 =	3(So, Sg, S(o)ei)	+0	+2(2Cr)
Japan	3 =	1(So)	+1(Sg)	+1(Ssi)
Philippines	11^+ =	9(Sowi, Sog, Sg, 6Vg)	$+0^+$({V})	+2(Cr, S)
Taiwan	5^+ =	3(Sow, 2Vg)	$+0^+$({V})	+1(Cl, Ssi)
AMERICA				
Bolivia	4^+ =	3(So, 2Vg)	$+0^+$({V})	+1(Cr)
Mexico	10^+ =	1(So)	$+6^+$(6Vg, {V})	+3(Cr, 2Ss)
Paraguay	3 =	2(So, Vg)	+0	+1(Cr)

and laws are bilingual. There is a "linguistic frontier" north
of which the official language of local administration is Flemish,
and south of which it is French; the capital, Brussels, is offi-
cially bilingual although largely French-speaking. The medium
of instruction in schools is the locally dominant language, with
provision for use of the other language depending on the number
of students requesting it (25 students per grade for Flemish, 6
for French). The other language is taught as a subject, generally beginning at the third year. A foreign language (English or
German) is required for six years in the secondary schools.
One university is Flemish, one French, and two bilingual. Latin
is used for religious purposes in the Roman Catholic Church,
and is required for six years in the Classical division in secondary schools (about 60%).

FINLAND is the easternmost of the Scandinavian countries,
bounded by Sweden and Norway on the west and the Soviet Union
on the east; its area is about 130,000 square miles, and the
population is about 4.5 million. About 90% of the inhabitants
are native speakers of Finnish, the remainder of Swedish; both
languages are official for use in Parliament, laws, and higher
education. The medium of instruction for lower education is
determined locally by percentage of population: schools in the
minority language must be provided if the number of speakers
in the community is over 12%, but are eliminated if the number
of speakers falls below 8%. Where one of these languages is
the medium, the other is taught as a subject in secondary schools,
i.e. from the 5th to the 12th year. Beginning with the 6th year,
a foreign language, usually English (60%?) or German (40%?),
is studied, and in the last three years a second foreign language
is added. Swedish is used for international communication with
the other Scandinavian countries.

ETHIOPIA, located in the eastern "horn" of Africa, covers

an area of about 450,000 square miles (including the federated
territory of Eritrea in the north), with total population perhaps
about 12,000,000. [4] The major languages spoken natively are
Amharic, the official language (3 to 5 million), Tigrinya (1.3
million), Galla (2.5 million). Of these, Amharic is used extensively for written purposes, Tigrinya somewhat less so, and
Galla is not normally used for writing. English is steadily increasing in importance, with most secondary and higher education now using it as the medium. Out of nearly a score of less
important languages, four are spoken by a quarter of a million
or more: Tigre, Gurage, Somali, and Sidama; of them Somali
is the chief language of neighboring Somalia, Tigre is also spoken in parts of the Sudan, and the other two are confined to
Ethiopia; Sidama is regarded by some as a group of closely
related languages. There are other languages spoken by smaller
numbers of people, totalling altogether possibly a million speakers
The language of the Ethiopian church is a Classical language,
Ge'ez, and (Classical) Arabic is the religious language of the
Muslims. Amharic, Tigrinya, and Ge'ez are all written in the
Ethiopic alphabet, which consists of about 30 consonant letters
which occur with different vowel diacritics and are written from
left to right; there is a special word-divider symbol.

MEXICO, one of the largest Latin American countries, is
bounded on the north by the U.S.A. and on the south by Guatemala;
its area is about 760,000 square miles, and the population is
about 35,000,000. About 90% of the population are native speakers of Spanish; the remaining 3,500,000 are native speakers of
Indian languages. Of about fifty Indian languages in the country
six (Nahuatl, Yucatec, Otomí, Zapotec, Mixtec, Totonac) have
over 100,000 speakers each, and together account for about half
of the speakers of Indian languages. Many, perhaps half, of the
Indian speakers are bilingual — sometimes in two Indian lan-

guages, more often in their native language and Spanish. A
number of the Indian languages are used as the medium of education in the first years of school and have primers published
in them; several are used somewhat more extensively for written purposes. The study of a foreign language is required in the
secondary schools and the most widely studied are English (80%?)
and French (20%?). Private schools exist with French or English as the medium of instruction. Latin is used for religious
purposes in the Roman Catholic Church.

NOTES

[1] For example, Greenberg's "index H" is being used by
Stanley Lieberson (1964, 1965) in his sociolinguistic analysis of
Canadian bilingualism, and Stewart's typology has been used in
studies of language situations in the Caribbean area.

[2] The students' national profile studies were part of the
work of courses in Sociolinguistics offered at the University of
Washington (Summers 1962, 1963) and Georgetown University
(1963-64).

[3] Possibly Galician should be added as a second minor
language, since it is generally classified linguistically as a dialect of Portugese which has been under strong Spanish influence
for a long time.

[4] Demographic estimates for Ethiopia vary widely; the
figures here are based on Ullendorff 1960.

REFERENCES

Ferguson, Charles A. "Diglossia," Word 15 (1959), 325-40. In this volume, pp. 1-26.

_____ "The language factor in national development," Anthropological Linguistics 4:1 (1962), 23-27. Reprinted in Study of the Role of Second Languages in Asia, Africa, and Latin America, ed. by Frank A. Rice (Washington, D.C., 1962), pp. 8-14. In this volume, pp. 51-59.

Greenberg, J. H. "The measurement of linguistic diversity", Language 32 (1956), 109-115.

Kloss, Heinz. Die Entwicklung neuer germanischer Kultursprachen (Munich, 1952).

Lieberson, Stanley. "An extension of Greenberg's measures of linguistic diversity," Language 50 (1964), 526-531.

_____ "Bilingualism in Montreal," American Journal of Sociology 71 (1965), 10-25.

Rustow, Dankwart A. "Political leadership in the emerging countries," 1963. Mimeographed. [A world of nations; problems of political modernization. Washington, D.C.: Brookings Institution, 1967.]

Stewart, William A. "An outline of linguistic typology for describing multilingualism," In Study of the Role of Second Languages in Asia, Africa, and Latin America, ed. by Frank A. Rice (Washington, D. C., 1962), pp. 15-25.

Ullendorff, Edward. The Ethiopians (London, 1960).

DISCUSSION

FERGUSON: What I want to present is an unsatisfactory solution to a problem that some of my students and I have been concerned with for several years: how to compare nations in some useful way in sociolinguistic matters. This grew out of a concern with educational and other problems related to language in developing countries. We wanted to know how to describe a nation in a way that would be useful for comparative purposes within linguistics or sociolinguistics, and also for correlation with economics, political science, and so on. After all, this is a very small universe of discourse—there are somewhere between 100 and 200 countries in the world—and we have other people's classifications of various kinds of political development, and so on. The procedure was to assign students term papers on the 'sociolinguistic situation' or 'language situation' of a particular country. The student was obliged to find out as much as he could about the sociolinguistic situation of that country from whatever sources of information were available, and then phrase his description in any way that he found useful. We subjected the papers to class discussion, and gradually, working through three courses in this way, we began to evolve a kind of format for a summary of language situations: a one-page summary in ordinary English like the four sample descriptions in this paper. But it is hard to compare these one-page summaries, no matter how clear and useful they may be, and so we were tempted to try to put this down in some kind of abbreviated notation. What I'm presenting here today is the kind of notation which has come out of these term papers and class discussions. Perhaps it is useful as a starting point towards giving a more satisfactory answer to this question of how to summarize the language situation in a country for comparative purposes within linguistics or sociolinguistics, and for correlating with other descriptions by economists or political scientists.

HYMES: Maybe in Mexico you should indicate when a distinctive region is associated with a language. There's a lot of difference between a hundred thousand speakers scattered around, as opposed to a hundred thousand in a block.

FERGUSON: That's true; if they're clustered in one place, obviously this in some sense makes them more important than if they are minority groups in a number of places.

DILLON: As a reference was made to Ireland, I feel challenged. I'm relieved to hear that notice is being taken of our situation, and I'm sorry to say that an estimate of 3% of Irish speakers in my opinion would be pretty high—it's nearer 1%. But the fact is that both Irish and English are recognized as official languages.

The Celtic group of languages raises all sorts of problems. In Ireland 1% of the people speak the language from birth. We have the fact that the language is one of the official languages of the country. But the curious thing is that, in the native-speaking areas, the language has no prestige; whereas, when you get to Dublin, the attitude is that it's our national language and our great pride. The contrast with Scotland is interesting. In Scotland, Gaelic is not the official language. But it isn't only the peasants who speak Gaelic—the lawyer speaks it, the teacher speaks it, the minister of the church speaks it—Gaelic is associated in peoples' minds with those in high positions. They hate Lowlanders, and they are proud of being Highlanders, and there are even some of them proud of the fact that they're descended from ancient Irish kings. There is quite a different attitude from that in Ireland. And of course the number of speakers is much higher—there are more than twice as many speakers of the Scottish dialect in Scotland as there are of Irish in Ireland. There are probably more speakers of Irish in Boston than there in Dublin.

What are you going to do with a language like Welsh?
Welsh is spoken by nearly a million people still. It's used in the
courts now; it's used in the schools; it's used in the University.
It's not used as an official language. Is it a major or a minor
language? I don't know where you'd put it in. What about Manx,
which is extinct, but is still recognized as an official language
on public occasions? There is then the question of Breton.
Breton is also widely spoken by nearly a million people. It is
permitted to be taught in the primary schools, although the
French hate it and do all they can to suppress it. But, I think,
in the Catholic private schools it may be favored, and of course
it's a literary language now. These are marginal cases, and I'm
wondering whether you considered them or what you do with them.

FERGUSON: Both Welsh and Breton we regarded as
minor languages, looking at the U.K. as a nation and at France
as a nation. But they are certainly on the borderline between
being minor and major languages.

DILLON: When I was last in Wales, there was a campaign going on—a sort of strike—by which students were parking
their cars in no-parking places in order to get summonsed by the
police — and to insist on their right of being summonsed in Welsh.

BRIGHT: When you were talking about Stewart's classification of types of languages, you mentioned some difference
of opinion on the definition of pidgin, and you gave your own definition of a pidgin language as a hybrid. Now I notice that Professor Kelley spoke of Bazaar Hindustani in his paper as pidgin, and
I assume that that is not a hybrid, but a grammatically simplified
form of Hindi. How then would you classify Bazaar Hindustani,
so far as you know the case, and what is the difference between
you and Stewart in your definitions of pidgin?

FERGUSON: On this point, Stewart is being careful; he didn't want to commit himself as to whether a pidgin had to be a hybrid or not. I don't know what his decision would be on Bazaar Hindustani, but by his definition as I understand it, he would probably allow it.

KELLEY: I would rather not commit myself on pidgin the way you do—that it should have one source lexically and another grammatically. I would prefer to leave the way open to hybridization, both grammatical and lexical. In the case of Bazaar Hindustani, I would expect certain lexical hybridization, because dialects of Bazaar Hindustani vary from place to place, and the source of loans is from the local dialect, very much as in Samarin's Sango.

PAPER: This paper illustrates the many kinds of information that we have never been able to get, or haven't even thought of getting. I wanted to bring up some other examples, because when I read the Mexico profile I thought something was omitted and I couldn't think of it until you were talking this afternoon. Then I remembered that Norman McQuown did his Spoken Turkish, during the Second World War, with a native speaker of Turkish in Mexico City. There is, furthermore, a large Yiddish speaking population in Mexico City. There is a Yiddish-language school system that is both the only school system that many children go to as well as a supplementary system; there is at least one newspaper, book publication, and so forth. I suppose a similar situation exists with Lebanese Arabic in Brazil.

FERGUSON: Or with Gujarati in Kenya, or something like that. I meant to mention that we don't distinguish in these formulas between so-called 'indigenous' languages and 'immigrant' languages, which is a distinction often made very strongly in the countries we are talking about. But if, let us say,

Yiddish in Mexico meets the other criteria, then it should have been put in. We knew that there were schools in Yiddish, and also schools conducted completely in French. Probably we didn't include them because the numbers were too small.

LAW: There's one thing which was left out of your formulas which is rather important to me—that is, the total number of languages reported for a particular area. We realize of course that such figures are inaccurate for many countries, because we are discovering new languages, and things of this sort. But I thought it might be worthwhile to try including it, and I would suggest you might consider including it as a denominator beneath your first number. That is, for Mexico it would be 10 over such and such a number; you are considering 10 languages out of the total number reported for the area.

FERGUSON: We did consider putting the total number of languages in somewhere, and the problem was really with the immigrant languages. In a country like Canada, for example, there are large numbers of immigrant languages. There are probably more speakers of Italian in Toronto than any city outside Rome. But the usual figures you get for the number of languages in a country don't include those languages. And I might say, while I'm mentioning immigrant languages, that this problem is not limited to the kind of immigrant groups that we have in the United States. Actually the best example we had of this was in Sarawak and North Borneo, where the percentage of Chinese is increasing rapidly; in fact, it has already reached about 30% of the population, and their birth rate is higher. So it seems that within a few decades the Chinese will far outnumber the Sea Dyaks, Land Dyaks, etc.; and yet Chinese is regarded as a foreign language, an immigrant language, both by the Chinese and the local people, even though the Chinese speakers are citizens.

HAUGEN: You might need to make provision for restoring other languages in your formulas, to give some of this other information that has been mentioned by so many speakers, and that we'd like to have in a complete survey of languages of the world. For instance, in Scandinavia, a minor language is Lappish, and Lappish doesn't get in by any of your formulas.

FERGUSON: It doesn't get in for Finland, here, for example.

HAUGEN: Nor for Sweden, or Russia, or even for Norway, although in Norway there are 30,000 speakers and it is taught in the schools. Both in Norway and Sweden there are professorships of the language in the universities. Here is a language that gets split between several countries and as a result falls out, so to speak, between the partitions of your grid. Faroese is another one, which is now a standard language and has been for a hundred years, but has a very low official status and only 30,000 speakers. Yet it has a literature, a good dictionary, and a professorship in Copenhagen. What do we do with it?

FERGUSON: If it has a substantial literature, then it could be regarded as a special language with a special status and would be called "S1" in this case.

HAUGEN: But it doesn't have a special status. It's rather a small areal language, like some of the ones that have been already mentioned. I think the concept of area is a very important one, for a population which has a sense of cohesion and national significance, and more and more people are going to develop it, I'm sure, in the next hundred years.

FERGUSON: Of course, if Faroese were spoken in India, it would be disregarded—30,000 people with a standard language off on a couple of islands somewhere. . .

P. IVIĆ: I am not so sure that the nation-wide group languages are of lesser importance than regional languages. Let's take the case of inter-war Poland. Yiddish was used by about 10% of the population—the Jews, scattered throughout the nation in practically all towns and cities. Thus Yiddish was a nation-wide reality; whereas the Byelorussian language, which was spoken by roughly the same number of people in Poland, was a regional reality.

I also question the definitions of the 'official language.' In some countries, like Yugoslavia, there are official languages which are really nation-wide, then there are those of provincial importance, and finally there are languages which are official only in certain communities. For instance the Slovak language, having about 50,000 speakers in Yugoslavia, is official in the communities where it is spoken. Should we treat it equally with Serbo-Croatian?

FERGUSON: We did decide to include languages which were regionally official, so to speak; but that raises the question that some official languages are more official, let us say, more widely used than others. And I know that Stewart is wrestling with that problem, too, not only in the case of 'official' but in some of these others. He is thinking of some sub-divisions or additional functions, when languages of one function or another are nation-wide rather than local. But by these formulas we would include the letter "o" beside a language which was used as a regional official language.

P. IVIĆ: Another point is, what do the words "widely used for religious purposes" mean? Here also we need more precision. In Yugoslavia there is an Eastern Orthodox population embracing about one half of the inhabitants and using Old Church Slavonic in churches, while about 40% of the people are Roman Catholics using Latin. Obviously, these two languages should be considered as widely used. But what about Arabic, used by the Moslems who make up some 10% of the population? And finally there is a small Jewish population using Hebrew for religious purposes. Where is the limit?

FERGUSON: I don't know how to answer that question. We speculated about what we would include for the United States as widely used for religious purposes, and I think we decided on Latin, Greek, Old Church Slavonic, Hebrew—but I'm not quite sure what our criteria were.

P. IVIĆ: Another intricate question is that of languages widely taught in secondary schools. Would it be proper to regard, e.g., four foreign languages which are all taught widely in secondary schools as a characteristic of the nation? In Yugoslavia there are four languages of this kind—English, Russian, French, and German; and the percentage of students is now about the same (in fact, in most schools the students have the choice of two out of four). Should all four be in the list?

FERGUSON: I agree that we should have more precise limitation. It so happened that in the fourteen countries we studied here it was relatively easy to decide which languages were relatively more important than others. In Spain, for example, almost everybody takes French in schools although you can take English or German. One could even exclude Greek from Belgium, for example, although many students study Greek there whereas you couldn't exclude Latin from the school system, since probably 60% of secondary school graduates in Belgium have had six years of Latin.

BRYAN: There is one aspect of the linguistic description of a country that you haven't touched on, and I'm wondering if you've neglected it as irrelevant, or as completely hopeless, that is whether the different languages are or are not related to each other. If you were describing the linguistic situation in Tanganyika, Swahili, the official language, and the other languages spoken there (some of them by large numbers of people, and some of course by only a few thousand) are mostly demonstrably related. And English is demonstrably not. Or in the Sudan, for instance, there are a very large number of languages, many of them demonstrably not related. Amharic and Galla are distantly related, but how distantly? Greenberg would relate them more closely than I would. Well, anybody who knows anything about African linguistic classification knows that there is at present a great debate on such matters between the British Africanists and the American Africanists. So some languages are not related, some demonstrably are, and others the linguists are still scrapping over. Are you going to try and cope with that situation at all?

FERGUSON: I should have mentioned that explicitly as one of the things unfortunately not covered in the formulas. Dialect diversity within a single language isn't shown. But even if we did include that in the formulas, I would prefer to put it in terms not of genetic relationship, but of some other measure of similarity, because what really matters here is the ease of learning the various languages, rather than some precise degree of relationship.

BRYAN: The fact of the matter is that the outlook of Swahili as the official language in Tanganyika is pretty good precisely because of its close relation to its neighbors.

McDAVID: I might mention one complicated system, dating from my Burmese avatar. As my informants of 1942-45 reported the situation, before the war English had official status in Burma. Among the people of the country, Burmese was the dominant everyday language; there was, besides, an ecclesiastical language, Pali, and a learned language, Sanskrit. In addition, under the British administration, before Burma was separated from India, all arms of civil administration were a part of the Indian civil service. In consequence, down to independence the Burmese civil service, railroads, and telegraph were largely manned by people of Indian descent, with Hindustani the operational language of these official functions; in the capital, Rangoon, there was more Hindustani spoken than Burmese. And in Burma, as elsewhere in southeast Asia, the Chinese proved themselves so enterprising that for all practical purposes Chinese was the language of finance and retail trade. In addition there were various ethnic minorities, of greater or less size, with more or less official recognition of their language. There was consequently some difficulty in calculating how extensively each of these languages was used.

But we can find an equally difficult situation closer to home, where it is exceptionally difficult to get accurate figures on the use of other languages than English in the United States. In an effort to discover what languages are used how extensively and by whom, Einar Haugen, Joshua Fishman and I have been pounding a number of tables. All we can say is that it is less difficult to get the figures for first-generation immigrant speakers than it is to learn the numbers of speakers of languages that have been long domiciled in this country, whether aboriginal or colonial or immigrant. According to the 1960 census, there are only twelve hundred native speakers of French in Louisiana, because the census office records only what it calls the "mother tongue of the foreign born." It presumes that every native-born American, wherever residing and of whatever parentage, is a native speaker of English. A further complication in this situation is that only one "mother tongue" is recorded for each speaker, and when in doubt the census-taker puts down the official language of the nation from which the immigrants came, so that Swiss, Luxemburgers, Belgians, and Ashkenazic Jews are not fairly described from a linguistic point of view. The simple-

mindedness of the census deprives us of information about many
of the interesting language situations with which we are concerned.

FERGUSON: It might interest you to know that as major
languages for the United States we agreed on English, German,
Italian, Spanish, Polish, Yiddish, in that order. That is, these
all fulfilled the criteria for major language, which came as a
surprise to those of us who were speculating about it.

On the question of the census, just try suggesting to the
Bureau of Census that they should add just one more question to
the questionnaires—say, what third language is spoken— and
you'll realize that there's pressure from a hundred and one groups
to get additional questions onto the census, all of which are said
to be vital to understanding how America functions. The Bureau
of the Census people are naturally slow to add questions.

FRIEDRICH: Dr. Dillon mentioned the Scotch Gaelic
and Dr. Haugen the Lappish case. It seems to me that your
criteria for ranking these languages and deciding whether to
include them were heavily behavioristic. That is, you were
looking for things that you could see and measure: do they use it
in a church, use it in parliament, things of that sort. This has
the virtues of objectivity, but also the weakness of avoiding
things that you can't measure in a certain way. It also will elicit
a cry of protest from people who think that some language matters a lot in their country. Now maybe the Norwegians feel that
Lappish matters a lot. I feel that way about Tarascan, which
just happens to fall out of your study because it doesn't have a
hundred thousand people; but this is a language of great symbolic significance within Mexico. It has a considerable status and
prestige. Also in the U. S. there is great difference in the symbolic statuses of languages. Some are quite large, but the people don't care very much; others have high standing in certain
ways. I think one could avoid the dangers of the subjective fac-

tor by perhaps working out a few standard questions which one would put to the people who are in a position to know, or to the population in question.

GARFINKEL: I have two comments. First, when I reflect on your reservations about your profile 'dimensions,' I'm struck by the fact that the properties you use as rules to analyze an actual linguistic community depend, for their character as 'appropriate interpretations' of an actual case, upon the existence of members' own knowledge of 'systematic' properties of their common linguistic practices, and on members' uses of these properties as rule-like bases for conducting their everyday affairs. In this way members' practical linguistic activities are measures which insure the 'appropriateness' with which your rules analyze a situation. However, no notice is taken of this characteristic of the linguistic community.

Second, in addition to your set of formulas for characterizing linguistic situations, there ought to be another section with the heading: "Practical advice to whomsoever might seek to insure the usefulness of the formulas to analyze the situations.' Such a section, and the practical advice it contains, are dictated by our task. For example, consider the rule, "5= 2(Sowi, So)" and the rest, for Belgium. Our task is to treat an actual linguistic situation in such ways as to make this rule a correct method for analyzing the actual situation. In order to accomplish this task and to assure its continued accomplishment, we depend upon the right to talk about and to make something of linguistic situations and methods for analyzing them. Professionals—linguists, anthropologists, sociologists—claim such rights from and assign them to each other by reason of association membership. From a knowledge of the practices that make up the ways of offering and claiming professional competence, we can make out the advice that professionals use, that they don't need to be told about, when it comes to seeing how a situation may be treated to make a rule right.

One piece of advice runs: "Read the rule like this, '5= 2 (Sowi, So), and so forth'; i.e., to see the rule, add and so forth." A second piece of advice: "Read the rule so as to include, as part of what it is talking about, any and all considerations of unless, considerations which Any Member knows need not and cannot be cited before they are needed, though No Member is at a loss when the need is clear." We saw that come up today.

A third item of advice runs: "In the course of seeing that a rule applies, the use of and so forth and unless can introduce any matter whatsoever, thereby raising questions of where any of it ought appropriately to begin or end. Read the rule, therefore, with the proviso "Let it pass," or "Enough is enough as Anyone knows." For example, here is Belgium. We have the question, "Does this rule apply?" Well, there is this, and this, and that, and so—well, "Let it pass, enough is enough, we have to get done."

Finally, I've been told of a practice for seeing that a rule applies, called "Factum valet." It is said to mean that an action otherwise prohibited by rule is to be treated as correct if it happens nevertheless.

I am not carping or finding fault. I'm quite serious. I propose that such practices—admittedly I've only given a rough and ready characterization of them—are part and parcel of what we are doing in "using a rule" or in recognizing that a rule applies, or when we're said to be following a rule.

FERGUSON: I wonder if, in presenting these alleged facts about various countries, I was misleading some of you into thinking that, if you asked a native of one of these countries, you'd get full agreement with the formula that I've presented here. I'm sure that for almost every one of the fourteen countries, there would be serious questions raised by people of the

country. But it might be very useful to attach to these some
statements—perhaps not quite along the line suggested by
Dr. Garfinkel, but certainly somewhat similar—statements
which would explain the attitudes of various segments of the
population on these particular questions, because these are also
part of the language situation. That is, whether a language is
used as a means of education or not is one important question.
Whether a large segment of the population believe it <u>should</u> be
used as a medium of education or not is another important question. And this second kind of thing is not in the formulas at all.

GARFINKEL: I suggest that the very features you treat
as shortcomings of your method, as troubles for which you seek
remedies, are essential characteristics of linguistic situations
and may be of critical interest in themselves. I'm arguing that
linguistic phenomena, in that they consist of members' common
ways of talking, are <u>methods</u> for producing organizations of
everyday activities. As methods of organizational production,
these common ways of talking are themselves also <u>features</u>
of organized activities of everyday life. In their character as
method and feature of organized everyday activities, linguistic
phenomena are essentially equivocal phenomena. As matters
stand right now, we are conducting studies of common linguistic
practices as if we only lack the good sense or wit or training or
mathematics to repair this equivocality, and that its repair
rather than its study is required to bring common linguistic
practices under the jurisdiction of rigorous methods of description. But I urge that this essential equivocality requires examination in its own right.

12 | Sentence Deviance in Linguistics and Language Teaching

Randolph Quirk's excellent paper, "Types of Deviance in English Sentences,"* asserts that the issues discussed in it "have an immediate relevance and a reasonably direct application to language learning and the teaching of English." It is the purpose of my paper to explore these issues and some closely related ones in order to see this relevance and possible application.

Although linguists have almost universally recognized the great variability of language behavior even within a single speech community, they have made their greatest advances in techniques of analysis and sophistication of theory by operating with language as though it were uniform or nearly so. One of the first steps in any kind of linguistic analysis is the delimitation of the range of behavior covered, whether this is done in terms of the identification of a particular speech community or context of situation or in terms of the specification of a corpus to be analyzed. Sometimes this essential preliminary delimitation, has been done carefully and explicitly, sometimes less carefully and without explicit statement, but it is always there, and it has often been the exclusion of troublesome "abnormal" language

_____

*A Common Purpose, ed. by J. R. Squire (Champaign, Illinois: National Council of Teachers of English, 1966), pp. 46-60.

material from consideration which has enabled the linguistic
analyst to achieve the precision and elegance he so prizes.

There can, of course, be no quarrel with a working
procedure which allows for such handsome results, and I would
assume that the main stream of linguistic analysis for some
time to come will continue to follow this procedure, seen in its
most explicit form possibly in the all-or-none assumption of
grammaticality made in some formulations of transformational
generative grammar.[1] Quirk's paper, however, illustrates
another trend in modern linguistics—the attempt to devise procedures and approaches which will do justice to the extreme
variability of human language behavior without losing the great
gains of the last century in linguistics.[2] Part of my paper will
deal with this trend in linguistics and some of its implications
and its problems.

Language Variability and Classroom Teaching

The contribution which linguistics has offered to language teaching, whether native language or foreign language,
has been largely concerned either with the transfer to language
teachers and textbook writers of certain of the linguists' attitudes toward language or with the use of linguists' precise
statements about the facts of particular languages in planning
courses or doing classroom teaching. It would be difficult to
deny the value of this contribution, even if it does not justify
the claims of some of the enthusiasts for a "linguistic method"
of language teaching and some of the believers in the magic of
courses in "applied linguistics." But insofar as the linguist's
perfectly legitimate working procedure of assuming a fictive
uniformity in language has been transferred as a basic assumption to textbooks and language teaching, some damage has been
done, or, let us say, the full potential contribution of linguistics has not been utilized. Also, insofar as linguists' descrip-

tions of particular languages, presented in the framework of
fictive uniformity, have led to poor pedagogical procedures
because of the need for students to acquire varying patterns of
language behavior, a disservice has been done. Accordingly,
a later part of my paper will deal—all too briefly—with pedagogical questions.

Up to this point we have had before us as examples of
the issues under discussion only the illustrations and test sentences of the Quirk paper. I would like to add an example of
deviance which may make clear the general nature of this problem for linguistics and for language teaching. In the Arabic
speaking world most uses of the language seem to cluster
around two norms, often called Classical Arabic (al-lugha al-
fuṣḥā) and Colloquial Arabic (al-lugha al-ᶜāmmīya). The
former is the vehicle of most Arabic literature and much formal speaking; the latter is the medium of informal communication.[3] Linguists following their usual working procedure of
assuming uniformity, have written excellent descriptions of
the Classical language and regional varieties of the Colloquial.[4]
It is also true, however, that speakers of Arabic in many situations use intermediate forms of the language or mixtures of the
two polar types. In a semiformal discussion of a technical
subject, for example, the speakers will use vocabulary, forms,
and constructions from both norms. Of the hundreds of linguistic studies of Arabic, only a handful have attempted a description of these intermediate or mixed forms of the language,[5]
and even these attempts have not been outstandingly successful.
What is more, almost all linguistically oriented teaching of
Arabic has concentrated either on Classical or Colloquial or
each in turn: there is no published textbook which gives the
student much guidance on the intermediate or mixed varieties.
Instructors of Arabic agree that one of the objectives of Arabic
teaching must be to give the students competence in using the
in-between kinds of Arabic, yet no one has offered a satisfactory, systematic way of doing so.

This example has been offered as a fairly dramatic
illustration of the basic issue suggested by Quirk's paper,
which may be summarized somewhat crudely in these statements: (1) Much human language behavior is highly variable
and full of "abnormalities." (2) Linguists do not yet know how
to analyze highly variable language behavior. (3) Language
teachers often need to teach such highly variable behavior in
order to reach their objectives.

Sentence Deviance

Let us examine four major types of sentence deviance,
some of them well represented in Quirk's material, others for
one reason or another excluded from his study. Although the
discussion here is limited to sentences, it must be noted that
analogous types of deviance exist at other levels such as phonology and larger-than-sentence units and in general would show
the same kind of relevance to linguistics and language learning.
The term deviance here, following Quirk's use, refers to sam-
ples of language which for any reason are not regarded by users
of the language as fully acceptable. It is not intended to suggest
that language material can always be fruitfully analyzed in terms
of norms and deviations from them.

Interference. Some deviance is related to knowledge
of other languages or dialects on the part of the speaker. Quirk's
illustrative sentence 2, I am living here since two years, is an
example of this. He says the sentence "manifests deviance of
which only a foreign learner is likely to be capable," and ex-
cludes this type as irrelevant to his discussion. This exclusion
is perfectly legitimate within the terms of Quirk's study, but
it must be acknowledged that this kind of deviance, customarily
called interference, is of great interest and importance for

linguists, psychologists, and language teachers concerned
with the process of language acquisition.

What psychological mechanism accounts for the kind
of interference shown in Quirk's sentence 2 ? Explanation of
this question is bound to produce hypotheses about language
behavior of direct value to the linguist who wants to construct
a general theory of human language. The extensive work on
contrastive analysis of languages is beginning to make some
progress here, but the field remains disorganized. [6] Linguists
have not yet even agreed on useful procedures for contrastive
analysis, and what is more serious, no one has yet provided
a coherent theory of interference which would bridge the gap
between even the most sophisticated contrastive analyses and
observed language behavior.

It is also possible that most of the deviance which we
will classify under other major types could also be fruitfully
studied as exemplifying interference. Such an approach would
see all variability in language behavior as the result of competing norms and mutual interference. At our present state of
understanding of this whole process, however, it seems more
profitable to limit the study of interference to the most obvious
cases and to leave extensions of the concept for later.

The relevance of this kind of deviance for the foreign
language teacher is indeed accepted now but we can point out
that English teachers in the United States also meet the problem of interference in two general cases: (a) with students who
have another language as their mother tongue, including in
particular several million Spanish speakers in the Southwest
and in New York and other urban centers, and (b) with students
whose home language is a variety of English so divergent from
the standard as to cause serious problems. In both these cases

it would seem that a study of interference as well as of the
relevant facts of the mother tongue would be of value to the
English teachers.

Dialects. Most linguistic research on the question of
variation within a language has been concerned with the notion
of dialect differences, especially those that can be shown on
maps. The systematic study of regional dialect variation
which began in Europe in the early nineteenth century had
already made a considerable contribution to the linguists'
understanding of language behavior before the structuralist
approach of the twenties and thirties began its spectacular
development. In recent decades we have seen the combination
of older work in dialect geography with the more recent insights
and methods of structural description,[7] and this promises still
greater contribution. Strangely enough Quirk does not even
allude to deviance related to regional differences in English.
His Operation and Judgment Tests would be quite applicable
to this kind of deviance. For example, I didn't visit him, but
I should have done would be rated much more acceptable by
millions of Commonwealth speakers than by North Americans
who prefer I should have or I should have done so. Or the use
of the auxiliary do with have would show striking regional differences in acceptability. We can only assume either that
Quirk was not interested in this kind of deviance or that his
subjects were too homogeneous by this dimension to make
study of it worthwhile.

Another kind of dialect difference is more closely
related to the problems Quirk is dealing with, that of social
dialects. Linguists have generally recognized that the linguistic differences in any speech community tend to correlate, in
part, with lines of social cleavage in the community, and the
same dialectological machinery of isoglosses, innovations,
waves, bundles, and so on can be used in studying social

dialect differences. Until fairly recently, however, relatively
little was done in social dialects compared to the work in
regional dialects, possibly because the latter are so universally
mappable, lending themselves more readily to geographic presentation. Another reason has probably been the lack of analyses of social stratification which were as clear and usable as
the facts of geography.

    This field cannot be ignored, however, by anyone
interested in questions of grammatical acceptability, since it
often happens that what is deviant in one segment of the speech
community is accepted as the norm in another segment. Quirk's
sample sentence 1, <u>Him and her don't want no cake</u>, would presumably have been rejected by most of his university subjects,
but I think it likely that there are subjects who would find such
a sentence acceptable and would reject a more standard version, although I am not sure that the Quirk techniques, requi-
ring command of the standard language, would be appropriate
for the kind of testing needed. This is simply another indication of how customary it is for linguists working on English to
limit themselves to the kind of English they personally use.
Apart from the pioneering work of Fries some decades ago
and isolated examples since then, published linguists' studies
of American English have dealt with the kind of English used
at universities, forgetting that in some respects it surely
represents a minority usage which might be regarded as un-
acceptable by many speakers. [8]

    I labor this point here only to emphasize that not all
differences in "grammaticality" are of the same type; they
frequently have a close relationship to differences in social
dialect and can best be analyzed in connection with systematic
study of social dialect phenomena. Quirk notes in two places
(p. 49 and p. 51) the relevance of the prescriptive tradition
to the problem of acceptability, but he nowhere notes the

probably greater importance of the whole structure of social dialects in which standard and prescriptive ideals are both embedded.

Register and style. The two kinds of deviance identified above generally characterize one group of speakers as opposed to another, and each individual speaker normally shows one kind of interference (e. g. Spanish interference with English) or speaks one regional or social dialect (e. g. educated middle class Chicago English). Some kinds of deviance, however, are part of the repertory of each individual in the sense that he sometimes finds one form appropriate and sometimes another. This includes such differences as the levels of formal, informal, and intimate,[9] as well as situational or status-and-role differences such as different varieties for the professor and student, parent and child, doctor and patient, and so on. Differences of this kind are referred to by many British linguists as differences in register, and the term is a convenient one. Quirk in his book The Use of English has presented this kind of variation very effectively in a popular way, and he seems to be referring to it by the phrase "medium deviation" in the final paragraph of his paper. The actual experiment he reports, however, seems to exclude this dimension from consideration. It would seem likely that explicit indication of appropriate register or context of situation would have affected the acceptability judgments in certain cases, and that future experimentation of this kind must take more explicit notice of register deviance.

Another kind of deviance is suggested by Quirk's terms "ordinary" and "difficult" in his final paragraph. This kind is very similar to the traditional notion of stylistic differences and deserves an important place in any systematic study of literature. This kind of deviance includes not only the notion of a distinct literary style or special styles appro-

priate to different literary genres, but also the individual stylistic differences which seem to occur at all levels, dialects,
and registers—literary and nonliterary. Like other kinds of
deviance, it needs continued investigation and has obvious pedagogical relevance.

Theory of Deviance

Before going on to comment about pedagogical application, it may be worthwhile to return briefly to the linguists'
assumption of uniformity mentioned before. Linguists not only
operate with an assumption of fictive uniformity which makes
analysis easier, but they also often seem to assume that all
variation can best be accounted for in terms of deviation from
the uniform language they describe. Perhaps the transforma-
tionalists make this assumption most explicitly with their
notion of a generative grammar of "all and only" grammatical
sentences, plus a set of rules for using that grammar to
account for deviant material.

There is no question that the norm-with-deviance
view is a useful model of language behavior, but it seems quite
probable that it is an inadequate model from a number of points
of view. There is, for example, the relatively trivial matter
that at certain points in any language there seems to be no
acceptable form or sequence—all is deviation. For example,
standard American English has no acceptable past participle
for wake; Quirk's sentence 22, Neither I nor he felt a thing,
has no acceptable present-tense equivalent.

Second, and more important, is the familiar difficulty
of determining the norm: just what should be regarded as
"grammatical" or "acceptable"? Whether the grammar is being
written for a single variety of a language or for the whole

language, the question arises whether the descriptive norm
should be based on informant reaction (the so-called "intuition"
of the native speaker) or on distribution-frequency measures,
or on criteria related to simplicity or accessibility of the description.   There are many techniques, statistical and otherwise,
for handling variation throughout a corpus or population without references to a norm.

Finally, human beings from a very early age produce
with great frequency a wide range of fragmentary utterances,
blends, hesitations, omissions, slips-of-the-tongue, and so
on.   Some of these phenomena are patterned and are very
likely learned in much the same way that the "normal" patterns
are learned; others may be of quite different origin.   In any
case, it seems quite clear that before the child has mastered
the basic grammar of his native language, he has already
"learned" how to misbehave with his language.   It seems to me
entirely plausible that a grammar which fails to account for
"all and only" the grammatical possibilities but can generate
an impressive array of abnormalities, i.e. nongrammatical
possibilities, could be considered a more powerful grammar
—and in some practical ways a more useful one—than a grammar which elegantly generates all the grammatical items but
fails to predict any abnormalities.

Pedagogy

Quirk's assertion of the pedagogical relevance of the
issues of his paper is well founded, and the discussion in the
first two sections of this paper amplifies and emphasizes it.
Two points can be made in this connection.   One is the great
need for additional information about deviance of all types in
English so that the data can be used in the preparation of
teaching materials and the planning of course content.   One
reason that students in American schools have not been taught

more about American dialect differences is that reliable information about such differences has rarely been available in the
form in which it could be used. This is even more true for the
other kinds of deviance.

The second point is the need for experimentation in
the teaching of variable language behavior. The Arabic example given previously is a clear indication of the need, but the
problem is there for almost any kind of language teaching.
Almost no consideration has been given to the problem of
teaching a student how to shift from one register to another,
or one style to another, let alone some of the finer problems
of perception and production related to the issues of Quirk's
paper.

NOTES

[1]Cf . N. Chomsky, Syntactic Structures (The Hague:
Mouton and Company, 1957), pp. 13-14.

[2]Cf. Word, XIII (1957), 477-8.

[3]For a further statement of the situation see C. A.
Ferguson, "Diglossia," Word, XVI (1959), 325-40. Repr. in
D. Hymes (ed.), Language in Culture and Society (New York:
Harper and Row, 1964), pp. 429-39.

[4]E.g., J. Cantineau, "Esquisse d'une Phonologie de
l'Arabe Classique," Bulletin de la Société de Linguistique de
Paris, XLIII (1946), 93-140; R. S. Harrell, Phonology of
Egyptian Colloquial Arabic (New York: American Council of
Learned Societies, 1957).

[5]E.g., H. Blanc, "Style Variations in Spoken Arabic,"
pp. 81-156 and R.S. Harrell, "A Linguistic Analysis of Egyptian Radio Arabic," pp. 3-77 in C. A. Ferguson (ed.), Contributions to Arabic Linguistics (Cambridge: Harvard University Press, 1960).

[6]Cf. J. H. Hammer and F. A. Rice (eds.), A Bibliography of Contrastive Linguistics (Washington: 1965).

[7]Cf. U. Weinreich, "Is a Structural Dialectology Possible," Word, X (1954), 168-280; and subsequent articles by Moulton, Stankiewicz, Ivić and others. Cf. also S. Saporta, "Ordered Rules, Dialect Differences, and Historical Processes," Language, XLI (1965), 218-24.

[8]For a useful recent collection of papers, see Roger Shuy (ed.), Social Dialects and Language Learning (Champaign, Ill.: National Council of Teachers of English, 1965), especially the chapters by Stewart and Labov.

[9]R. C. Pooley, Teaching English Usage (New York: Appleton-Century-Crofts, 1946) especially chapter III, Levels in English Usage; M. Joos, The Five Clocks, International Journal of American Linguistics, 28.2 (April 1962).

13 | St. Stefan of Perm and Applied Linguistics

Dedicated to Roman Jakobson

The fourteenth-century Russian Orthodox bishop of Perm, St. Stefan, "Apostle of the Zyrians", is almost completely unknown today among both hagiographers and specialists in applied linguistics. [1] Yet this unusual man dealt with all the major problems of linguistic development in a non-literate society and devised solutions well worth consideration today by workers in applied linguistics facing the same problems in the developing countries of Asia, Africa, and Latin America. Similarly, his missionary strategy deserves study by church historians and theologians of Christian mission, not only in terms of success and failure but also in terms of the religious background from which it sprang and its subsequent fate.

Culture change related to socio-economic development is often tied to the spread of religious systems, and in the case of two major world religions, Buddhism and Christianity the use of local languages and the invention of new alphabets have sometimes received explicit ideological approval as a policy

in missionary expansion.[2] St. Stefan's efforts will be examined
here as a case study in the general area of language aspects of
national development.[3]

1.1 St. Stefan.[4]—Stefan was born about the year 1335 in
Ustjug, a town in the area of the Zyrians or Komi[5] where there
had been a settlement of Russians as early as 1212. He was
apparently Russian in origin and culture, but from early childhood he was familiar with the living conditions, character,
and language of the Komi who lived around him. In 1365 he
entered a monastery at Rostov where he spent thirteen years
in study and training, including the study of Greek. He was
strongly influenced by the great Sergius of Radonezh, probably
the most loved of the Russian saints, and is accounted one of
his important disciples. Among his fellow monks Stefan was
admired for the unusual holiness of his personal life and his
sensitivity to the feelings and wants of others. Finally he was
ordained to the priesthood and returned to his homeland to pro-
claim the gospel to the Komi. As he set himself to this task
he found great resistance among the Komi, stemming partly
from their loyalty to their own customs and the traditional
shamanistic religion of the people and partly from the growing
opposition to the Russians, who had begun to settle in the
region as early as the eleventh century but were now beginning
to take a position of economic and political dominance.

Stefan's attitude toward the Komi form of paganism
was uncompromising: he fought the resistance movement led
by Pam, the chief shaman, and he steadily replaced the local
shrines and their pagan decorations by Christian churches with
images of saints. On the other hand, he sympathized with the
Komi in their opposition to the Russians: he made extensive
use of the Komi language and he often took the side of the
Komi in controversies with the Russians. He invented an
alphabet for the Komi language and translated major parts of

the liturgy into Komi, thus giving Komi the oldest literary
monuments of any Uralic language except Hungarian, and he
introduced the use of Komi in public worship and in the schools
which he established. [6]

Whether by virtue of these policies or by his demon-
strated bravery and his model Christian life—contrasting
sharply with that of many of his fellow Russians—Stefan was
remarkably successful in his missionary work, and during
his lifetime he saw the majority of the Komi baptized into the
Orthodox Church. In 1383 he was made the first bishop of
Perm, with seat in Ust'vym. Stefan visited Moscow on a number of occasions, and died there in 1396. He is commemorated
in Orthodox Churches on April 26, presumably the date of his
death, and his sainthood has also been recognized by the
Roman Catholic Church even though he lived after the great
schism between East and West.

1.2 After St. Stefan. [7]—With the death of Stefan the Komi
people began their history of five centuries of loyalty to the
Orthodox Church, love and reverence for the name of St. Stefan,
and pride in the early possession of a literary language of
their own. Stefan's successors, however, were not of his
calibre, and neither Russians nor Komi carried his linguistic
work much further. [8] The history of Old Permian literature is
mostly the copying and recopying of translations made by
Stefan himself or shortly after his time. The next burst of
literary activity was not until the nineteenth century, when
Komi nationalist stirrings gave rise to some new works;
because of the czarist prohibition of any written use of the
Komi language apart from religious purposes, the works seem
all to have been devotional materials, new translations from
the Gospels, and the like. A knowledge of the script remained
alive for three centuries, perhaps more among Moscow copyists
of manuscripts than among the Komi people themselves.

Gradually, however, the script was abandoned and the language
was transliterated in Old Church Slavonic characters.   Then
the use of the language in written form or even for the celebration of the liturgy also disappeared and the church became
Russified.

The Russian Orthodox Church, in spite of the success
of St. Stefan's work and the use of national languages elsewhere
in Eastern Orthodoxy, apparently did not again try the use of
local languages until the nineteenth century, when with the
missionary work of such men as Makary Glucharev, Innokenty
Veniaminov, and Nikolai Kasatkin, the liturgy was translated
into Tatar, Chuvash, Finnish, Japanese, Chinese, Aleut, and
other languages. [9]

With the revolution of 1917 and the socio-political
changes it brought, a new government language policy was
instituted.   Although the goals of the intended culture change
were different, the Lenin policy of using national languages[10]
represented a return to Stefan's ideas.   By 1925 the territory
of the northern Komi had been made an Autonomous Region
(later an Autonomous Republic) and the territory in the south
a National District.   A writing system for Komi was devised,
based on the Russian cyrillic alphabet, each political entity
was given a literary language based on the Komi spoken in it,
and the two official literary languages were adopted for use in
the educational system and the 'mass media' of books, press,
radio, and so on.   The previously existing parish schools
which were conducted in Russian were abolished.   Information
is not readily available on the present use of Komi in the work
of the Orthodox Church.

2. 0 The basic linguistic question to be answered by the agent
of culture change is: What language shall be chosen as the
principal means of communication (hereafter PMC) in the

process of change ?[11] Various answers to this question have
been given, and arguments on their relative merits are still
heard among contemporary specialists on education in developing countries. If, as in the case of Stefan, the answer is the
choice of a previously unwritten local language, three additional questions must be answered: What variety of the language
shall be chosen as the standard ? What kind of writing system
shall be used ? What kind of literature shall be produced ?
These more technical questions have also received different
answers, but it may be hoped that modern workers in applied
linguistics will develop a body of knowledge and experience
which can serve as the basis for more rational decisions than
have been possible in the past.

2.1 Choice of language. —Regardless of the initial means of
communication, whether by interpreter, the use of a common
second language, or gestures and the learning of the local language, sooner or later the decision must be made which language to use as the PMC. The easiest choice for the missionary[12] is to use his own language, teaching it to the people he
is dealing with and then proclaiming or explaining his message
through it. This choice has often been made, and indeed it has
many practical advantages, the chief of which are the immediate utility of written and recorded materials in the missionary's
language which do not require translation, the possibility of
using additional missionaries without special language training,
and the possibility of more advanced study by promising local
individuals at the institutions of the missionary's home country.
If the missionary's language also happens to be a major world
language, other advantages are also apparent. A variant of
this choice is the use of a language which the missionary knows
as a second language but which is not his native language.
This is most commonly the choice either (a) when the missionary is the agent of a group which uses a different language, or

(b) when a particular language is closely tied to the religion
the missionary is bringing or is the regular medium of education in his home society.

A possible example of (a) was the use of English by
the German clergymen sent by the missionary societies of the
Church of England in the eighteenth century to such places as
India and East Africa.[13] The best known case of (b) is the
expansion of Western Christianity to northern Europe in the
fifth to eleventh centuries, when the individual missionaries
often learned the local language for initial contacts and preaching, but chose Latin as the PMC. This use of Latin regardless
of the local language has remained typical of the Western
Church up to the Reformation and of the Roman Catholic since
then, with few exceptions. The Eastern Churches, on the other
hand, have generally assumed that when the gospel was taken
to a new people the local language would be chosen.[14]

The second possible choice is that of a local language,
either the native language of the community or a local lingua
franca. If the society in question already has a written language
with some degree of standardization, the missionary's problem
is one of mastering this form of the language, possibly with
adaptations for the new uses to which the language will be put.
As an example of this we may cite the work of the Baptist
missionary to Bengal, William Carey, and his associates,
whose use of the Bengali language for prose works for education and instruction was the beginning of modern Bengali literature. Written Bengali at that time was used chiefly for certain
kinds of poetry and when used at all for prose was in a heavily
Sanskritized form far removed from the spoken language.
Here the missionaries' choice of neither Sanskrit nor English
as the PMC was decisive for the future of the Bengali language
and the Bengali speech community.[15]

In regions of extreme multilingualism the missionary
may find it advisable to choose one local language out of many
to serve as the PMC. At times this choice has been for an
existing local lingua franca, i.e. a language which is already
learned as a second language and used for intercommunication
among speakers of different languages, typically for purposes
of trade. A good example of the choice of a local lingua franca
was the policy of the Spanish friars to use Nahuatl as the PMC
in the evangelization of highly multilingual Mexico.[16] Sometimes, however, the choice has been based on the simple accident of the location of the initial missionary activity in the area.
An example of language choice in a multilingual situation was
the decision by Lutheran missionaries in New Guinea. The
missionaries were faced with a large number of languages each
with a small number of speakers, and after some years of consideration and the production of materials in about a dozen languages, the three languages of Kate, Yabem, and Graged were
chosen as PMCs for several dozen speech communities.[17]
This process of reduction of PMCs will probably proceed further in New Guinea with the increasing use of Neo-Melanesian
(Pidgin English) as a lingua franca and the recent government
emphasis on English. Some missionary-linguists object to the
choice of lingua francas and insist that every speech community
no matter how small should have the gospel presented in their
own language, and this has become the general policy of the
Wycliffe Bible Translators and the Summer Institutes of Linguistics, which constitute the largest single group of workers
using applied linguistics for religious purposes.[18]

In closing the discussion of this point it is worth noting
that in recent years many specialists in education in developing
countries have expressed strong preference for the use of the
vernacular, i.e. the local primary language, as the medium of
instruction at least at the lower levels. A number of reservations have been expressed however, and it seems clear that

further experimentation and comparative case studies are
needed to determine the critical factors to be considered in
making this kind of choice. [19]

2.2 <u>Choice of standard</u>. —The choice of a previously unwritten language to serve as a PMC involves the choice of one
particular variety of the language in preference to others. If
the language in question is relatively homogeneous, i.e. dialect variation is at a minimum, this problem is unimportant,
but it often happens that the dialectal variation is considerable
and the choice of a particular variety as the norm may have
repercussions on a number of levels. The two policies most
often adopted are (a) to choose the dialect most highly regarded
by the whole speech community, i.e. an incipient standard, or
(b) to choose the dialect at the point of entry of the outside
influence in the community, as representing the dialect which
will naturally tend to be the one used by bilingual and bicul-
tural individuals. It must be noted in connection with (a) that
an incipient standard may not be the variety which informants
assert is the 'purest' or the 'best' but one which is spreading
rapidly by the processes of migration and urbanization; an
example is the urban Wolof of Senegal.

    Stefan seems to have adopted policy (b), basing his
language mostly on the variety of Komi spoken along the lower
course of the Vyčegda River. This was essentially the kind
he himself had learned in his childhood in the Russian settlement, and incidentally is not far geographically from the
present-day political center of the Komi Autonomous Republic.
The linguistic evidence seems to show, however, that the
Komi language was more nearly uniform at that time than it
is now and that the lines of dialect difference did not coincide
very closely with modern boundaries. [20] The various examples
of texts in Old Permian show slight dialect variations among
themselves, suggesting that there was no rigidly codified

norm or true standard at that time, and the religious publications of the nineteenth century also show some dialect variation.

When the two literary languages were created after
the Revolution, one was based on the Komi of Syktyvkar, the
capital of the Komi ASSR, and the other on that of Kudymkar,
the capital of the Permyak National District. The former is
called Zyrian-Komi or simply Komi, the latter Permyak-Komi.
These two literary languages are very close together and it is
hard to see any linguistic reason for keeping them separate,
although there may be political or cultural justification for
doing so not apparent to the outsider.[21]

In many speech communities the question of choice of
a preferred variety is a much more complex question, and at
times missionaries have adopted a third policy (c) to create a
common language which is not based on any one dialect and
minimizes the features which separate the dialects. Although
something of this sort happens to some extent in the formation
of any standard language, its conscious adoption as a policy
has usually led to many difficulties. One of the most often
cited examples of this kind of policy is the attempt to create a
standard Ibo in the face of complex dialect variation.[22]

2.3 Choice of writing system. —One of the basic issues
involved in language planning in a non-literate society is the
nature of the writing system to be introduced. Beyond the
fundamental choice between syllabary and alphabet, there is
the choice between the use of an existing system and one spe-
cially invented for the language. Within these major choices
there are a host of details, such as the use of symbol sequences
and diacritics, the degree of morphophonemic information to
be incorporated, and features of punctuation. This whole issue
has been examined somewhat more systematically than other

linguistic questions in national development, and many of the relevant sociolinguistic factors have at least been identified.[23]

The typical view of missionaries today seems to be that one should choose the alphabet which is used for the national language of the country and the spelling conventions should be such that they would provide an easy transition to the national language. This also seems to be the considered judgement of Soviet linguists, who have preferred modified versions of the cyrillic alphabet for minority languages in the USSR. In the language planning activity after the Revolution and on into the twenties Arabic script was sometimes used and a number of roman alphabet orthographies were devised, but these were all replaced by cyrillic orthographies in the forties. One difference between Soviet and SIL practice has been in the spelling of loanwords from the national language: the Soviets have generally preferred to have Russian loanwords spelled in the minority language just as they are in Russian regardless of the discrepancies in pronunciation and orthographic conventions, while the SIL workers generally prefer a spelling of Spanish or Portuguese loans which is consistent with the pronunciation and orthographic conventions of the borrowing language. Russian practice in this respect has now shifted, but the earlier practice was like that followed in the language development activity associated with the spread of Islam. In most languages written with the Arabic script, Arabic loanwords, including proper names, are spelled as they are in Arabic regardless of their pronunciation in the borrowing language, a procedure which facilitates the study of Arabic or other Islamic languages but causes trouble for the monolingual who is learning to read his own language.

Stefan's choice of writing system is of special interest. He invented an alphabet, called Abur, which was clearly based on his knowledge of Greek and Church Slavonic, but he deliberately made the forms of the letters sufficiently different from either so that the Komi could regard the writing system as distinctively theirs and not an alphabet used for another

language. It even seems likely that he gave some of the letters
an appearance suggestive of the Tamga signs in use among the
Komi as property markers and decorations.

In the creation of new writing systems in the early
centuries of the Church's expansion to new peoples in the East,
the usual pattern was to use the letters of the Greek alphabet
as a base and add new letters as required by sounds not present
in Greek. This was, for example, the procedure followed in
the creation of the Coptic alphabet, Bishop Wulfilas' invention
of the Gothic writing system, and in the creation of an alphabet
for Slavic by St. Cyril and St. Methodius although this last was
perhaps made especially distinctive. In some cases, however,
the originator of the new alphabet had reasons for wanting to
emphasize the distinctiveness of the new writing system. A
good example of this was the creation of the Armenian alphabet
by St. Mesrop in the fifth century. St. Mesrop clearly felt that
the Armenian people needed an alphabet that would not only be
adequate to represent the sounds of their language but would
also be distinctly different from the Greek and Syriac alphabets
in use by the surrounding peoples.

In all these cases the invention of the new alphabet
has been based on some kind of phonological analysis of the
language to be served, as indeed the original invention of the
alphabetic system of writing in the Eastern Mediterranean in
the second millennium B.C. may be regarded as the first
attempt at phonemic analysis and notation; for some practitioners
of modern linguistics the procedures of 'phonemics' are still
primarily an attempt to provide a consistent and natural notation for languages.[24] The chief limitation on the phonemic
principle in the later alphabet inventions has been the orthographic conventions of the source alphabet. St. Stefan's, for
example, provided two letters for the phonemically distinct
o's of Komi but failed to do so for the e's, and this reflects

the existence of two o's in the Greek alphabet (omicron and omega, pronounced alike at that time) and only one e (epsilon; the eta was then pronounced [i]).

When the inventor of a new alphabet is a religious figure it is to be expected that some reference will be made to supernatural elements in the process. Among Christian linguist-saints this has generally been limited in contemporary reports to an acknowledgement of the help of prayer, but later generations have often found a miracle in the achievement and have added details of divine intervention and revelation. A good example is the work of St. Mesrop. The earliest biography of the saint recounts his study with Greek and Syrian scholars, a two-year period of experimentation with children using a preliminary form of the alphabet, and the final designing of all the variant forms of the letters with the aid of a Greek scribe. In the account of the Armenian historian Movses of Khoren who lived at a somewhat later period, although his dates are uncertain, ". . .to the eyes of his soul was revealed a right hand writing on a stone so that the stone kept the trace of the lines as on snow. . .And rising from prayer he created our letters".[25] Although St. Stefan was much revered, no such accretions of legend about his invention of the Abur seem to have developed.

2.4 Choice of literature. —When the missionary has chosen the language, decided on the standard variety, and devised the writing system, his final question is what kind of material to produce in the language. Christian missionaries have generally produced primers for teaching the alphabet, and then the books that they felt were most important for the spread of the Christian faith, regardless of what other needs or desires of the people may have been. It is interesting to compare in this connection the somewhat different priorities assigned by different branches of Christendom. The Orthodox Churches typically issue first translations of basic parts of the Divine Liturgy, including, of course, selections from the Bible which are found in it. Roman Catholic missionaries usually produce first devotional materials and catechisms, and Protestant missionaries tend to turn their attention first to translation of the Bible, especially the New Testament and Psalms.[26] The Lutheran linguist-reformers of the sixteenth century who started new orthographies and standard languages in Europe in connection with the spread of the Reformation, such as Michael Agricola for Finnish and Primož Trubar for Slovenian, typically worked first on the New Testament and Luther's Small Catechism, then the Psalms, the liturgy, and the Augsburg Confession.[27]

Stefan's choice of literature seems to have been in accordance with the tendencies of Eastern Orthodoxy. Almost all the extant documents of Old Permian are translations of the liturgy, and the major exception is the existence of inscriptions on icons, which in the Orthodox tradition are essential elements of public worship. After giving the briefest introduction to the writing system—a number of lists of the letters and even letter names are extant—Stefan apparently felt that the most important task of the written language was to enable the Komi to follow the Orthodox pattern of public worship. It is reasonable to assume that Stefan was also interested in questions of doctrinal instruction, private prayer, and practical ethics, but these were related to the liturgy, with its treasury of Scripture readings and ancient hymns and prayers.

3. In the fourteenth century St. Stefan of Perm undertook to convert to Christianity a non-literate society of some thousands of people. In meeting the language problems involved in this undertaking he made the following decisions. He chose the local language as the principal means of communication. He chose as the basis for its standard the dialect whose speakers

had the greatest contact with the Christianizing culture. He
invented a writing system which was essentially phonemic and
distinctively different in the shape of its letters from any other
known system. He chose as the first publication in the language
the books most necessary for conducting the proper rites of the
Church.

In all these decisions the good saint acted without
benefit of a sociolinguistic theory or frame of reference, and
without any recorded body of previous sociolinguistic experience which he could consult. One must admire St. Stefan's
clearcut decisions and successful implementations of them but
equally one must bewail the fact that a present-day agent of
culture change faced with language problems in a non-literate
society still has no sociolinguistic theory and very little in the
way of recorded and analyzed case histories to give guidance.
We have not progressed much beyond St. Stefan's competence
of five centuries ago.

Without attempting to chart any of the future courses
of sociolinguistic inquiry related to national development, it
seems only reasonable to suggest that an immediate step of
considerable practical value and—one might hope—ultimately
of significance for the growth of sociolinguistic theory would
be the preparation of an inventory of the several hundred docu-
mentable examples of linguistic innovation of the kind described
here. Such an inventory should include not only information on
the questions of linguistic choice discussed here but also information on such relevant questions as the size of the speech community and its attitude toward language; it could also include
some crude measures of success or failure such as time elapsed
before first major literary figure or first indigenous periodical.
One feels that Stefan would have welcomed the existence of such a
collection of information, and it even seems likely that

such strange professional colleagues as Soviet linguists implementing Lenin's policies and SIL workers intent on
spreading Christianity could cooperate in the compilation and
use of the inventory. If it were not for the fact that Soviet
scholars and evangelical missionaries would equally reject the
formulation, although for different reasons, one would be
tempted to see St. Stefan of Perm as the patron saint of workers in the applied linguistics of national development and ask
his blessing on their research and its application.

NOTES

[1] Roman Jakobson in his important article, "The
Beginning of National Self-Determination in Europe", The
Review of Politics (1945), 29-45, referred to the work of
St. Stefan as part of the East European heritage of linguistic
nationalism. In Constantin de Grunwald's Saints of Russia
(London, 1960), however, Stefan rates only three lines, on
p. 83. In the interesting survey by W. Wonderly and E. Nida,
"Linguistics and Christian Missions", Anthropological Lin-
guistics 5,1 (January, 1963), 104-144, his name does not even
appear. The most convenient acccunt of him available in
English is probably Alban Butler's Lives of the Saints, 2nd
edition (London, 1956), Vol. 2, 167. —This paper was presented at the Conference on Language Problems of Developing
Nations held at Airlie House, Warrenton, Va., November 1-3,
1966, under the sponsorship of the Social Science Council's
Committee on Sociolinguistics, with financial support from the
National Science Foundation.

[2] For example, Theodcre Balsamon, Patriarch of
Antioch in the twelfth century, wrote, "Those who are wholly
orthodox, but who are altogether ignorant of the Greek tongue,

shall celebrate in their own language; provided only that they
have exact versions of the customary prayers translated on to
rolls and well written in Greek characters". Quoted in Cyril
Korolevsky, Living Languages in Catholic Worship, translated
by Donald Attwater (London, 1957), 15.

[3] Cf. C. A. Ferguson, "The Language Factor in
National Development", Anthropological Linguistics 4, 1
(January, 1962), 23-27, reprinted in Frank A. Rice, editor,
Study of the Role of Second Languages . . . (Washington, 1962),
8-14. On the need for case histories, see Alfred S. Hayes,
editor, Recommendations of the Work Conference on Literacy
. . . (Washington, 1965), 14.

[4] The chief source for information on the life of
Stefan is the biography written by his contemporary, the monk
Epiphanius the Wise. The nineteenth century Russian edition
of V. G. Družinin, Žutie Svjatogo Stefana Episkopa Permskogo
Napisannoe Epifaniem Premudrym (St. Petersburg, 1897) has
been reprinted photomechanically, with an English introduction
by Dmitrij Čiževskij on the literary position of Epiphanius
(The Hague, Mouton, 1959). There seems to be no English
translation except for a small part which appears under the
title, "The Panegyric to St. Stefan of Perm", in S. A. Zenkov-
sky, editor, Medieval Russia's Epics, Chronicles, and Tales
(New York, 1963), 206-208.

[5] The general name for the whole people and their
language is Komi, and this will be used throughout the paper,
but the name Zyrian or Zyryenian has also been used, especially to refer to the northern population and their speech.
The name Permian is used especially to refer to Stefan's
literary language (Old Permian) and as an inclusive term for
Komi and Udmurt, which constitute a branch of the Finno-
Ugric language family.

[6] The best account of Old Komi (= Old Permian) is that of the prominent Komi linguist V. I. Lytkin, Drevneperm-skij jazyk; čtenie tekstov, grammatika, slovar' (Moscow, 1952). There is a lengthy, informative review of this in German in Acta Linguistica (Hung.), 4 (1954), 225-249, by D. Fokos-Fuchs.

[7] No comprehensive work on the history of the Komi people has been available to me. The account here is based on scraps of information from a variety of sources. Doubtless it can be corrected in detail, but I hope it is reliable in its general outline.

[8] One name stands out among his successors, Jona, who was bishop from 1456 to 1470. Jona carried the Christian-izing of the Komi to the southern population in what was then called Great Permia, baptizing the prince, who took the name Michael. With the subjugation of Prince Michael by the forces of Moscow the whole Komi people came formally into the poli-tical structure of the Moscow state, and the bishops came to live more in Russian Vologda than in Komi Ust'vym.

[9] For a convenient account in English of these three missionaries, see Stephen Neill, A History of Christian Missions (Penguin Books, 1964), 440-449. Glucharev, whose life work was among the Kalmucks in the Altai plateau of Central Asia, wrote a penetrating book, Thoughts on the Me-thods to be Followed for a Successful Dissemination of the Faith, in which he advocated the use of local languages and the development of popular education on the widest scale, but his views were generally ignored by his contemporaries.

[10] Cf. V. I. Lenin, O Prave Nacij na Samooprede-lenie, numerous editions and translations.

[11] The expression 'principal means of communication' is used here to refer to the language used for formal instruction, for meetings related to culture change (planning and implementation of change, carrying on of new institutions), and for publication. The possibilities are, of course, more complex than this phrasing of the question suggests. For example, the choice may be made to use one language for early years of primary school and another as the medium for secondary and higher education. Possibilities of this kind will be ignored here partly for simplicity of presentation and partly because not so many alternatives are likely to have been considered in the Permian situation.

[12] Hereafter the term 'missionary' will be used as the most appropriate term for the present study, but it must be remembered that the missionary is only a special case of the conscious agent of culture change, which includes conquerors, colonizers, technical assistance personnel, and even social science experimenters.

[13] Cf. J. Richter, Allgemeine evangelische Missionsgeschichte, Vol. 1: Indische Missionsgeschichte, 2nd ed. (1924).

[14] Cf. Christine Mohrmann, "Linguistic Problems in the Early Christian Church", Vigiliae Christianae 11 (1957), 11-36, esp. 17-19, and Koralevsky, op. cit. Chapter 1.

[15] Cf. Edward C. Dimock, "Literary and Colloquial Bengali in Modern Bengali Prose", in Charles A. Ferguson and John J. Gumperz, editors, Linguistic Diversity in South Asia (Bloomington, 1960), esp. 51-58.

[16] Cf. Robert Ricard, The Spiritual Conquest of Mexico, translated by Lesley Byrd Simpson (Berkeley and Los Angeles, 1966), 45-60, for discussion of the language

problem; the use of Nahuatl in treated pp. 45-51 and 290;
G. F. Vicedom, Church and People in New Guinea (London,
1961), 49-54.

[17] Cf. A. C. Frerichs, Anutu Conquers in New
Guinea (Columbus, Ohio, 1957), Chapter 10: Language and
Literature, esp. 163. For further discussion of the New
Guinea language situation, see S. A. Wurm, "Papua-New
Guinea Nationhood: The Problem of a National Language",
Journal of the Papua and New Guinea Society, 1966.

[18] For an impassioned statement of this view see
Kenneth L. Pike, "We Will Tell Them, But in What Language",
His, October 1951, 8-11, 14; reprinted in Kenneth L. Pike,
With Heart and Mind (Grand Rapids, Mich., 1964), 124-130.

[19] For a persuasive statement of the preference for
the vernaculars, see The Use of Vernacular Languages in Education (= UNESCO Monograph on Fundamental Education No. 8)
(Paris, 1953), and for some of the reservations, see the thought-
ful review of this book by William Bull, International Journal
of American Linguistics, 21 (1955), 228-294; reprinted with
added bibliography in Dell Hymes, editor, Language in Culture
and Society (New York, 1965), 527-533. For a thorough discussion of the alternatives and a set of definite recommenda-
tionf for the New Guinea area, see S. A. Wurm, "Language
and Literacy" in E. K. Fisk, editor, New Guinea on the Threshold (Canberra, 1966), 135-148.

[20] "In any case, the old Komi (Old Permian) literary
language, created in the fourteenth century by the missionary
Stefan on the basis of the Lower Vyčegda dialect, was still
equally close to the Vyčegda and Kama Komi, and it was not by
chance that the Permian (Ust'vym) bishops spread Christianity
by this language also among the Kama Komi". V. I. Lytkin,

editor, <u>Komi-Permjackij Jazyk</u> (Kudymkar, 1962), 26.

[21] "The Permyak-Komi and Zyrian-Komi languages are particularly close to each other; therefore in scientific literature they are not counted as two languages, but as the two main dialects of the one Komi language", <u>ibid.</u>, 5.

[22] For a detailed discussion of the linguistic problems in Ibo, see Ida C. Ward, <u>Ibo Dialects and the Development of a Common Language</u> (Cambridge, 1941). An example of the creation of a standard based on careful analysis of dialects and a kind of reconstruction of a logical ancestor to them is reported by Einar Haugen, "Construction and Reconstruction in Language Planning: Ivar Aasen's Grammar", <u>Word</u>, 21 (1965), 188-207; see also his "Linguistics and Language Planning", in William Bright, editor, <u>Sociolinguistics</u> (The Hague, 1966), 50-72.

[23] The best general account of the factors involved in the creation and change of orthographies is Jack Berry, "The Making of Alphabets", in <u>Proceedings of the Eighth International Congress of Linguists</u> (Oslo, 1957), 752-764. See also Sarah C. Gudshinsky, <u>Handbook of Literacy</u> (Glendale, California, 1957); Andrée F. Sjoberg, "Socio-Cultural and Linguistic Factors in the Development of Writing Systems for Preliterate Peoples", in William Bright, op. cit., 260-276; William A. Smalley and others, <u>Orthography Studies</u> (London, 1964). An instructive case study is provided by Paul Garvin, "Literacy as a Problem in Language and Culture", in <u>Report of the Fifth Annual Round Table Meeting on Linguistics and Language Teaching</u> (= <u>Georgetown University Monograph Series on Language and Linguistics No. 7</u>) (Washington, 1954), 117-129.

24 Cf. Kenneth L. Pike, Phonemics: A Technique for Reducing Language to Writing (Ann Arbor, Michigan, 1947).

25 Cf. Koriun, The Life of Mashtots [Mesrop], translated by Bedros Norehad (New York, 1964). There is a very informative introduction translated from the modern Armenian introduction to Koriun by a Soviet scholar, the late Manouk Abeghian. The quotation from Movses of Khoren is from his History of the Armenians, translated [into modern Armenian] by Stephan Malkhastian (Erevan, 1961), 325-326.

26 In the choice between 'practical' books of instruction for everyday behavior and ideological documents which attempt a conversion to new viewpoints, the modern Russian linguists seem to have been more like the Protestants in preferring the ideological, since translations of the works of Marx, Lenin, etc. are often among the early publications for newly-literate communities.

27 Cf. Jaakko Gummerus, Michael Agricola, der Reformator Finnlands (Helsinki, 1941), 40-67.

14 | Language Development

Discussions of language problems of developing countries cover a wide range of problems such as national multilingualism, language education policies, and languages as symbols of group identity. Many of these issues can be dealt with by the conceptual frameworks used in the study of social organization, political systems, or economic processes. Some questions, however, relate to the state of a language itself, as shown by observations that such and such a language is "backward" or "inadequate" or that a particular language needs "purifying," "reforming, " "modernizing," or some other forms of improvement. This kind of issue is closer to the conceptual framework of linguistics, although not commonly dealt with by professional linguists, and it may be useful to offer a linguistic perspective on it.

1. <u>Linguistic structure</u>. The traditional twofold task of linguistics is to make statements that hold true for all languages everywhere and at all times (a general theory of language) and to make statements about particular varieties of language under particular conditions (characterization of languages, e.g., grammars, language histories, etc.). In

either case linguists have been concerned with what kinds of
sequences are "pronounceable" in a given language (or in all
languages), what kinds of sequences are grammatically possible
in a given language (or in general), and what kinds of sequences
are meaningful in a language (or in general). Although the
range of possible variation remains within the definite limits
of the general characteristics of languages, now commonly called
"language universals" (Greenberg, 1966a, 1966b; Uspenskij,
1965), there is an astonishing diversity of possible structures
as exemplified by the thousands of different languages
now in existence and the several hundred for which there is
historical documentation. Accordingly, it has often been
tempting to regard one kind of linguistic (phonological-gramma-
tical-semantic) structure as being in some way superior to or
more advanced than others. As time has passed, however,
linguists have increasingly become convinced that there is no
simple scale of superiority in structure and no simple evolutionary line along which known linguistic structures could be
placed. In this fundamental sense there is as yet no convincing
evidence that the total structure of one language is better than
that of another in that it is easier to acquire (as a first language),
less ambiguous, more efficient for cognitive processes, or
more economical of effort in oral use, let alone more "logical,"
"expressive," or the like (Ray, 1963, Ch. 10).

     The three great world languages—Russian, Chinese,
and English—differ greatly in structure. Russian has
a relatively stable vowel system, a pervasive feature of palatalization, and a complex inflectional morphology. Chinese
has a phonology and lexicon largely based on the syllable, it
has distinctive tone, and it has almost no morphological
machinery. English has a very variable vowel system and is
somewhere between the other two in morphological complexity.
There is at present no known way to rate the respective structures of the three languages as wholes. [1]

The assumption is now standard in linguistics that all
known languages apparently constitute roughly the same kind
of symbolic behavior system, in spite of this great variety,
and that there are at the present time no "primitive" languages
exemplifying the type of earlier stage in language behavior that
must have existed hundreds of thousands of years ago (Hymes,
1961, 75-76).

2. <u>Features of development</u>. If judgments of back-
wardness or limited development of a language cannot be made
on the basis of linguistic structure, how can they be made?
The view adopted here is that there are at least three dimensions relevant for measuring language development: graphization— reduction to writing; standardization—the
development of a norm which overrides regional and social
dialects; and, for want of a better term, modernization—
the development of intertranslatability with other languages in a range of topics and forms of discourse characteristic of industrialized, secularized, structurally differentiated,
"modern" societies.

Hymes (1961) offers a more comprehensive approach
for evolutionary study of language; here we follow a more
limited approach comparable to developmental studies in
political sociology or economics rather than the evolutionary
approach of anthropology. Ferguson (1962) uses two dimensions:
(a) "utilization in writing," which combines graphization and
modernization, and (b) standardization. Haugen (1966) offers
a four-way matrix of development form-function-society-
language giving (a) selection of norm, (b) codification, (c)
elaboration of function, (d) acceptance; of these, elaboration
corresponds roughly to modernization, and the other three
aspects of standardization. Fishman (1968) emphasizes that the
processes of language development are not single events but
involve repeated elaboration and recodification. Sjoberg (1964)

offers a suggestive but oversimplified matching of stages of
language development with preliterate, preindustrialized
civilized, transitional, and industrialized nations.

2.1 <u>Graphization</u>. The regular use of writing in a
speech community, like such other innovations as the use of a
steel knife in a stone-age society, has repercussions throughout the culture and social organization. The relative perma-
nence of written records makes possible the transmission of
more material from generation to generation; the transporta-
bility of written records makes possible communication with a
larger number of people; and the immediate fixing in written
form makes possible more complex sequential thought on the
part of individuals. In this essay, however, we are
concerned with the effect of writing on the development of
language itself.

The first point to be made is that <u>the use of writing
adds another variety of language to the community's repertory</u>.
The vocabulary, grammatical structure, and even the phonological structure of the language as used in writing begin
immediately, as it were, to have a life of their own. Linguists
like to point out that speech is primary and writing secondary
and that written language is always in some sense a representation of speech. Although this is true in a general way, and is
worth repeated emphasis to correct widespread misconcep-
tions, the fact is that writing almost never reflects speech in an
exact way, written language frequently develops characteristics not found in the corresponding spoken language, and it
may change along lines quite different from changes in the
spoken language. After the spread of writing, varieties of
the spoken language can no longer be described <u>in vacuo</u>; they
will interact with the written form to a greater or lesser
degree, and the linguistic analyst must note spelling pronun-

ciations, lexical displacements, and grammatical fluctuations
which originate in or are reinforced by written usage.

It is remarkable that communities, as they begin the
regular use of writing, generally do not feel that ordinary,
everyday speech is appropriate for written use. Sometimes
this may be because the community already makes use of a
classical language, but sometimes it merely transfers to the
new medium some of the attitudes already present in the community toward the language of higher levels of discourse such
as formal speeches, religious rituals, and the like. It may be
assumed that all speech communities show linguistic differentiation along a casual/ noncasual dimension (Voegelin, 1960),
and many communities will regard the new use of writing as
far along toward the noncasual end, only much later coming
to recognize the value of written representation of casual
speech. Two well-described examples of this tendency may
be found in the beginnings of modern Bengali prose and the
early use of modern English as a regular means of written
communication (Das, 1966, pp. 17-22; Jones, 1953, Ch. I).

It is sometimes asserted that the existence of a
written variety inhibits language change, thus constituting an
important influence for uniformity through time comparable
to the kind of regional and social uniformity implicit in standardization. Evidence on this point is conflicting and the
question merits systematic study (cf. Zengel, 1962).

The second point to be made is that the use of writing
leads to the folk belief that the written language is the "real"
language and speech is a corruption of it. This attitude seems
to be nearly universal in communities which have attained the
regular use of writing. It is only the occasional perceptive
observer, or in more recent times the professional linguist,
who sees the relationship in other terms. To the extent that

after the passage of time the written form of the language proves to be the more conservative, the spoken may be regarded with some justification as derived from it, but the picture is invariably more complicated than this, since isolated relic areas may be less innovative than the written language, or the original dialect base of the written language may have been a highly divergent variety of the language.

The importance of this folk belief for language development lies in the way it limits the kind of conscious intervention in the form of language planning that the community will conceive of or accept. Much time and effort is often spent on questions of orthography and language reform, in the tacit assumption that changes in the written language will be followed automatically by changes in speech. Some reforming zeal is also expended on bringing pronunciation in line with existing written norms. Insofar as these various efforts are part of a standardization process which responds to the communicative needs of the speech community, they may result in actual change, especially if they do not conflict with the basic phonological and grammatical structure of the language, but often the efforts fail, at least in part because the beliefs do not correspond to the realities of the written-spoken relationship.

2.2 Standardization. Language standardization is the process of one variety of a language becoming widely accepted throughout the speech community as a supradialectal norm—the "best" form of the language—rated above regional and social dialects, although these may be felt appropriate in some domains. The process of standardization in language is often mentioned in works on general linguistics and many books on the history of particular languages deal with the process, but general treatments of standardization are rare (cf. Kloss, 1952, Ch. I; Guxman, 1960; Ray, 1963). The concept of standardization also includes the notions of

increasing uniformity of the norm itself and explicit codification of the norm. It is sometimes extended also to include
such notions as the introduction of writing, the expansion of
lexicon, and even the choice of one language instead of another
as an official or national language, but it will not be understood
in these senses here.

Various aspects of the process of standardization can
be documented for scores of languages in the past and it is in
progress in many languages today. While standardization is
recognized as a dimension in language development as viewed
here, there are a good number of instances where a language
has been highly standardized and has then regressed to a
state of dialect diversity without a standard and may even have
been restandardized on a different basis later. This is
especially clear with languages with a very long written
history such as Egyptian, but other cases are also well-known
(Pulgram, 1958, Ch. 23). Such regressions, comparable to
returning from a high level of technology to a lower one, are
known in other aspects of cultural evolution, and do not invalidate the developmental viewpoint.

Although at this point in history there can be no cer-
tainty about the nature of the final achievement of standardization as a stage in language development, it seems possible to
interpret the various forms of standardization as moving
toward an ideal state when the language "has a single, widely
accepted norm which is felt to be appropriate with only minor
modification or varieties for all purposes for which the language is used" (Ferguson, 1962, p. 10). If this interpretation
is followed, a number of special types of language standardization can be viewed as way-stations in the developmental process. Examples of these special types include diglossia,
where the supradialectal norm is not used for ordinary conversation, as in Arabic and Tamil (Ferguson, 1959), and

multimodal standardization, where competing supradialectal
norms exist, as in Eastern and Western Armenian (Garibian,
1960), Hindi-Urdu (Gumperz and Naim, 1960), Norwegian
Bokmal-Nynorsk (Haugen and Chapman, 1964, pp. 365-366).

The process of language standardization is not well
understood and needs both case studies and attempts at generalization so that some testable hypotheses can be advanced, but
at least two points can be made on the basis of present knowledge. First, there are many paths of standardization and a
number of sociolinguistic variables to be investigated in connection with the different paths. Second, in most of the well-
known cases of language standardization in Europe since the
Rennaissance, a number of features keep recurring, although
they are not all present in each case:

1. The basis of the standard was the speech of an
educated middle class in an important urban center.
2. The standardizing language was displacing another
language from its position as normal written medium.
3. One writer or a small number of writers served
as acknowledged models for literary use of the standardizing
language.
4. The standardizing language served as a symbol of
either religious or national identity.

Some of these features are also evident in language standardization in other parts of the world and at other times, but the
examination of other cases would probably require adding some
features to the list.

2.3 Modernization. The modernization of a language
may be thought of as the process of its becoming the equal of
other developed languages as a medium of communication; it
is in a sense the process of joining the world community of
increasingly intertranslatable languages recognized as appro-

priate vehicles of modern forms of discourse. This view of
modernization—and indeed the very term itself—should not
disguise the fact that this process is not really new or
"modern": it is essentially the same process that English
went through in the fifteenth century or Hungarian in the nineteenth when the language was extended to cover topics and to
appear in a range of forms of discourse for which it was not
previously used, including nonliterary prose and oral communication such as lectures and professional consultation.
Two important forms of discourse in contemporary modernization are the news and feature stories of the press and radio.

The process of modernization thus has two aspects: (a)
the expansion of the lexicon of the language by new words and
expressions and (b) the development of new styles and forms of
discourse. The second aspect has less often been discussed
than lexical expansion and would repay study. Interestingly
enough the new forms of discourse which must be developed
seem in themselves to be less distinctive for the speech community than the more literary forms (oral or written)
preceding them. Thus the poetic structures (meter, rhyme,
assonance, allusion, stanza-form, etc.) of a given language
may be highly distinctive and difficult to transfer to other languages, whereas the structures of nonliterary prose (paragraph-
ing, ordered sequences, transitions, summaries, cross-
references, etc.) tend to be universal and highly translatable.

Lexical expansion is required in order to treat new
topics, and this seems to take place most effectively when the
tempo of change is not too fast, the practitioners who need the
vocabulary are involved in its creation, and there are sufficient lines of communication among the users of the new terminology to achieve consistency. In this area, too, there has been
little systematic study. The efforts of language planners
generally focus on the production of glossaries and dictionaries
of new technical terms and on disputes about the proper form

of new words, when the critical question seems to be that of
assuring the consistent use of such forms by the appropriate
sectors of the population. When the lexical expansion of
modernization actually takes place, it may not be at all in
accord with the carefully prepared glossaries of the planners.
Probably the use of new terms and expressions in such places
as secondary school textbooks, professional papers, and conversation among specialists is far more important than the
publication of extensive lists of words. Case studies of rapid
lexical expansion in recent times should be made to determine
the factors accounting for success in cases like Japanese and
Hungarian and relative lack of success in cases like Hindi and
Arabic.

On the issue of the source of new vocabulary and the
methods of word creation, one important point seems to be
that a technical vocabulary can be equally effective whether it
comes from the language's own processes of word formation
or from extensive borrowing from another language. The issue
of purism can be a critical one in the sense that feelings may
be strong and disagreements sharp, but it seems almost
totally irrelevant to the final success of the lexical expansion
process. Of the two examples cited, Hungarian followed
almost exclusively the path of internal creation, whereas Japanese
used extensive borrowing from English as well. This issue is
important for social psychological research in finding the
factors involved in the attitudes adopted, and it has a kind of
importance for linguistic research in that it may involve
changes in word structure and the distribution of sounds, but
it seems of less importance for understanding the process of
language development itself (cf. Ray, 1963, pp. 36–44 and references).

3. Summary. Among the many language aspects of
national development that could be the object of study and

measurement, it is possible to isolate the question of the
degree of development of a particular language. Language
development in this sense is viewed here as having three
conceptually distinct components: (a) graphization, the use
of writing; (b) standardization, the use of a supradialectal
norm; and (c) modernization, the development of vocabulary
and forms of discourse.

Graphization adds to the language a new variety, which
in relation to the spoken varieties tends to be slower to change,
is generally regarded by the users as more fundamental, and
can serve as a better means of standardization and modernization.

Standardization brings to a language the kind of integration and uniformity needed for large-scale communication,
but there are various paths of standardization, and analysis of
these and the relevant social variables is needed.

Modernization provides the language with the specialized subvocabularies and forms of discourse corresponding
to the highly differentiated functions the language must
fulfill in a modern society.

Finally, all three components of language development
can be the object of language planning (Haugen, 1966, and references) although the factors making for success and failure in
such planning are not clear.

NOTES

[1]This does not, of course, exclude the possibility that particular features of particular languages may be rated as more regular, easier to acquire, etc. For example, the representation of the grammatico-semantic category of number (singular-plural) is very complex and irregular in Russian, much simpler in English, and very simple and relatively unimportant in Chinese. It is reasonable to assume—and there is some confirmatory evidence—that children learning these languages acquire the notion of plurality at roughly the same ages but that it takes the Russian child longest to attain full mastery of the plural inflection, the English-learning child less time, and the Chinese child least. There is no way to weight this isolated phenomenon against the total structure of the language. Children seem to master the basic structures of their languages at roughly the same age, no matter what language they are acquiring.

REFERENCES

Das, Susirkumar. 1966. Early Bengali Prose. Calcutta: Bookland.

Ferguson, Charles A. 1959. Diglossia. Word, 15:325-340. In this volume, pp. 1-26.

Ferguson, Charles A. 1962. The Language Factor in National Development. Anthro. Ling., 4(1), 23-27. Reprinted in F. A. Rice (ed.), Study of the Role of Second Languages, Washington, Center for Applied Linguistics, 1962, pp. 8-14. In this volume, pp. 51-59.

Fishman, Joshua A. 1968. Sociolinguistics and the Language
    Problems of the Developing Countries. In J. A. Fishman
    et al. (eds.), Language Problems of Developing Nations,
    New York: John Wiley & Sons, pp. 3-16.

Garibian, A. S. 1960. Ob armjanskom nacional'nom literaturnom
    jazke. In M. M. Guxman (ed.), Voprosy formirovanija
    i razvitija nacional'nyx jazykov, Moscow 1960, pp. 50-
    61.

Garvin, Paul, and Madeleine Mathict. 1960. The Urbanization
    of the Guarani Language—A Problem in Language and
    Culture. In A. F. C. Wallace (ed.), Men and Cultures,
    Philadelphia: University of Pennsylvania Press, pp.
    783-790.

Greenberg, Joseph H. 1966a. Language Universals. In
    T. A. Sebeok (ed.), Current Trends in Linguistics III.
    The Hague: Mouton, pp. 60-112. (Reprinted separately
    with slight revisions by Mouton.)

Greenberg, Joseph H. (ed.). 1966b. Universals of Language,
    2nd ed. Cambridge: MIT Press.

Gumperz, John J., and C. M. Naim. 1960. Formal and
    Informal Standards in the Hindi Regional Language
    Area. In C. A. Ferguson and J. J. Gumperz (eds.),
    Linguistic Diversity in South Asia, Int. J. Amer.
    Ling., 26(3), Pt. III (Bloomington, Ind.).

Guxman, M. M. (ed.). 1960. Voprosy formirovanija i
    razvitija nacional'nyx jazykov. Moscow.

Haugen, Einar. 1966. Dialect, Language, Nation. Amer.
    Anthro., 68, 922-935.

Haugen, Einar, and Kenneth G. Chapman. 1964. Spoken
    Norwegian, rev. ed. New York: Holt, Rinehart and
    Winston.

Hymes, Dell H. 1961. Functions of Speech: An Evolutionary
    Approach. In F. Gruber (ed.), Anthropology and
    Education. Philadelphia: University of Pennsylvania
    Press, pp. 55-83.

Jones, R. F. 1953. The Triumph of English. Stanford,
    Cal.: Stanford University Press. (Rep. paper 1966.)

Kloss, Heinz. 1952. Die Entwicklung neuer germanischer
    Kultursprachen von 1800 bis 1850. Munich: Pohl.

Pulgram, Ernst. 1958. The Tongues of Italy: Prehistory
    and History. Cambridge, Mass.: Harvard University
    Press.

Ray, Punya Sloka. 1963. Language Standardization. The
    Hague: Mouton.

Sjoberg, Andree F. 1964. Writing, Speech, and Society:
    Some Changing Relationships, in Proc. 9th Intl. Cong.
    Ling. The Hague: Mouton, pp. 892-898.

Uspenskij, B. 1965. Strukturnaja tipologija jazykov. Moscow.

Voegelin. C. F. 1960. Casual and Noncasual Utterances within
    Unified Style. In T. A. Sebeok (ed.), Style in Language,
    57-68. Cambridge: MIT Press, pp. 57-68.

Zengel, Marjorie Smith. 1962. Literacy as a Factor in
    Language Change, Amer. Anthro. 64, 132-139.

15 | Contrastive Analysis and Language Development

In giving a course called Contrastive Analysis at a university or Linguistic Institute the instructor often starts with a disavowal: he says he is not sure that there is such a field as contrastive analysis, or if there is such a field, he is not sure what the methodology is, that is, how one should set about doing contrastive analysis. Consequently, it made me feel rather good this morning to listen to speaker after speaker reaffirm the existence of a field, or at least a set of procedures, that might be called contrastive analysis. Even more, the speakers reaffirmed the value of such research and study either for 'pure' linguistics or for pedagogical application. That is more or less the position that I take—contrastive analysis is, in some sense, fundamental to all of linguistics and has important implications for language teaching and other 'applied' problems.

Two of the fundamental goals of linguistics are the development of a general theory of human language behavior and the development of appropriate procedures for the full characterization of any language. For both of these goals contrastive analysis is a basic tool. Progress toward the development of a general theory can come by various routes, but certainly at some point it will be necessary to compare grammars of different languages in detail in order to discover the underlying similarities and to distinguish these from the superficial similarities and differences which give each language its distinctiveness. Also, it is possible to make useful attempts at the characterization of a particular language (i.e. writing a grammar of it) without explicit reference to other languages, but since one of the purposes of such characterizations is to show the ways in which the language differs from all other languages, it is necessary at some point to utilize contrastive analysis in one form or another.

Contrastive analysis is also fundamental to other goals of linguistics, such as the characterization of the history of particular languages or their spread of dialect variation at a given point or through time. In fact, since de Saussure it has been customary for many linguists to regard the description of diachronic change as essentially the comparison of successive structural stages, i.e. a set of contrastive analyses. These points have all been presented and argued effectively elsewhere; the purpose of the present paper is to point to the relevance of the notion of contrastive analysis in the study of child language development.

1. Diachronic Stages. In his 1941 book on child language,[1] Jakobson made clear the notion that a child's language is always a coherent system (although with more marginal features and fluctuation than adult language) and that the development of a child's language may profitably be regarded as a succession of stages, just as the history of a language may be. In fact, the study of child language may be regarded as only a special case of diachronic linguistics, viz. the study of a succession of stages $x_1, x_2, \ldots, x_n$ of linguistic structure when x_1 is $\emptyset$, while in other cases x_1 is a full-fledged language.[2] This would suggest that techniques of contrastive analysis

useful in one variety of diachronic linguistics might be helpful in the other, or, at least, should be tried in both.

I think that the structural diachronic view of child language has been clear but has rarely been acted on; that is, people have rarely performed explicit contrastive analyses of successive stages of a child's language development. In the last several years, however, a number of people have begun to write grammars of successive stages of children's language. In particular, I am referring to the work of Roger Brown and his associates, who have described the grammatical structure of three children at five successive stages.[3] In each case they write a rather explicit, careful transformational-style gram- mar and then point out how moving from one stage to the next involves the addition of rules, or the change of rules. It would be quite instructive for us to take this kind of example to illustrate contrastive analysis of diachronic stages in child language development, but the presentation of a full grammar —even of a two or three year old child—is a considerable undertaking and a simpler illustration may suffice to make the point clear.

As an example of this kind of contrastive analysis, a succession of phonological charts of three stages of the lan- guage of a French-learning child, Jacqueline, are presented.[4] The first stage represents the period (13th to 16th month) during which she had a two-word vocabulary—words for 'mama' and 'papa' which may be analyzed as utilizing three phonemes / m b a / . The second stage selected is nine months later, when she had acquired all the phonemes of French except for / r z ž ẅ ñ / .[5] The phoneme inventories of these three stages appear in the charts of Table 1, accom- panied by a corresponding chart of adult French.[6]

Two difficulties are involved in determining the phoneme inventories here. One is the problem of phonemic

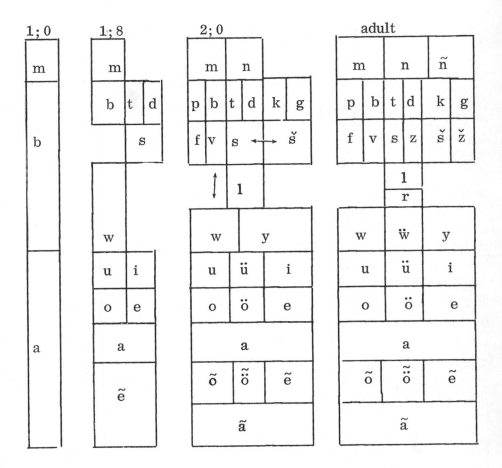

TABLE 1. Diachronic Stages. (French) Consonant inventory
of Jacqueline Bloch at successive stages. (Based
on O. Bloch, 'Notes sur le langage d'un enfant')

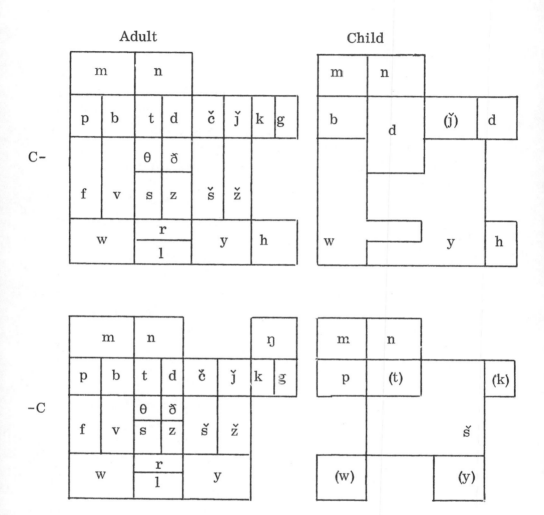

TABLE 2. Model and Replica. (English) Initial and final
consonants of Hildegard Leopold at age 1; 10.
(Based on W. Leopold, Speech Development of
a Bilingual Child, Vol. 2)

analysis when the vocabulary is very small and the child's repertory of contrasts is difficult to elicit. The chief justification for the recognition of phonemes or phoneme-like elements in the speech of a child with only two items in his vocabulary is that the principle of contrast has been established (at least at the utterance level if not at syllable or phonemic-segment levels) and that the sound types present are the predecessors to sound types more clearly identifiable as phonemes later.

The second difficulty is in retrieving the necessary information from the published studies. Even when a careful diary-like study provides sufficient information to make reasonable judgments about contrasts, it is generally written in a sound by sound, word by word chronological framework rather than as a synchronic description of total structure at given points in time. In this particular case, however, it was possible to extract sufficient information about the selected stages.

The child was late in beginning to speak. It was not until the thirteenth month that she said her first two words, and it just so happened in this particular case that she said something like 'papa' and 'mama', a choice of words that would be pleasing to many language investigators. To be more exact, the phonetic facts were apparently something like [baba˙] and [mɛm ɛ̃] (cf. French papa, maman) with both words at first showing variation between one and two syllable pronunciations, perhaps [ba]~[baba˙] and [mɛ̃]~[mɛm ɛ̃]. It is clearly possible to analyze these two utterances—the only two possible sentences in this stage of the language—as consisting of / m b a/ in appropriate combinations, with /a/ representing a generalized vowel phoneme. The inventory seems to consist of a vowel versus two non-vowels, and in the non-vowel category, a nasal opposes a non-nasal. It is tempting to view the

gradual development of Jacqueline's French as a development
from those three beginning categories, as we see the vowel
category split up into more vowels, the non-vowel nasal category into more nasals, and the non-nasal /b/ in a quite complicated way into all the obstruents of the language.

The next period selected was the following October,
nine months later—Jacqueline was born at the end of January
1910. It is not quite clear how large a vocabulary she had
because her father seems to say in one place in the article
20 words, and in another place 40. My count through the text
found at least 21 words attested, hence the estimate of between
20 and 40. The phonological pattern, on the whole, is pretty
clear, as presented here. It is interesting to note that the
labial stop phoneme is characteristically voiced /b/ and yet
in the apical range there is both a /t/ and a /d/. I think
that Jakobson, for example, might have been surprised at
this kind of development. It is worth pointing out here, although it is not made explicit in this kind of chart, that the
/b/, which is quite common, represents a number of different
consonant phonemes in the adult language, and the /d/, which
is much rarer, represents in one case, at least, an initial d,
while in another two cases represents an initial s. The spirant phoneme /s/ here, which is at the beginning of the development of the spirant system, is interesting in that it is
limited at this time to medial position. Little Jacqueline
acquired during October the two words is(i) meaning 'here'
and apsi meaning 'thank you', although using /d/ for initial
s, as in dodo 'pail' (cf. French seau, baby talk 'seau-seau').
The semivowel /w/ represents the beginning of the development of the French semivowel system, and we may remark
that in languages with some kind of /w/, this is very often
acquired quite early, contrary to the expectations of Jakobson's
theory. The vowel system already consisted of five oral
vowels and one nasal vowel at this stage.

The next stage selected was the following January.
The reason mid-October was selected for stage two was that
it was just at that point that a voiced-voiceless distinction was
starting and if I had tried to make a sharp analysis of the next
month or so, it would have been very difficult to decide whether to put in t and d, p and b, and so on, because there was
a great deal of fluctuation: in some words there was consistency, but in others free variation. By the end of the following
January, she had definitely separated out t and d, p and b, k
and g, and there was at least an incipient f-v contrast. There
are only one or two comments that are worth making here about
the chart of the third stage. First, it is necessary to show that
the v and w are in a state of variation. They have not yet really
emerged as contrastive elements at this stage. The predominantly [w] in pronunciation, with [v] and [w] variants, has as
sources both /v/ and /w/ in the adult language. The s-š
situation is far more complicated and is really difficult to un-
ravel. Two elements are indicated in the chart because it
seems quite certain that in some words there were clear preferences for an š pronunciation, although these do not always
agree with the source in the parent language and there was a
great deal of fluctuation. In fact, the phonetic variants of the
/š/ ranged from a palatalized [t] through [š] to various kinds
of palatalized [s]. By this time, Jacqueline had acquired all
the nasal vowels.

Stage three is about the point at which the father's
description stopped, but we can assume that Jacqueline grew
up to speak adult French, and I took the liberty of continuing
the chart to the full set of phonemes that we might expect from
an adult speaker. We notice here that there are only five additions. As Jakobson predicted, /r/ is one of the last consonants to be acquired. The f-v contrast will finally become
stabilized. The /ž/ which was just about to come in at the
end of January (previously variation between [ž] and [y]) is

well-established and the palatal ñ̲ and the third semivowel are
acquired. We do not have to belabor any of these points, because I am not trying to propound any particular theory of
development, and I am not trying to defend a particular analysis of
Jacqueline's speech. I am trying to point out that it is possible to
make successive structural analyses of a child's speech and
to look at the whole process of language development as a set
of changes from one structure to another; doing so might con-
ceivably offer us some useful insights into the phonological
structure of a particular language and into the processes of
child language development. Also, the particular formulation
used here is not what I am trying to defend, although I think
that it is useful and I would be prepared, within certain limits,
to defend it. But there are other equally good, and perhaps
better ways of presenting a succession of structural analyses,
such as sets of rules comparable to those offered by Roger
Brown for the grammatical level. I would be a little doubtful,
however, in our present state of understanding of the phonological component of transformational generative grammars,
about recommending that kind of analysis for successive stages
of the development of phonological structure.

2. <u>Model and Replica.</u> The second kind of contrastive
analysis that I would like to offer at this time is quite different.
For a long time people have described child language development in terms of deviations ('mistakes') from or successive
approximations to the adult norm. One of the great forward
steps made in the study of child language development in the
last few years was the decision to study the child's language
on its own terms, and it was by doing so that important advances in understanding childhood grammar have come. What
I am suggesting here, however, is in effect a return in some
ways to the earlier attitude. Not only should we compare the
child's phonology or grammar or his whole range of language
behavior at the thirteenth month, the twenty-second month,

or at whatever seem to be appropriate intervals, but it is also useful to compare the child's grammar at any particular point to the adult grammar, and I would like to do that for reasons similar to those justifying the study of a succession of stages. It throws some light on the question of language structure in general—that is, how the adult language works. For example, I have discovered a number of things about English which I did not know before by comparing the child's English at a certain point with the adult's. And also, once again, it may throw light on the kind of processes at work in the child's acquisition of language.

As an illustration of this second kind of contrastive analysis, what I have called 'model and replica', I have taken Leopold's study of his daughter Hildegard.[7] Once again, it is difficult, in reading through the thick second volume of the four-volume study, to reach an understanding of the structure at a particular stage in Hildegard's development. Leopold's study is explicitly structural, it has detailed phonetic description, and it is exhaustive in the sense that all vocabulary is observed, transcribed and referred to its source language(s). In spite of this, it is difficult to stop at any one point and say what the total vocabulary is, or the grammatical structure, or the phoneme inventory. Once again I made the effort, and it turned out, to me at least, to be rewarding. The particular stage selected was the 1;10 period partly because the very next month, which happened to be the last month to which Leopold carried his detailed study, Hildegard did many new things with her phonology, and we have some new contrasts and obviously incipient contrasts. But for the month 1;10, an analysis of phonemic contrasts and the correspondences with the adult language turns out to be fairly feasible and instructive. The girl's total vocabulary at this point was about 300 words.[8] The table here gives a chart of the adult possibilities for initial consonants, a chart of the adult

possibilities for final consonants, and a chart of the
corresponding structures in Hildegard's speech. Medial consonants are not included, chiefly because of the complexity of
the situation. It seems that Hildegard in many cases introduced
a new contrast in medial position, rather than in initial position
as one might have expected. Also, there was a great deal more
fluctuation in that position, making it much more difficult to
draw a chart which is clear and presents the situation accu-
rately.

          Let us look at the initial consonant contrastive struc-
tures. Here I must explain the conventions that are involved
in this kind of presentation. In the previous contrastive charts,
I was trying to show by one particular set of conventions something about the phonological structure of the child's speech at
that time, with no attention paid to the model. Here the chart
for the adult is intended to reflect the structure of the adult
language, but the child's chart is not directly related to the
structure of the child's language. The boxes in the child's
charts are intended merely to show the relationships between
the child's sounds and the corresponding source sounds in the
adult speech. If the box labeled n on the child's chart is in the
same place and has the same shape and size as the box labeled
n on the adult chart, this means that adult /n/ has the child's
/n/ as its regular correspondence in the child's speech. Incidentally, the notion of regular, systematic correspondences is
of interest itself. It was possible at this stage, 1;10, for
Leopold in every case to decide on the 'normal' correspondence.
In many cases, there are complications and exceptions, but it
is possible in every one of these cases for Leopold to make a
judgment as to the one normal correspondence. In checking
my judgment against his by examining the words as cited in
the full vocabularies, I found that my judgment agreed with his
in every case.

Reading down the chart, we see that adult words beginning with p or b had corresponding words in Hildegard's speech beginning with the single phoneme /b/ , a voiced labial stop. Reading further down that same column, we see that words with initial f, v or w all had the /w/ as their equivalent in Hildegard's speech. As we look at the next column /n/ was representative of n, and the voiced apical stop /d/ was the child's phoneme corresponding to adult t d and the interdentals. Going further down that line, it is interesting to observe that initial s and z when they are represented at all in the speech of Hildegard are represented by /y/ . The adult r is represented by /w/ . Initial l is much more problematic—it occurs in only a few words, and it is difficult to assign a normal representation to it, but this seems to be /y/ . If we look at the extension of the box of /d/ , it turns out that the initial /d/ for the child corresponds to the adult ǰ as well as the two apical stops. It might seem a little surprising that the child uses /d/ for adult ǰ but not for č. Hildegard had many words such as /duš/ for juice, but only rare words such as choo-choo corresponding to adult initial /č/ . This latter sound is reflected by a fluctuating but predominantly voiced affricate in the child's speech. All I can say is that this is not at all unusual—many children seem to split adult /č/ and /ǰ/ this way.

Let us now look at the charts of final consonants and note some of their special features. The blank boxes mean that the normal correspondence was zero. That is, at this age, final f and v had no counterparts in the child's language; they were simply omitted. Similarly, final r and final l had no equivalents in the child's language; they were simply omitted. The parentheses around the /t/ and /k/ suggest a situation difficult to present from a classical phonemic point of view: the /t/ and /k/ were just becoming contrasting elements at this time. There are some words which prefer /t/ , others /k/ , and still other words that are in a state of flux. Unfor-

tunately the choice does not correspond exactly to the source
items, since sometimes the adult language has a /t/ where
the child has a /k/ and vice versa. But generally, however,
the final /t/ is represented by a final /t/ and a final /k/ by
a final /k/. It is interesting here that final /k/ is coming
into the language before initial /,k/ appears. In initial position
/k/ and /g/ are represented by /d/.

The /w/ and /y/ are put in parentheses here because
they occur only as the second part of the diphthongs au, ai, and
oi. While some analysts prefer to recognize these as the equivalents of initial /w/ and /y/ , it seems more appropriate
here either to regard the second element as a vowel or to
regard the diphthongs as single units. If we disregard the y
in parentheses, it is then immediately apparent that /š/ in
final position covers roughly the same territory that /y/ covers
in initial position, that is, they have roughly the same sources
in the model language. In Hildegard's speech at this point, you
will notice that in initial position she generally has voiced
sounds, and in final position voiceless ones. Insofar as there
is a voicing contrast, it is beginning to develop in the medial
position. From looking at this diagram and considering the
phonetic similarity of [y] and [š] it becomes clear that /y/ and
/š/ are voiced-voiceless counterparts in Hildegard's speech,
a conclusion which is not made explicit in Leopold's study.
And, having once observed the y-š relationship in Hildegard's
speech, as a result of this model-and-replica contrastive analysis, we can then look elsewhere for similar phenomena, and
it turns out that y and š often function as voiced-voiceless counterparts in child language.

3. Implications. This paper has presented some evidence for the usefulness of contrastive analysis in the study of
child language development, both by the contrasting of successive
stages much as in the history of a language and by the contrasting of adult and child language. In both cases the contrastive

analysis suggested here is systematic and explicit, whatever
approach to grammatical and phonological analysis may be
followed. It seems likely that there are important linguistic
implications for these two kinds of contrastive analysis of
child language. The first kind would tend to deepen our knowledge of child language development and, indeed, of diachronic linguistics in general. The second would help us toward
a better knowledge of model-replica processes—processes
which are relevant not only in the child's acquisition of a first
language but very likely also at least to some extent in the
acquisition of a second language in childhood or later. Both
kinds of contrastive analysis show some promise of helping
us in the formulation of a general theory of language.

This whole Round Table discussion is supposed to be
about contrastive linguistics and pedagogical implications,
and therefore a sentence or two about pedagogical implications
is in order. One kind of pedagogical application that should be
possible here would be that of helping along the process of
child language development. It is true that a number of workers
in psycholinguistics have expressed their amazement that
child language development seems to take place almost no matter what you do, and that the processes tried experimentally
so far to explain the miracle such as expansion by the adults
or direct imitation by the child, etc., seem impressively inadequate. I would say, however, that even though we maintain
an attitude of amazement and wonder at the fact that children
do learn their language in spite of what their teachers, parents,
etc. may do about it, it should still be possible to help the
child acquire his native language, i.e. to simplify or speed up
the process by some technique or other, and it would seem
natural to make the same kind of assumption here as in language teaching in general: other things being equal, it is
likely that the teacher or course planner can do a better job if
he has accurate explicit knowledge of the structure of the

learner's language and the target language. In the second
place, there might well be some pedagogical implications here
for second language teaching, in terms of a better understanding of the model-replica process and in terms of understanding
successive stages of acquisition of language. In this last instance there could be relevance in both directions since the
study of the stages of acquisition of a second language may contribute to the understanding of first language acquisition.
Finally, it is just conceivable that these two kinds of contrastive analysis might give us some clues on how to improve our
techniques in the kinds of contrastive analysis that were talked
about this morning, such as the comparison of Spanish and
English for the purpose of teaching adults one or the other as
a foreign language. In summary, the use of contrastive analysis in the study of child language development may be of value
for linguistics proper and may have valuable pedagogical appli-
cations.

NOTES

[1] Jakobson, Kindersprache, Aphasie und Allgemeine
Lautgesetze (Uppsala, 1941), to appear as Child Language,
Aphasia and Phonological Universals (The Hague, 1968).

[2] For a discussion of several kinds of diachronic analysis, cf. C.A. Ferguson, 'Linguistic Theory and Language Learning' Georgetown University Monograph Series on Languages and
Linguistics. 16:115-122, esp. 116-120.

[3] R. Brown, U. Bellugi, and C. Cazden, 'The child's
grammar from I to III', 1967 Minnesota Symposium on Child
Psychology.

4 The child is Jacqueline Bloch, whose linguistic development was discussed in considerable detail by her father O. Bloch, 'Notes sur le langage d'un enfant', Mem. Soc. Ling. Paris 18: 37-59 (1913); id., 'La phrase dans le langage d'un enfant', Journal de Psychologie 21:18-43 (1924).

5 In the source articles there is no discussion of such contrasts as é:è, è:ê, o:ô, a:â which are present in orthoepic French but are absent in the French of many native speakers. These contrasts are omitted from consideration here as are such phenomena as the 'mute e' and 'h aspirée.'

6 For the use of charts of this kind to present phoneme inventories, cf. C. A. Ferguson and M. Chowdhury, 'The phonemes of Bengali,' Language 36:22-59 (1960) esp. 29-30.

7 W. F. Leopold, The Speech Development of a Bilingual Child 4 vols. (Evanston, Ill., 1939-49) esp. Vol. 2 Sound Learning in the First Two Years (1947).

8 It is to be noted that Hildegard seems to have had a single phonological system for all her words, whether of German or English origin, and almost all her sound types could be explained from English models. Cf. W. F. Leopold, 'A child's learning of two languages' Georgetown University Monograph Series Languages and Linguistics 7:19-30 esp. 20-23.

16 | Contrasting Patterns of Literacy Acquisition in a Multilingual Nation

National multilingualism, the use of different language codes by substantial segments of the population of a country, is a well-recognized phenomenon, and a number of lines of research on it are currently being pursued. A less well-recognized socio-linguistic phenomenon is the coexistence within a nation of different approaches to the acquisition of literacy, not in the limited sense of different methods of instruction within a single framework of national purpose but in the sense of fundamentally different patterns which represent different aims, utilize different methods, tend to apply to different segments of the population, and have different outcomes. Thus, in a given nation there may be a contrast between a 'traditional' literacy with its goals and procedures, on the one hand, and a 'modern' literacy with different goals and procedures, on the other. Or a nation with a predominant and universally acknowledged pattern of literacy may have a different pattern, followed by a religious minority or by the majority but as a supplementary literacy for particular religious purposes. This phenomenon of national diversity in styles of literacy is the subject matter of the present paper.

In some ways this phenomenon could be better treated
as a small part of different total patterns of education in a
nation, and treatments of it in this more general context can
doubtless be found. The purpose of the present paper, however,
is to focus more narrowly on the actual processes of the acquisition of the ability to read, since it is at this point that the
insights and methods of linguistics can be of greatest value in
the analysis and characterization of the different patterns. The
findings on this limited phenomenon may then prove of relevance
for larger-scale treatments of educational processes.

The phenomenon of varied patterns of literacy acquisition within a nation can be found in many African countries, and
it deserves study from a number of points of view. Here a
single country will be examined, Ethiopia, and a single technique
of analysis will be used, contrastive presentation of basic facts
assembled in terms of a check list of questions. The data have
been obtained from interviews, published studies, and observation of behaviour in literacy learning situations.

Ethiopia has a number of patterns of literacy acquisition,
each with distinctive aims, methods, and results, and each followed by substantial numbers of people. It also has intermediate,
ill-defined patterns, and a number of minor patterns in terms of
number of people involved. Three fairly well-defined major
patterns will be examined here. Several preliminary observations must be made: first, the overwhelming majority of
Ethiopians do not become literate at all; second, there seems to
be at present no widespread well-defined pattern of learning to
read Amharic in the schools, although Amharic is the national
language, it is the medium of instruction in primary education,
and almost every educated Ethiopian is literate in it. Third,
the majority of Ethiopians do not have Amharic as their mother
tongue, but speak one of the other two major languages (Galla or

Tigrinya) or one of the seventy-odd minor languages of the country.

The three patterns of literacy acquisition to be studied are church school pattern, adult campaign pattern, and Quranic school pattern. Each is examined in terms of five questions: (1) What are the apparent goals ? (2) What is the nature of the writing system to be mastered ? (3) What language or languages are involved ? (4) What methods of instruction are employed ? (5) What is the setting in which instruction takes place ?

I. CHURCH SCHOOL PATTERN

Goals

The traditional church-school literacy training provides a basic competence for participation in the services of the Ethiopian Orthodox Church, and completion of the training gives a particular status in the society or marks a particular stage in an individual's life (Dawit däggämä, 'he repeated David'). This training may serve as the first stage in the comprehensive traditional system of church education; more often at the present time it serves as preparation for entry into a government school or other educational institution. The traditional church education is described in Haile Gabriel (1966) and Imbakom (forthcoming): briefer accounts appear in O'Hanlon (1946), Pankhurst (1966), and Girma (1967). The most detailed description of the Ethiopian writing system is Cohen (1936); some additional information appears in Wright (1964).

This pattern of literacy acquisition is essentially acquisition of the ability to read aloud material written in Geez, the classical liturgical language of Ethiopia. The process involves memorization of the characters and their pronunciation, in the traditional order, reading of traditional selections from Scripture and liturgical texts, and memorization of certain texts. Ability to write the characters is secondary, and literacy in Amharic, the national language of Ethiopia, is a by-product of the process. Typically instruction is by a priest (the school is commonly called yä-qés temhert bét, 'priest's school'), at a site in the vicinity of a church, and the pupils are boys about 5-8 years of age.

Writing System

The Ethiopian writing system consists of a core of 33 characters, each of which occurs in a basic form and in six other forms with diacritical additions representing vowels, a total of 231 different characters. These do not constitute 231 unrelated items to be learned since: (a) the basic shapes show similarities; (b) one feature is in effect a diacritic for palatalization; and (c) each diacritical vowel addition shows some kind of basic invariance, ranging from the unvarying small loop to the right for é to the various largely unpredictable shapes for e. In addition to the 231 there are nearly 40 characters which contain a special feature usually representing post-consonantal w; of these, 20 are often listed as a kind of appendix to the alphabet proper and the others are not commonly listed. There is no capital/lower-case distinction, and the use of different type fonts or styles is not well developed. The writing goes from left to right.

Punctuation and numerals constitute additional components in the writing system. Core elements of punctuation are a word-divider and a full stop (consisting of two dots and four dots respectively); recent additions include equivalents for comma, colon, and question mark. The numeral system consists of 20 characters (1–10, 20–100, 1,000) used in a positional notation without a zero, always accompanied by horizontal strokes above and below each character.

Language

The subject-matter language of traditional church schools is Geez, and the medium of instruction is normally Amharic. The same writing system is used for Geez, Amharic, and Tigrinya, and in rare instances for other languages of Ethiopia. The traditional pronunciation of Geez uses only Amharic phonemes, and the sound-symbol correspondences are identical for Geez and Amharic. Tigrinya preserves several consonants lost in Amharic but originally present in Geez; apparently Tigrinya speakers who study in church schools usually learn the Amharic pronunciation of Geez rather than using a Tigrinya pronunciation of the extra consonants. For Geez, as for Amharic, a written text provides an unambiguous guide to the consonants and vowels of the corresponding oral rendition, with the exception of two features: (a) gemination of consonants, which is of considerable frequency and grammatical significance in both Geez and Amharic, and (b) absence of vowel in consonant clusters, which is represented by the same characters as consonant + /e/ . For the speakers of Amharic these features are relatively unimportant, in spite of fairly frequent spelling ambiguities, because the context is usually sufficient to make the proper identification. For Amharic speakers reading Geez and for non-Amharic speakers reading Geez or Amharic these features are more troublesome and are the occasion for corrections by the teacher.

Since there were more consonant phonemes in Geez than there are in Amharic, and Amharic words related to Geez

tend to be spelled similarly to their Geez counterparts, Amharic
orthography is in a many-to-one relationship with Amharic pronunciation, i.e. the Amharic speaker who wants to spell a word
he knows must select the appropriate h̲, s̲, s̲, or vowel carrier
(see table). Contemporary Amharic spelling exhibits considerable variation on these points and several others, and various
suggestions have been made for standardization of the spelling
(see Cowley, 1967, for discussion and further references).

Geez spelling and pronunciation; Amharic spelling		Amharic pronunciation
አ ዐ	(ʾ ʿ)	φ (vowel carrier)
ሀ ሐ ኀ ከ	(h ḥ ḫ x)	h
ሰ ሠ	(s š)	s
ጸ ፀ	(ṣ ẓ)	ṣ

Method

The method of instruction varies from place to place,
and modernizing elements are entering, but the traditional procedures are as follows:

(1) The pupils are shown the letters in the arbitrary
traditional order: hä̲ hu̲ hi̲ ha̲ hé̲ he̲ ho̲; lä̲ lu̲ li̲ lé̲ le̲ lo̲, etc.,
left to right on the chart, and memorize them in this sequence.
The pupils 'read' the characters aloud one by one as the pointer
indicates them, and they do this over and over again until the
whole set of 231 or 251 is learned. At this stage the pupils may
have, in effect, memorized the letters by their position, and a
pupil may be bewildered by having a particular letter pointed out
for naming outside the sequence.

(2) A second traditional order of the alphabet (the abugida) is then used for further drilling to make certain that the pupils know all the letters independently of their position in the sequence. This second order is closely related to the usual order of letters in Semitic (and Latin) alphabets. It is generally believed, however, that this order does not continue the probable order of South Arabic letters, which were the starting-point of the Ethiopian syllabary, but was introduced at a later date by someone familiar with another alphabet (see Getachew, 1966-67).

(3) Next the fidälä hawareya, 'apostles' alphabet', consisting of the first several verses of the 1st Epistle of John, is 'read' and memorized. This passage seems not to have been selected for its simplicity or ease of comprehension, nor for the distribution of different characters within it. The purpose behind the selection was very probably that the passage would serve as a preparation for reading the Gospel and Epistles of John and the Book of Revelation, which are favourite parts of the Bible in the Ethiopian Church. The text is first read letter by letter (the quter style), then in a singsong manner by pairs of letters (the ge'ez style). Next the pupil reads out in a slow sing-song way short phrases of two or three words (the wärd näbab style), paying special attention to gemination, word connections, and accent. Finally, he reads connectedly (the qum näbab style).

(4) The next stage consists of learning to read and/or memorize selections from Scripture and the prayers and songs of the Church. The actual selection of texts varies from school to school, depending on the decisions of the teacher and the availability of manuscripts at the particular church. Typically, certain commonly recited prayers and hymns such as the Praises of Mary and the Lord's Prayer are learned, but the training may also include selections from the Gospel of John or other texts.

(5) Additional selections of Scripture are then read
and re-read. The most important of them, which forms a part
of all church school literacy training, is the book of Psalms
(Mäzmurä Dawit 'Psalms of David'). When the pupil has gone
through the entire 151 psalms to his teacher's satisfaction
(usually three or four times through) the pupil is 'graduated'
and his family traditionally has a feast of celebration at which
the boy reads or recites some of the psalms or other material
he has learned. Up to this point little or no attempt has been
made to explain the meaning of the material or to teach the
Geez language as such.

(6) Traditionally writing is not taught as such during
this period, but some teachers now give instruction in writing.
The traditional method, formerly used at a more advanced
level of study, uses reed pens, ink made by the pupils from
leaves and soot, and slabs of wood or bone on which to write.
The traditional instruction in writing usually takes about three
or four months. Some pupils may learn to write by observation
or self-instruction. Many pupils, by the time they have finished
their Dawit, have acquired enough competence in writing and
reading the Ethiopian syllabary to write letters in Amharic for
illiterates.

Setting

In general, every parish church and every monastery
has a school associated with it. In addition, many wealthy
people have a teacher in the household to conduct classes, and
there are also teachers who offer instruction independently.
The usual setting is outside, with the pupils sitting on rocks in
a rough circle. Much of the teaching is done by the more advanced students, and students of all levels are mingled in the

same 'classroom', each moving at more or less his own pace. Recitation is often simultaneous. The schools average about 30 pupils per teacher, but the number of pupils may be as high as a hundred. The teachers are priests, monks, or laymen (däbtärä) with Church education. Many of the teachers at this level do not have a clear understanding of the content of the Geez material they are teaching.

II. ADULT CAMPAIGN PATTERN

The adult campaign pattern of literacy acquisition consists of acquiring the ability to read (with understanding) and write Amharic material. The writing system has already been described in the preceding section, but the methods of teaching are quite different. Some indications of the methods can be found in Alphabetization (1966), Djaletta (1964), Getachew (1962-63), 'Notes on a New Method. . .'(n. d.), and in the introduction to various primers.

The principal agencies sponsoring adult literacy campaigns have been the Ministry of Education, UNESCO, various missions, churches, church-related organizations (e. g. Yemissrach Dimts, Sudan Interior Mission), and the National Literacy Campaign. Other agencies have also been involved, both governmental and non-governmental (e. g. Ministry of Community Development, National Lottery, Philips Co.). Although the various agencies may have somewhat different aims, and the various instructional materials differ in a number of ways, there is a fundamental similarity in aims and methods.

The pupils in adult literacy campaigns may be of almost any age, but are predominantly 15-45. They may be of any native language, but are predominantly non-Amharic speaking;

of any religion but predominantly Christian or under Christian
influence, often non-Orthodox. The teachers are sometimes
volunteers, often high-school students, and the classes take
place in buildings intended primarily for other purposes, most
often schools or churches.

Method

        The adult campaign pattern differs from the church-
school pattern in having clearly delimited lessons presented in
a primer or charts or both, each lesson treating a selected
portion of the writing system. The selection of lesson material
is based either on the shape of the letters, the frequency of
occurrence of the letters, or both. Some primers start with the
full set of basic characters and then gradually add the various
vowel 'orders'. Others start with a small group of similarly
shaped letters of high frequency and progress towards the less
regular and less frequent. Some emphasize the use of real
words from the first lesson, many have pictures, either to
illustrate words to be learned or to be associated with the shape
of the first letter of a key word. One system has even used
colour coding of the various vowel orders. Whatever the details
of the methods, all are based on the notion that the material to
be learned should be presented systematically and in small units.

        The adult campaign pattern also differs from the church-
school pattern in providing teachers' manuals with discussions
of method and justification for the particular approach followed.
One set of materials even has a special book for inspectors who
travel from class to class to make sure the work is going properly. Another difference between the more traditional church-
school pattern and the adult campaigns lies in the nature of the
'follow-up' material, i. e. the reading matter provided for the

pupils when they complete the first step of literacy acquisition.
In the church-school pattern the material is chosen for its
value in religious education, without regard for its usefulness
in preserving or extending competence in reading and writing.
In the adult campaign pattern, however, follow-up material is
often prepared expressly for the newly literate and is intended
to improve his reading skills. Some of this material has a
religious flavour, and in the opinion of the producers it may be
directly related to a Church message, but much of it is not
obviously religious in content.

Setting

Adult literacy classes are generally conducted in classroom settings, often in school rooms after hours, but sometimes in other facilities which approximate classroom characteristics. The teachers are people with some degree of modern
education in Amharic, often high-school students or high-school
graduates. A large proportion of adult literacy teachers are
unpaid volunteers, but the more successful programmes generally have paid part-time teachers, and there exists a small
corps of experienced full-time teachers and inspectors in various literacy programmes. A number of these people have had
specialized training in literacy work, ranging from a few days
orientation to intensive workshops in foreign literacy centres.

III. QURANIC SCHOOL PATTERN

Goals

The Quranic school literacy training provides a basic
competence for Muslim religious observances and may also

serve as the first stage in the comprehensive system of Muslim education, which reaches its culmination in study at a Muslim centre outside the country. More often at the present time it serves as a preparation for entry to a government school or another educational institution. The system of Muslim education in Ethiopia is described briefly in Trimingham (1962). The Arabic writing system is described in Mitchell (1953), where particular attention is paid to the techniques of writing, and Blachère (1952, pp. 58-65), where its historical development is summarized.

This pattern of literacy acquisition is essentially acquisition of the ability to read aloud and write certain kinds of material in Arabic. The material consists chiefly of parts of the Quran and the prescribed forms of daily prayer.

Writing System

The Arabic system consists of a core of 28 characters, most of which show variations in shape, depending on whether they are connected to the left, the right, both, or neither. Six characters never connect to the left, and no characters connect at word boundaries, which are thus marked by space. The variation in shape per character ranges from essential invariance in the case of a letter like < w > to four quite different shapes for   < h > . Several sets of characters have similar or identical forms, except for diacritical marks consisting of various numbers of dots over or under the letter. In addition to the core characters there are about a dozen special signs which are used as diacritics to indicate short vowels (otherwise not marked), gemination of consonants, presence of glottal stop, certain endings, and other features. These additional signs, referred to collectively as taškīl, are not usually present in written Arabic texts, although they are generally used in texts of the Quran. There is no capital/lower-case distinction, but there are several different styles of script. The writing goes from right to left.

Punctuation and numerals constitute additional components in the writing system. The most important item of punctuation is a sentence marker, but equivalents of the comma, question mark, and other European signs of punctuation are increasingly used. The numeral system is a decimal notation in a one-to-one correspondence with the so-called Arabic numerals used in Europe, but the shapes of the numerals are quite different.

Language

The subject-matter language of traditional Quranic schools is Arabic, and the medium of instruction is usually the mother tongue of the group (e.g. Galla, Somali) or Amharic. For a very small minority of the pupils Arabic is the mother tongue. For a substantial number of other pupils some form of spoken Arabic is familiar as a lingua franca. For some pupils, also, the Quranic school is an important part of the process of acquiring a spoken use of Arabic. It must be noted, however, that most of the pupils do not learn spoken Arabic and acquire only a very limited ability to use written Arabic. It must also be noted that the difference between the forms, syntax, and lexicon of written Arabic and of spoken Arabic is very great (Ferguson, 1959), considerably greater than between written and spoken Amharic and roughly comparable to the difference between Geez and Amharic.

The sound system of the Arabic language differs from

the sound systems of the various mother tongues of Ethiopian
Muslims. No other language in Ethiopia has a set of 'emphatic'
consonants, like those of Arabic, although a number have glot-
talized consonants which sometimes serve as counterparts in
phonological adaptations in loan words, etc. Some languages
of Ethiopia have velar spirants and pharyngeal sounds like those
of Arabic, others do not. No other languages of the country
seem to have interdental spirants like those of Arabic.

For (Classical) Arabic a written text provides an
unambiguous guide to the consonants, but without the taškīl the
short vowels, gemination of consonants, and the distinction
between long vowels and diphthongs are not shown. The Arabic
writing system with full taškīl is fundamentally similar in
nature to the Ethiopian syllabary, but there are important differences: connected versus separate letters, difference in
direction of writing, usual omission of taškīl versus obligatory
vowel diacritics.

Method

In the most traditional schools the pupil uses a wooden
plate (lawh) on which he writes and erases. The Arabic letters
are taught in the traditional ABC order, first by name then by
sound with each vowel mark (e.g. a, ba, ta. . .; 'a, 'i, 'u. . .)
and with some of the other special signs. Many of these sequences are recited in special singsong manners. The pupils
then progress to words. The first connected text is usually the
fātiḥa, the opening sura of the Quran, which is used on many
occasions. This is followed by other passages from the Quran,
prayers, and other items of religious importance. In those
schools which use textbooks the commonest beginning work is
a primer printed in Singapore (Qāᶜida Baghdādiyya) which

includes practice material in letters and words, the fātiḥa and
other Quranic material, and instructions for ritual prayers and
ablutions.

After the earliest stage most emphasis is given to the
memorization of the Quran and other religious texts, particular
attention being paid to correct recitation (tajwīd, including both
pronunciation as such and musical tone, since all these texts
are chanted in accordance with traditional practice. Relatively
little attention is given either to the meaning of the material or
to the structure of the Arabic language.

Setting

In general, every village mosque has some kind of
Quranic school associated with it. In addition, some of the
towns and cities have separate Islamic schools, varying in
nature from very traditional to quite modern. The former are
usually conducted by a local imam or a visiting shaykh who
offers his services. The latter are run by a founder-director
or by a board of interested citizens. The pupils in all these
schools are nearly 100 per cent Muslim, although a few non-
Muslims can be found. A high proportion of the teachers speak
Arabic either as their mother tongue or as a second language;
of these many seem to be Hararis, whose native language is
Adare but who are multilingual from an early age, in three or
more of the following: Adare, Arabic, Amharic, Galla, Somali,
French, English, Italian.

IV. TRENDS

The characterizations of the three preceding sections attempted to give a picture of each pattern of literacy acquisition in its most typical form at the present time. Each pattern has also, of course, a history which deserves separate study, and each pattern shows tendencies of change which are important to understand either for assessment by planners and policy-makers or for the formulation of general hypotheses on the processes of national development. This section presents six apparent trends.

Expansion

Since two of the three patterns of literacy acquisition are traditional in nature and aimed at goals not clearly related to national development, it might be supposed that they are diminishing in numbers of people involved and in general importance. This does not seem to be the case. Although no figures can be presented, it seems clear that the number of pupils following the traditional patterns is increasing, and although the function of these patterns in the 60's may be shifting and certain features of methods and materials may be changing, their importance does not seem to be diminishing. The adult campaign pattern, as might have been expected, is also increasing, and new elements of both diversification and co-ordination of efforts are appearing. In short, for some years to come all these patterns will probably continue to expand, and no new pattern of school reading instruction is likely to emerge.

Modernization

All three patterns show strong trends of modernization

in teaching methods and in the instructional materials utilized.
In the church schools in Addis Ababa, for example, it is
almost impossible to find copies of the traditional manuscripts
in use. Printed single sheets are now usually available, con-
taining the fidel in both traditional orders, the numbers, the
beginning of the first Epistle of John in Geez, and in addition,
the Roman alphabet and Arabic numerals, an advertisement for
the printing press, and a picture of the Emperor. Also several
printed editions of the Dawit are available, some including also
devotional material (all in Geez), and there is even an authorized
edition of the Psalms with parallel Geez and Amharic. All these
materials are increasingly used in traditional church schools,
especially in Addis Ababa, and although most of the schools in
the provinces are much less modernized, the trend is unmistakable.
The greatest modernization in methods is the tendency to teach
writing at an early stage; schools can now be found in which the
priest-teacher is trying to teach a skill which he himself has
not mastered, since in his own training writing had not been
emphasized.

The Quranic schools show similar kinds of modernization. In Addis Ababa the traditional wooden boards seem nowhere
to be in use, and even the most traditional school visited by the
author had wooden benches, a blackboard, and a few books,
although the basic classroom technique was memorization from
oral models. The most important change taking place is the use
of modern printed textbooks in Islamic schools; in place of the
Singapore primer, primary school textbooks from Egypt and
Lebanon are increasingly used. These textbooks are intended
in their country of origin for speakers of Arabic, while in
Ethiopia the pupils may have little or no knowledge of Arabic
when they come to school, but the use of pictures, graded lessons, exercises, etc., is clearly an example of modernization.

One Islamic school in Addis Ababa has even printed its own first- and second-grade primers for Arabic instruction ('Abid, 1950), and there is also a beginning book in Arabic with text in Amharic, printed in Asmara (Sayyid Ibrahim, 1959-60).

The adult campaign materials from the beginning had a 'modern' appearance, but even here examples of further modernization can be found, such as new and improved wall charts and follow-up readers with colour illustrations. The most striking example is the consideration being given by one mission group to make use of a cassette-type magnetic tape set with accompanying printed materials for pre-literacy and literacy work in non-Amharic-speaking areas.

Governmentalization

All three patterns of literacy acquisitions have been chiefly non-governmental in sponsorship, financing, and actual operation. Each pattern now shows signs of becoming more closely connected with the government. A considerable number of church-run schools now follow the government curriculum and receive from the Government the usual financial support in terms of teachers' salaries, etc. These schools are included in the Ministry of Education's statistics on schools, and although they may vary considerably in the nature of the instruction offered, they are basically equivalent to government schools rather than traditional Church schools. The pupils attending them may indeed have first acquired literacy at a priest's school. Although this governmentalization represents an addition to traditional schools or a replacement of church education beyond the beginning stage, it is bound to have ever stronger effects on the traditional systems themselves, and clearly is an example of close connection with government.

Quranic schools are similarly moving towards governmentalization, although at a much slower rate. Direct governmental sponsorship exists in at least one Islamic school: the
primary school associated with the mosque in Addis Ababa,
which follows the government curriculum (plus Arabic and
religious studies), has government-supplied teachers, and is
government financed. In a few other schools the Government
supplies some teachers although no other financial aid. In
many Islamic schools in the towns and cities, as opposed to
the situation in rural areas, the most important trend to
governmentalization is the increasing use of the government
curriculum, so that sixth-grade students are prepared for the
national sixth-year examination. Up to the present there are
apparently no Islamic schools as such beyond the sixth grade,
except for a single school in Asmara affiliated to an Egyptian
university, and Muslim students must attend government or
private secondary schools where no Arabic or Muslim religious
studies are offered.

Tying to National Development

The two traditional patterns of literacy acquisition were
not explicitly related to national development—indeed, the concept of national development is itself a recent notion in the
Empire—and the adult campaign pattern in many instances was
conceived of as contributing to Christianization or to spiritual
growth within Church congregations. Increasingly, however,
in both governmental and non-governmental circles, all three
patterns are regarded as contributing to national socio-economic
developments, and changes in operation and methods are initiated with this new goal explicitly used as justification. The
Government in its development planning assigns a place to literacy instruction. (Cf. Second Five Year Development Plan,

p. 268, 'Action against Illiteracy' and also p. 260, 'as far as
reducing the rate of illiteracy and the extension of basic primary education are concerned, the contribution of the church
schools cannot be ignored'.)

The most striking explicit tie between literacy training
and national development, as might be expected, is being made
in the adult campaign pattern. The connection was already
recognized in earlier campaigns (cf. Djaletta, 1963), but recent
trends emphasize it even more. The recently inaugurated
UNESCO-sponsored Work-Oriented Adult Literacy Project ties
the teaching of literacy directly to agricultural and industrial
development projects.

Decline of Traditional Higher Education

The two traditional patterns of literacy acquisition have
served as preparation for traditional systems of higher education, within the Orthodox Church schools of various kinds or
Islamic schools. In the past only a small percentage of those
who had completed the literacy training went on to higher education, but at the present time even this number is rapidly declining. The Islamic schools above the beginning level of Quranic
school are in the process of disappearing in Ethiopia, and the
practice of going outside Ethiopia to an Islamic country (e.g.
Sudan, Egypt, Aden) for higher education has decreased sharply.
At the present time Quranic schools generally feed into government or other non-Islamic schools.

The traditional higher schools of the Ethiopian Orthodox
Church are of various kinds, each devoted to a special kind of
study, including: religious music; Geez language and literature
including the composition of poetry; the books of the Old and

New Testaments, including commentaries; the writing of the Church fathers; works on monastic life; the mathematics and astronomy related to the calculation of the Ethiopian Church calendar; and the specialized arts and crafts within the Church. Students normally attend several different schools, following their own interests; it has been estimated (Imbakom, forthcoming) that it would take about thirty years to complete study in all the different kinds of schools. At the present time all these kinds of schools exist, and there are hundreds of students in them, but the attendance is declining, and one observer has predicted that within a generation these higher schools will have disappeared.

V. PEDAGOGICAL IMPLICATIONS

The specialist in language teaching or the teaching of reading will be disconcerted by at least two features of the three Ethiopian patterns of literacy acquisition described here. In the first place he will be surprised to find that the majority of Ethiopians first become literate, by these methods, in a language which they do not speak. The language of literacy may be a classical language of limited functions in the society (e. g. Geez or Arabic) or it may be the national language of Ethiopia (Amharic) for a non-Amharic speaker. The first reaction of the specialist would be that the normal pattern of literacy acquisition should be in the mother tongue of the learner, but where this is not possible special teaching methods and materials should be used. Generally in Ethiopian literacy acquisition there is no explicit recognition of the difference between mother-tongue literacy and literacy in another language, apart from Eritrea and some scattered mission programmes. Before passing judgment, however, the specialist might well investigate

the importance of such factors as strength of motivation for
literacy acquisition, religious values associated with literacy,
and the special status of the national language. In the only
experiment related to this question which has been reported
for Ethiopia the non-Amharic speakers made somewhat better
progress in literacy acquisition than the Amharic speakers
using the same materials (adult campaign pattern).
(Cf. Brooks, 1966.)

        The second surprise for the specialist would be the
very great emphasis placed on memorization, especially in the
two traditional patterns. A reading teacher from the United
States, for example, would be astonished to hear 3- and 4-
year-old children reciting or singing from memory hundreds
of lines of text in languages they do not speak or understand.
The first reaction is likely to be one of disapproval, both because of the apparent irrelevance of the subject matter and
because of the apparently excessive use of memorization as a
teaching technique. Here again further investigation might be
in order. The memorized material may have high relevance
in terms of ability to participate in religious ceremonies or to
exhibit one's skills to admiring adults, and even in terms of
the child's own pleasure in rhythmical verbalization, comparable in some ways to nursery rhymes with nonsense material
in them. Finally, the excellent pronunciation achieved by many
of the children in this kind of memorization may even suggest
its usefulness for second-language teaching at the early ages.
For example, some children observed by the author used phonological features of Arabic in their recitation which they did not
have in their mother tongue, including post-velar and interdental consonants and the distinction between long and short
vowels. There is certainly opportunity here for careful pedagogical experimentation, and some of the results might even
have theoretical significance in understanding the essentially

mysterious processes of child language development and literacy acquisition.

REFERENCES

The works listed below were consulted in the preparation of this paper. They are arranged in alphabetical order by author, by first names for Ethiopian authors, and surnames for non-Ethiopian authors. All Ethiopian and Muslim calendar dates have been converted to the Gregorian calendar, e. g. 1968-69 is put for 1961 Eth. Cal. Where an Ethiopian author's preference for Amharic spelling is known, this is used; otherwise the transliteration system of the Journal of Ethiopian Studies is followed (cf. Wright, 1964). The same transliteration is used for Amharic titles.

Abīd, Muḥammad. 1950. Mabādi' al-Qirā' a ar-Rashīda (Principles of Correct Reading), Vols. 1 and 2. Cairo: Dar Al-Maaref.

_____ 1966. Alphabetisation and Adult Education by Radio. (Foreword by Dr. R. A. J. van Lier). Eindhoven, Netherlands: N. V. Philips.

Blachère, R. 1952. Histoire de la Litterature Arabe, Vol. I. Paris: Adrien-Maisonneuve.

Brooks, Kenneth G. 1966. The Campaign against Illiteracy in Ethiopia. Report prepared for UNESCO. (Mimeo.) Addis Ababa.

Cowley, R. 1967. "The Standardization of Amharic Spelling," J. Ethiopian Stud. , pp. 1-8.

Cohen, Marcel. 1936. 'Ecriture,' in Traité de Langue
    Amharique, pp. 17-28. Paris: Institut d'Ethnologie.

Djaletta Jaffero. 1962. Inspectors' Training Manual, Yemis-
    srach Dimts Literacy Campaign. Mimeo. bd. in
    heavy paper. Addis Ababa. (2nd ed., 1964).

_____ 1963-64. Amareñña Manbäbiya (Amharic
    Reader), 1st Book. Addis Ababa: Central Printing
    Press.

_____ 1963. Follow-up Work Training Manual.
    Yemissrach Dimts Literacy Campaign. Mimeo. bd.
    in heavy paper. Addis Ababa.

_____ 1964. Teachers' Manual. Yemissrach
    Dimts Literacy Campaign. Mimeo. bd. in heavy
    paper. Addis Ababa.

Ephraim Isaac. 1964?. Ethiopia's Problem of Illiteracy.
    Pamphlet. Cambridge, Mass. (?).

Ferguson, Charles A. 1959. 'Diglossia,' Word, XV, pp. 325-
    40.

Getachew Haile. 1966-67. "The Problems of the Amharic
    Writing System." A paper prepared in advance for
    the Interdisciplinary Seminar of the Faculty of Arts
    and Education. Mimeo. Addis Ababa: Haile Sellassie
    I University.

_____ 1962-63. Teachers' Manual. Addis
    Ababa: National Literacy Campaign.

Girma Amare. 1967. "Aims and Purposes of Church Educa-
    tion in Ethiopia," Ethiop. J. Educ., I, 1, pp. 1-11.

Girma Amare. 1963. "Memorization in Ethiopian Schools,"
J. Ethiopian Stud. , I, pp. 27-31.

Haile Gabriel Dagne. 1966. "Struktur des Kirchlichen
Schulwesens," in Versuch einer Erziehungsreform in
Äthiopien. Unpubl. Ph.D. Thesis. Free University
of Berlin.

_____ 1968. "The Entoto Speech on Church
School Training," Ethiop. J. Educ. , II, 1, pp. 11-14.

_____ (n.d.). Hullu Yemmar. (Each one Learn).
Manual of the National Literacy Campaign Association.
Addis Ababa: Commercial Press.

Imbakom Kalewold. (Forthcoming). Traditional Ethiopian
Church Schools. (Tr. by Menghestu Lemma with pre-
face by R. K. Pankhurst). New York: Teacher's
College Press.

Hagner, Olle. 1952. Kunama Aurabu Kolattama Kida Kitaba.
Eritrea: Evangelical Mission (printed by Svantessons
Boktrykeri, Hässkholm, Sweden).

Mitchell, T. F. 1953. Writing Arabic. London: Oxford University Press.

Muhammad 'Abdurrahmán. 1964. At-Tadríj lil-Madáris al-
Athyūbiyya (Primer for Ethiopian Schools). Vol. 1.
Addis Ababa: Jam'iyyat Nashr al-Thaqáfa.

Mulugéta Sämruna and Asräs Däjäné. 1964-65. Manbäbenna
Mäṣaf Bä-Radiyo (Reading and Writing by Radio).
Addis Ababa: Instructional Materials Production
Center.

_____ (n. d.). "Notes on a
New Method of Teaching Amharic Reading and Writing. "
(Addis Ababa ?).

O'Hanlon, Douglas. 1946. "Ethiopian Church Schools, " in
Features of the Ethiopian Church, pp. 13-21.
London: S. P. C. K.

Pankhurst, Richard K. 1962. "The Foundations of Education,
Printing, Newspapers, Book Production, Libraries,
and Literacy in Ethiopia, " Ethiopia Observer, pp.
251-53.

_____ 1966. "Ethiopia, " in David G. Scanlon
(ed.), Church, State, and Education in Africa, pp. 23-
58. New York: Teacher's College Press.

_____ (1932 ?). Qā'ida Baghdādiyya. Singapore:
Maktaba wa-Maṭba'a Sulaymān Mar'i.

_____ 1959-60. Sayyid Ibrahim Yáarabeñña
Qwanqwa Astämari (Arabic Language Teacher).
Asmara: Fioretti Press (?).

_____ 1962. Second Five Year Development
Plan. Addis Ababa: Imperial Ethiopian Government.

_____ 1966-67. Se'lawi Fidäl (Picture Primer),
1st Book. Addis Ababa: Ethiopian Publishing S. C. ,
Berhanena Selam.

Tafarra Wondimagnehou. 1955-56. Andäññaw Yanbab Mäṣhafé
(My First Reading Book). Asmara: Ministry of Education and Fine Arts.

Trimingham, J. Spencer. 1962. Islam in Ethiopia, London:
Frank Cass. (2nd printing, 1965).

_____ 1962-63. Yä-Amareñña Fidäl Mämariya.
(Amharic Alphabet Manual). Addis Ababa: National
Literacy Campaign Organization.

_____ 1968. Yä-Arua Mämariya (Anyuak
Primer). Also Anyuak title. Bilingual Anyuak-
Amharic. No authors, date, or place of publication
indicated. (Addis Ababa ?).

_____ 1967 ? Yä-Wangél Fidäl: bä-Qällal
Mängäd Kä-Fidäl esk-Anbab (Gospel Alphabet; from
Alphabet to Reading by an Easy Way). Addis Ababa:
SIM Press (?).

Wäldä Ab Wäldä Mariam. (n.d.). Tegreñña Nejämmärti
(Tigrinya for Beginners). Asmara: Education
Department, Brit. Mil. Aden.

Wright, Stephen. 1964. "The Transliteration of Amharic."
J. Ethiopian Stud., II, 1, pp. 1-10.

17 | Absence of Copula and the Notion of Simplicity: A Study of Normal Speech, Baby Talk, Foreigner Talk, and Pidgins

The purpose of this paper is to examine one feature of human language in a general typological framework in order to obtain some insights into the notion of grammatical simplicity. The feature in question is the presence in some languages, or special varieties or registers of a single language, of an overt connecting link, or COPULA, between nominal subjects and complements in equational clauses of the type X is Y[1] as compared with the absence of such a link in other languages or other varieties of the same language. Thus, English My brother is a student and Japanese Ani wa gakkusee desu differ from Russian Moj brat student (om) or Arabic 'Axī tilmīðun by having a copula (is, desu) which has no overt equivalent in the latter two languages. Similarly, English Your mother is outside or has gone out may correspond to baby talk Mommy bye-bye with no copula, or French La machine est grande 'The machine is big' corresponds to Haitian Creole Machin-nâ gro.

1. Normal speech. It may safely be assumed that all natural languages have grammatical machinery for equational

clauses, but the details vary considerably from one language
to another. There has been very little systematic study of
clause types across languages, and future investigations may
show the inadequacy of the crude classification used here, but
it seems helpful for the purposes at hand. There seem to be
two main types of language as far as equational clauses are
concerned. Type A has a copula in all normal neutral equational
clauses; the absence of the copula is limited to certain set
expressions or signals a particular style or registers, such as
proverbs (e.g. Nothing ventured, nothing gained). In such languages the copula generally functions very similarly (i.e. has
similar patterns of allomorphs, exhibits similar grammatico-
semantic categories, occurs in similar constructions) to the
members of the major word class of verbs. It generally differs
from verbs, however, in certain respects, in some languages
so much as to constitute a separate word class, in other languages in such a way as to belong to a distinct subclass of
verbs ("auxiliaries"). In Indo-European languages of type A
the copula typically has a unique pattern of suppletion (e.g.
Latin es-~ fu-). In type A languages the copula often appears
also in existential clauses of the type There is/are X, although
they may have special constructions with the copula (e.g. English
there is/are), or not use it at all (e.g. French il y a), in such
clauses.

     Type B languages normally have no copula in equational
clauses. The copula is invariably absent in a main clause when
both members of the clause (subject and complement) are present, the clause is timeless or unmarked present in time, the
complement is attributive (i.e. adjectival rather than nominal),
and the subject is third person. In many type B languages the
absence of a copula goes beyond these minimum limits. For
example, probably in most type B languages the copula is absent

with first and second person subjects as well as third (e.g. Russian
Ja student 'I am a student'), although in some the absence is limited
to the third person (e.g. Hungarian Én diák vagyok 'I am a
student' but Ő diák 'He is a student').[2] In many type B languages the copula is absent also when the complement is a
noun or pronoun, as in the Russian and Arabic examples
previously cited, although in some the absence is limited to
adjectival complements (e.g. Haitian Creole Chwal yo parésé
'The horses are lazy' but Chwal yo sé étalô 'The horses are
stallions' McConnell 1953 p. 20). Again, many type B languages have no copula in either main or dependent clause but
some have it only in dependent clauses, e.g. Bengali Se chatro
'He is a student' but Se jodi chatro hɔě . . . 'If he is a student
. . .' (Sableski 1965).

In all type B languages there seem to be conditions
under which a copula must be used. The most widespread
such condition is when a tense other than present is called
for. Thus, English My brother was a student has Russian
and Arabic equivalents with an overt was in Moj brat byl student,
'Axī kāna tilmīðan.[3] Also, most type B languages seem to
use a copula if only one member of the equational clause
(subject or complement) is present, or if because of an
inverted word order the copula would be in an "exposed"
position.[4] Thus, Haitian Creole Machin nâ gro 'The machine
is big' but Sé gro 'It is big'; Chwal yo nâ châ 'The horses are
in the field' but Koté chwal yo yé? 'Where are the horses?'
Finally, in type B languages when emphasis is put on the
semantic link, as in definitions and exclamatory pronounce-
ments, a copula equivalent is used, either a special verb (e.g.
"stands", "is found") or a pronoun (e.g. "he", "they"), or a
verb "to be" which is normally used in other tenses or in
existential clauses. Thus, Russian čto jest'istina? 'What is
truth?'

In type B languages there is often a special negative construction used in equational clauses without copula and not elsewhere in the language. Thus Arabic and Bengali have special negative copulas, lays-~las- and nɔ-~ no- respectively, which are used only here: Arabic Laysa (lastu) tilmīðan 'He is not (I am not) a student'; Bengali še chatro nɔě 'He is not a student', Ami chatro noǐ 'I am not a student.' Some, however, have the same negative formative in these clauses that appears in the negation of verbal predicates (e. g. Russian Ja ne student, Haitian Creole Machin nâ pa gro.).

Type B languages typically have a different verb or verb equivalent for existential clauses, e. g. Bengali ach- 'exist, be' Russian jest' 'there, is/ are', Haitian Creole gê, and sometimes they have still another special form of clause negation for this, e. g. Bengali neǐ, Russian net, Haitian Creole nâ pwê. Bengali illustrates the full range of possibilities here (cf. Sableski):

eta boǐ   this is a book

eta boi nɔě   this isn't a book

ekhane boǐ ache   there are books here

ekhane boǐ neǐ   there aren't any books here

2. Simplified speech. It may be assumed that every speech community has in its verbal repertoire a variety of registers appropriate for use with particular statuses, roles, or situations. It may further be assumed that many, perhaps all, speech communities have registers of a special kind for

use with people who are regarded for one reason or another
as unable to readily understand the normal speech of the
community (e. g. babies, foreigners, deaf people). These
forms of speech are generally felt by their users to be
simplified versions of the language, hence easier to understand, and they are often regarded as imitation of the way
the person addressed uses the language himself. Thus, the
baby talk which is used by adults in talking to young children
is felt to be easier for the child to understand and is often
asserted to be an imitation of the way the children speak.
Such registers as baby talk are, of course, culturally transmitted like any other part of the language and may be quite
systematic and resistant to change. Unfortunately they have
not been studied very much; for summary and references,
cf. Ferguson 1964.

     Another register of simplified speech which has been
little studied, although it seems quite widespread and may
even be universal, is the kind of "foreigner talk" which is
used by speakers of a language to outsiders who are felt to
have very limited command of the language or no knowledge
of it at all. Many [all?] languages seem to have particular
features of pronunciation, grammar, and lexicon which are
characteristically used in this situation. For example, a
speaker of Spanish who wishes to communicate with a foreigner
who has little or no Spanish will typically use the infinitive of
the verb or the third singular rather than the usual inflected
forms, and he will use mi 'me' for yo 'I' and omit the definite
and indefinite articles: mi ver soldado 'me [to-] see soldier'
for yo veo al soldado 'I see the soldier'. Such Spanish is felt
by native speakers of the language to be the way foreigners
talk, and it can most readily be elicited from Spanish speaking
informants by asking them how foreigners speak. [5]

Similarly, Arabs sometimes use a simplified form of the language in talking to non-native speakers, such as Armenian immigrants. This form is sometimes referred to as the way Armenians talk and can be elicited by asking for Armenian Arabic. It is characterized by such features as the use of the third person masculine singular of the imperfect of the verb for all persons, genders, numbers, and tenses (e.g. ya^{c}rif 'he knows' for "you know", "I know", etc.) and the use of the long forms of the numbers 3-10 with a singular noun instead of the normal contracted form of the number with a plural noun (e.g. tlāte sā^{c}a for tlat sā^{c}āt 'three hours'). Some Armenians and other non-native speakers of Arabic do sometimes use these expressions, but it is not clear whether this comes as a direct result of interference from their own languages or results at least in part from imitation of Arabs' use of foreigner talk.

In both baby talk and foreigner talk the responses of the person addressed affect the speaker, and the verbal interaction may bring some modification of the register from both sides. The normal outcome of the use of baby talk is that as the child grows up he acquires the other normal, non-simplified registers of the language and retains some competence in baby talk for use in talking with young children and in such displaced functions as talking to a pet or with a lover.

The usual outcome of the use of foreigner talk is that one side or the other acquires an adequate command of the other's language and the foreigner talk is used in talking to, reporting on, or ridiculing people who have not yet acquired adequate command of the language. If the communication context is appropriate, however, this foreigner talk may serve as an incipient pidgin and become a more widely used form of speech.

Baby talk and foreigner talk are not the only forms of simplified speech. English, for example, has special usages for telegrams and formal instructions which resemble baby talk and foreigner talk in omitting definite article, pre- positions, and copula, and the resemblance of these usages to early childhood language behavior has been noticed (Brown and Bellugi 1964 pp. 138-9). The conventional nature of these usages, which native speakers explain as being more economical of space, time, or money, is shown by their use where the limitations are irrelevant, as with instructions printed on a package where there is plenty of empty space or choices of wording in telegrams where either wording is below the number of words allowed at minimum cost.

3. Simplicity. The notion of simplicity in language and lan- guage description has been a perennial issue in linguistics as in other disciplines, and there is little agreement on what constitutes simplicity. Some recent work in linguistics has been concerned with a "simplicity metric" in evaluating alternative grammars or partial grammars. The notion of simplicity in language itself, however, is only indirectly related to this. In the present paper we are concerned with the concept of simplicity in language, i. e. the possibility of rating some part of a language (e. g. a paradigm, a construction, an utterance, a clause type, a phonological sequence) as in some sense simpler than another comparable part in the same language or another language. For sample statements of this sort, cf. Ferguson 1959 pp. 333-4.

The notion of simplicity in language is important in several ways, since it may be related to theories of language universals, language acquisition, and language loss. Jakobson

and others have assumed that, other things being equal, the
simpler of two comparable features is likely to be the more
widespread among languages of the world, the earlier
acquired in child language development, and the later lost
under pathological conditions. Even though the last of these
assumptions may offer great difficulties because of the
varied nature of pathological conditions, there seems to be
some validity for the first two. [6] Accordingly, the creation
of taxonomies involving the dimension simple-complex and
investigation of these across many languages offers promise
in the development of the general theory of language.

    Also, any full-scale description of a language should
identify simple vs. complex (i.e. primary vs. derivative)
along a number of dimensions and thus offer predictions about
possible orders of acquisition of the respective features.
This process of prediction and empirical confirmation offers
an opportunity for checking the validity of grammars which
goes outside the linguists' intuitions about languages. For
examples of predictions of this kind, cf. Ferguson 1966. [7]

    The present paper suggests an additional approach
to the study of simplicity in language, viz. the investigation
of simplified registers, such as baby talk and foreigner talk,
which give some indication of what folk grammatical analysis
rates as relatively simple or easy versus complex or difficult.

4. Hypotheses. Even on the basis of the largely impressionistic and anecdotal accounts of simplified speech now available, it is possible to hazard some universal hypotheses.
For example, "If a language has an inflectional system, this
will tend to be replaced in simplified speech such as baby
talk and foreigner talk by uninflected forms (e.g. simple

nominative for the noun; infinitive, imperative, or third
person singular for the verb)." Several such hypotheses
might even be subsumed under a more general hypothesis
of the form: "If a language has a grammatical category which
clearly involves an unmarked-marked opposition, [3] the unmarked term tends to be used for both in simplified speech."
This general hypothesis may raise more problems than it
solves at this point in our understanding of grammatical
systems, but it illustrates the kind of hypotheses which may
be generated in the study of language universals. A fairly
specific kind of universal hypothesis is the central point of
this paper.

In pairs of clauses differing by presence and absence
of a copula in a given language, speakers will generally rate
the one without the copula as simpler and easier to understand. Also, studies of child language development seem to
show that children, apart from some marginal cases, first
make equational clauses without a copula and only later—if
the language has a copula—acquire the construction with the
copula. Thus, even though the linguistic analyst may find
that in the full normal speech absence of the copula is to be
regarded as a deletion and hence grammatically more complex than its presence, and even though languages which lack
a copula in equational clauses may have quite complicated
patterns of allomorphy and distribution of synonyms in verbs
"to be", it seems wise to make the assumption that other
things being equal absence of the copula is simpler than
presence of the copula.

Therefore, given that languages can be classified
into two types according to their equational clauses, type A
with copula and type B without copula, then:

Hypothesis 1. In languages of type A, the copula in equational clauses will tend to be omitted in simplified speech such as baby talk and foreigner talk.

Although this hypothesis says nothing about equational sentences in languages of type B, it predicts that speakers of a language of type A will tend to omit the copula when they are attempting to simplify their speech. Specifically it predicts that simplified registers in regular use in the speech community will tend to omit the copula, e. g. baby talk, foreigner talk, telegraph language, newspaper headlines. Going a step further, the hypothesis would suggest that a pidgin language whose lexical source was a type A language would tend to omit the copula.

The wording of the hypothesis in terms of possibility ("will tend to") rather than in absolute terms ("will") is based on the existence of empirical data showing considerable variation in the extent to which the copula is actually omitted. For example, in French baby talk the copula seems to be omitted much less often than in English baby talk, although être as an auxiliary is often left out (Papa parti 'Daddy bye-bye'). Also, of the Portuguese based creoles used in the Far East in the sixteenth century some apparently had a copula while others did not (Whinnom 1965).

A further subhypothesis can be made with regard to the degrees of likelihood of omission of the copula under different conditions. This hypothesis is based on the descriptive statements made about type B languages, although their relation to the notion of simplicity is unclear.

Hypothesis 2. In simplified speech of languages
of type A, the copula is more likely to be omitted under each of the following conditions than
otherwise:
    main clause
    subject and complement both present
    non-emphatic
    timeless or unmarked present
    third person subject
    adjectival complement
    non-exposed position.

The presentation of these two hypotheses constitutes
in effect the outline of a research project to examine the
omission of copulas in baby talk, foreigner talk, and pidgins
to find the extent to which the hypotheses would be discon-
firmed, confirmed in principle, or even quantified. Some
encouragement as to possible results comes from recently
presented evidence (Labov 1967) that certain varieties of
English which frequently omit the copula do not do so in
clauses where the standard language does not permit contraction, i.e. in instances of emphasis, exposed position, or
absence of one member of the clause.

5. Concluding observations. For the linguist interested in
typology and language universals this paper suggests the
usefulness of a taxonomy of copula and copula-like constructions
in the world's languages and the elaboration of hypotheses of
synchronic variation and diachronic change in this part of
language. The copula seems of particular interest because
of the universality of equational clauses, the widespread
patterns of polysemy and suppletion and possible exceptions
to general hypotheses of the status of markedness in grammar.

For the linguist interested in child language development, the paper repeats earlier suggestions that the notion of simplicity may be a useful one in accounting for the development of grammar in the child, repeats the point (Ferguson 1964) that baby talk is largely initiated by adults on the basis of existing patterns, and suggests further that the telegraphic style used by young children may in part be based on the fact that adults in their attempt to simplify their speech (i.e. use baby talk) tend to omit items such as the copula, prepositions, articles, and inflectional endings.

For the linguist interested in pidgins and creoles, the most important suggestion of the paper is probably the view that the foreigner talk of a speech community may serve as an incipient pidgin. This view asserts that the initial source of the grammatical structure of a pidgin is the more or less systematic simplification of the lexical source language which occurs in the foreigner talk register of its speakers rather than the grammatical structure of the language(s) of the other users of the pidgin. Such a view would not, of course, deny the grammatical influence of the other language(s), but would help to explain some of the otherwise surprising similarities among distant creoles by setting the starting point in a universal simplification process. It differs from the view held by some scholars from Schuchard to the present that "the Europeans deliberately and systematically simplified and distorted their language to facilitate communication with the non-Europeans " (Goodman 1964 p. 124) by emphasizing the conventional, culturally given aspect of the linguistic simplification and by recognizing with Bloomfield the interaction "between a foreign speaker's version of a language and a native speaker's version of the foreign language" (quoted in Goodman 1964 p. 12).

NOTES

[1]The equational clause type includes a number of
semantic (and in some languages grammatically distinct)
sub-types such as identity (Her father is the President of
the University), class membership (Your friend is a fool),
attribution of a property (The towel is wet). For the purposes of the present article these distinctions are generally
disregarded, and the terms "equational clause" and "copula"
are used to refer to any or all of them unless otherwise
specified. For discussion of equational clauses, see Elson
and Pickett 112-113; sample definitions in specific languages,
cf. Sableski 1965; Sebeok 1943.

[2]It has been pointed out that in those early Indo-
European languages which have equational clauses without
copula, this is normal only in the third person. Cf. Meillet
1906-08, p. 20.

[3]Bally called attention to this feature of languages
without copula in a more general discussion of zero and
ellipsis. Bally 1922 pp. 1-2.

[4]For the term "exposed" cf. Hall 1953 p. 66 fn for
latter read former.

[5]For examples of this kind of Spanish, see Lynch's
novel El Inglés de los Güesos in which an Englishman is
portrayed as using this kind of foreigner's Spanish; e.g.
p. 184 Osted moi buena conmigue . . . Mí no olvida nunca.
'You very good with me . . . Me not forget(s) never.'

[6]On the question of order of acquisition, it is, of course, necessary to recognize that other things are not equal and that acquisition may run not only from simple to complex but from less effort to more effort, from heavy affect to light affect, or from high frequency to low frequency, and that interference from other parts of the language or another language may be involved.

[7]The possibility must be noted that the speaker may, in the case of language development, reorganize his internal grammar in such a way that what was previously primary may become derivative and vice versa. Thus a speaker who learns Handschuh as a monomorphematic lexical item meaning 'glove' may later identify it as Hand 'hand' plus Schuh 'shoe' in a compound-word construction. Similar reorganizations of grammatical constructions make it hazardous to relate a line of derivation or the ordering of a set of rules to an actual developmental sequence, but the grammar will surely offer clues which can be checked against empirical data.

[8]For an extensive discussion of marked:unmarked categories in grammatical universals see Greenberg 1966 pp. 25-55.

REFERENCES

Bally, Charles. 1922. Copule zero et faits connexes. Bull. de la Soc. Ling. de Paris 23. 21-6.

Brown, Roger W. and Bellugi, Ursula. 1964. Three processes in the child's acquisition of syntax. Harvard Educ. Rev.

34.133-51. (Repr. in New directions in the study of language, ed. by E. H. Lenneberg. Cambridge, Mass., 1964).

Elson, Benjamin and Pickett, Velma. 1962. An introduction to morphology and syntax. Santa Ana, California: Summer Institute of Linguistics.

Ferguson, Charles A. 1959. Diglossia. Word 15.325-40. (Repr. in Language in culture and society, ed. by Dell Hymes. New York, 1964). In this volume, pp. 1-26.

_____ 1964. Baby talk in six languages. American Anthropologist 66:3:Part 2. 103-14. In this volume, pp. 113-34.

_____ 1966. Linguistic theory as behavioral theory. Brain function, ed. by E. C. Carterette, pp. 249-61. Berkeley: University of California Press.

Goodman, Morris F. 1964. A comparative study of Creole French dialects. The Hague: Mouton and Co.

Greenberg, Joseph H. 1966. Language universals. The Hague: Mouton and Co.

Hall, Robert A., Jr. et al. 1953. Haitian Creole. Menasha, Wisconsin: American Anthropological Association.

Labov, William. 1967. Contraction, deletion and inherent variability of the English copula. Paper read at the LSA Annual Meeting. [Language 45. 715-62 (1969)].

Lynch, Benito. 1955. El Inglés de los Güesos. México: Libro Popular.

McConnell, H. Ormande and Eugene Swan. 1953. You can learn Creole. 2nd ed. Port-au-Prince, Haiti: Impr. de l'Etat.

Meillet, A. 1906-08. La phrase nominale en indo-européen. Mem. de la Soc. Ling. de Paris 14. 1-26.

Sableski, Julia A. 1965. Equational clauses in Bengali. Language 41. 439-46.

Sebeok, Thomas A. 1943. The equational sentence in Hungarian. Language 19. 162-64.

Whinnom, Keith. 1965. The origin of the European-based Creoles and Pidgins. Orbis 15. 509-27.

18 | The Role of Arabic in Ethiopia: A Sociolinguistic Perspective

As I understand the purpose of my paper in this discussion of second language learning in formal education contexts, it is to call attention to the wide variety of multilingual situations in which bilingual education may take place. It seems clear that hypotheses or conclusions about second language acquisition will be affected by such factors as the nature of the linguistic environment, the relative dominance of the relevant languages in the society, their degree of standardization—indeed by the whole range of issues involving the respective roles of the languages and their means of acquisition outside the educational system. Some of the other speakers at this Round Table have already emphasized the variety of multilingual situations, but the presentation of one particular setting—Arabic in Ethiopia—may still be of value, since the kinds of decisions needed for the teaching of Arabic in the schools of Ethiopia are different in many respects from those needed in more familiar situations.

1. National sociolinguistic profile formulas

One method of presenting the sociolinguistic setting of a

language is to include it in a formula representing the sociolinguistic profile of a nation or other political entity. (Ferguson
1966, Uribe Villegas 1968). This method differs from others
in that it selects a political entity rather than any other demographic, societal, cultural or psychological framework, and in that
it uses a particular taxonomy of language types and functions
(Stewart 1968). This method makes no strong claims for pre-
dictive value and omits important sociolinguistic data relevant
for assessment of the "roles" of languages in a nation; it does,
however, offer a convenient way of making gross sociolinguistic
comparisons among nations and it seems to have considerable
heuristic value in suggesting lines of investigation and data collection often overlooked in the establishment of national language
policies.

Briefly summarized, the method consists of (1) identifying the number of major and minor languages and languages of
special status in the nation and (2) representing them in an ad-
ditive formula using capital and lower case letters standing for
language types and functions respectively. A third, more informative, expansion of the formula specifies the languages by
name, so that a separate key can provide information on degree
of linguistic distance among them and dialect diversity within
them; if necessary, information can be added on the diversity
of writing systems used. A sample national profile formula in
alternative expansions might read
(1)   2Lmaj + 6Lmin + 1Lspec
(2)   (Sow + Sei) + (5Vg + Sge) + Crl

Formula (1) states that in the nation in question there
are two major languages, six minor languages and one language
of special status. Expanded formula (2) specifies the major
languages as two Standard languages (S) one of which is official
(o) and also serves as an important lingua franca within the

country (w) and the other is used extensively in education (e)
and serves as the nation's means of communication with other
countries (i). It further specifies the minor languages as five
vernaculars (V) which primarily serve to identify their speakers
as members of particular ethnic or other sociocultural groups
(g) and one standard language which not only serves this function
but is also used in education. Finally, it specifies the language
of special status as a Classical (or dead Standard) language used
chiefly for certain religious (r) and literary (l) purposes. Further
details of the method, with more precise defining criteria for the
various categories, can be found in the articles cited.

2. Language situation in Ethiopia

Like many other nations of Africa, Ethiopia is a highly
multilingual country, although it differs from most other African
nations in having an indigenous language constitutionally recognized as its official language. The currently available body of
data is not adequate for definite identification of the major and
minor languages of the country, but an approximation can be
made on the basis of the present estimates of the Language Survey
of Ethiopia, subject to correction as more extensive and accurate
information becomes available.
The Ethiopian profile formula reads:

     (1)   5Lmaj + 13Lmin + 3Lspec

     (2)   (3S + 2V) + (13V) + (1C + 1S + Arabic)

     (2a)   (Sowe + Sie + Sgw + Vgw + Vg) + (13Vg) + (1Cr

                                        + 1Sw + Arabic)

Lmaj:	(in approximate order of sociopolitical importance)		
	Sowe	Amharic	(Ethio-) Semitic
	Sie	English	Indo-European (Germanic)
	Sgw	Tigrinya	(Ethio-)Semitic
	Vgw	Galla	E. Cushitic

Lmin: (in alphabetical order)

V_1g	Afar	E. Cushitic
V_2g	Anyuak	Nilo-Saharan
V_3g	Beja	N. Cushitic
V_4g	Chaha Gurage	(Ethio-)Semitic
V_5g	Derasa	E. Cushitic
V_6g	Gumuz	Nilo-Saharan
V_7g	Hadiyya	E. Cushitic
V_8g	Janjero	Omotic
V_9g	Kefa	Omotic
$V_{10}g$	Kembata	E. Cushitic
$V_{11}g$	Sidamo	E. Cushitic
$V_{12}g$	Tigré	(Ethio-)Semitic
$V_{13}g$	Wellamo	Omotic

Lspec:

Crl	Geez	(Ethio-)Semitic
Sw	Italian	Indo-European (Romance)
Arabic	Arabic	Semitic

Amharic is a standard language, with a writing system
of its own (the Geez syllabary with a few additions) and literature
going back to the 14th c.; it serves as the medium of instruction
in all government primary schools, the primary language of oral
and written communication in the government and the armed
forces and the only Ethiopian language whose function as a lingua
franca is national in scope; it is declared in the Constitution of
1965 as the official language of the Empire.

English is the medium of instruction in all government
secondary schools and higher education; it is an important spoken
and written medium in government communication; it is the language of upward socio-economic mobility. It has been publicly recognized by the government as the nation's second language, and
serves as its chief medium of communication with other countries.

Tigrinya is a standard language, using essentially the same writing system as Amharic; it has a small literature, and the publication of newspapers in Tigrinya antedates that of Amharic. Formerly the medium of instruction in primary schools in the Eritrea region, in which it is being replaced by Amharic, it still serves as a lingua franca in many parts of that area.

Galla is a vernacular with considerable dialect diversity which does not seem to be moving toward standardization; it is not normally written but is spoken as a mother tongue by more people than any other language in Ethiopia. In certain parts of the country it serves as a lingua franca.

Somali is a vernacular spoken over a large but sparsely settled area. It has considerable dialect diversity, but mutual intelligibility is high and there is some trend toward standardization. It has a large oral literature but is rarely written; in neighboring Somalia where it is the mother tongue of 90% of the country, Arabic or European languages are used for writing. (Andrjzewski 1962).

The minor languages are all vernaculars used by ethno-linguistic communities of at least 100,000 members. Most are clearcut languages, but several, e.g. Wellamo (-Gofa-Gemu-Kullo- . . .) and Gumuz (-Sese-Disoha-Dakunza-Sai- . . .) might be regarded as dialect clusters. Afar is often considered together with the closely related language Saho. Chaha Gurage may not be spoken by 100,000 but it is included as probably the most important representative of the cluster of languages called Gurage which taken together may have nearly a million speakers.

Geez is a classical language known from inscriptions as far back as the 4th century B.C.; its periods of literary flowering were between the 7th and 13th centuries, long after it had ceased

to be a spoken language. Today it serves as the liturgical
language of the Ethiopian Orthodox Church; it is the vehicle of
traditional Ethiopian ecclesiastical and historical literature and
is still used for the composition of poetry. Geez uses a syllabary
of some 250 characters derived from the writing system of South
Arabic inscription.

Italian has no official or publicly recognized status in
the nation, but there are several thousand for whom it is their
mother tongue and there is a fairly active Italian press. In its
standard form (with some dialect differences brought from Italy)
it serves as a lingua franca among some sections of society,
particularly in the Eritrea area. In a pidginized form it serves
as a lingua franca at a different level in scattered areas of Ethiopia. The use of Italian seems to be declining in favor of English and Amharic.

3. Varieties of Arabic

Arabic, as a great world language spoken by some hundred millions of people over the enormous area from Morocco
to the Persian Gulf and attested in literature for nearly a millennium and a half, offers a bewildering range of variation. First
there is the Classical written language extending from pre-Islamic
poetry to modern technical journals: this variety shows essential
the same sound system and morphology but with considerable
variation in vocabulary, syntax, and forms of discourse. Next
there is Colloquial Arabic, the chain of regional dialects which
constitute the Arabs' mother tongue today. The extent of variation among these dialects is greater than that between what are
recognized in other circumstances as separate languages (e.g.
Norwegian and Swedish), but the speakers of these dialects have
a strong sense of linguistic unity, and a speaker of Arabic recog-
nizes that speakers of other dialects are also speaking Arabic.

These two varieties, Classical and Colloquial, exist side by side in the Arabic speech community in a diglossia relationship (Ferguson 1959a, Gumperz 1962, Fishman 1968).

Among the regional dialects some may be regarded as "prestige dialects" (cf. Johnstone 1967, xxix-xxx), notably those of important urban centers such as Cairo, Beirut-Damascus-Jerusalem, Baghdad (Muslim variety), northern Moroccan cities. Arabic speakers within the areas of influence of these prestige dialects may in the course of their lives adjust their own dialect in the direction of the prestige dialect or even be bidialectal (e.g. Blanc 1964).

Intermediate between the two varieties or sets of varieties, relatively "pure" Classical and Colloquial, there are many shadings of "middle language". These intermediate forms, some highly fluctuating and transitional, others more stable, represent two tendencies: classicization, in which a dialect is modified in the direction of the classical, and koinoization, in which dialects are homogenized by the modification or elimination of features which are felt to be especially distinctive of a particular regional dialect (Blanc 1959).

Some of these intermediate varieties may be viewed collectively as a "pan-Arab koine" (cf. Johnstone 1967, xxv-xxx), and indeed the Arab world seems to be developing such a koine for at least the third time in its known history (pre-Islamic poetic koine, koine of early centuries of the Muslim era, modern koine cf. Ferguson 1959b).

Finally, in certain areas and under certain social conditions where Arabic has been used for limited purposes by people of other mother tongues, it has developed pidginized forms in which the lexicon and overt grammatical categories of the language have been drastically reduced. The best known examples are the Turku of the Lake Chad area and Central Africa and the "Bimbashi" Arabic which spread southward from the Sudan (Heine 1968 and references).[2]

4. 0. Arabic in Ethiopia

Having reviewed the method of sociolinguistic profile
formulas, the general language situation in Ethiopia, and the nature of sociolinguistic variation within Arabic, our task is now to
identify the kinds of Arabic and their respective functions in Ethiopia in such a way that this information can be represented in the
total profile formula for the nation.

Since at least as far back as the fourth millennium B. C.
there has been traffic and communication across the Red Sea,
between southern Arabia and the coast of eastern Africa including
the Ethiopian area.   And since at least the seventh century of the
Christian era, this has involved the appearance of speakers of
Arabic (as opposed to South Arabian languages) on African soil.
This process of temporary and permanent immigration of Arabic
speakers from Yemen and the southern coast of Arabia has continued into the 19th and 20th centuries.   The immigrants have
brought both language and religion, and Arabic and Islam have
spread to African populations, partly separately and partly in
close connection.

Also, peoples further south along the East African coast
and inland who have become Muslim, as a result of influence from
Yemen and southern Arabia, have moved northward, bringing with
them the use of Arabic for various purposes within their basically
non-Arabic-speaking-society.   The best example may be the constantly expanding population of Somali tribes all of whom have bee
Muslim since the beginning of the 16th century.

Since at least as far back as the second millennium B. C.
there has been traffic and communication between Egypt and the
Ethiopian area.   With the coming of Christianity into Ethiopia in
the fourth century, religious ties with the church in Egypt formed
a special line of communication and in medieval times a large par

of the literary production in Geez consisted of translations from Arabic works used by the Coptic Christians of Egypt. In the 19th century, Egyptian political influence extended down the Red Sea onto the Eritrean lowlands and the city-state of Harar, and this also directly affected the spread of Arabic and Islam, separately and together.

Finally, since at least the 19th century there has been movement of Arabic-speaking Muslims from the Sudan into Ethiopia. In addition to groups of Arabic mother tongue many have been speakers of other languages who used Arabic as a lingua franca.

This rapid and drastically oversimplified historical account of the spread of Arabic into Ethiopia cannot do justice to the complex story, which deserves research and study in itself, but it can give some indication of the varied strands of influence involved in the present-day use of Arabic in the nation. One aspect of Arabic influence on Ethiopian language—the presence of Arabic loanwords—has received treatment in a number of studies by Leslau (e.g. Leslau 1957).

4.1. Arabic as mother tongue

It is not possible to estimate with any high degree of accuracy the number of native speakers of Arabic resident in Ethiopia, although it must run in the tens of thousands. The total number is, however, relatively small, and by this criterion Arabic cannot be included in the Lmin of the formula.

The varieties of Arabic in use by the mother tongue speakers are roughly comparable to those in use in other parts of the Arabic-speaking world, i.e. there is a diglossia situation in which the speakers acquire the Colloquial in childhood and then

superpose some amount of Classical Arabic for written and formal
oral use. The kinds of Colloquial in use in Ethiopia seem to cluster
around two norms one of which may be labeled "Yemeni", the other
"Sudanese". Neither of these two varieties is homogeneous in
Ethiopia and there is fluctuation and use of intermediate varieties,
but Arabic speakers generally recognize the existence of the two
major types, which differ in pronunciation, certain details of
morphology, and in a considerable number of lexical items, including some items of basic vocabulary. The two varieties in any
case are to a high degree mutually intelligible.

As an illustration of the nature of the difference, we may
cite material elicited from two Ethiopian speakers of Arabic. Both
had essentially the same sound system but differed, for example,
in their reflexes of Classical / q ð θ / :

Classical	"Yemeni"	"Sudanese"
/ q /	/ q /	/ g /
/ ð /	/ ð , d /	/ d /
/ θ /	/ θ , t /	/ t /

In matters of morphology, for example, the "Sudanese"
had the ending -ta for the 1st and 2nd person singular of the past
tense while the "Yemeni" had -t for both, but in some styles of
speech used -tu for the 1st person and -ta for the 2nd. Or, the
equivalent of 'this' was da after the noun for the "Sudanese" and
hāða before the noun for the "Yemeni". On the standard 100-word
list of basic vocabulary used in the Survey, the two informants had
different words on about 30 items, although this may be misleading
since for a number of these the other word would also have been
familiar either as a synonym or from Classical use. Examples
of the differences:

	"Yemeni"	"Sudanese"	"Classical"
foot	xuff	riǰil	riǰl
man	raǰul	zōl	raǰul
sit	ǰalas	ga ᶜad	ǰalisa, qa ᶜada

water	mōya (masc.)	mōya (fem.)	mā?
what	ʔēš	šunu	mā

4.2. Arabic as religious language

Every Muslim in the world, regardless of mother tongue,
learns at least a few expressions in Arabic, such as greetings
(e.g. some version of As-salāmu ᶜalaykum 'Peace be on you'),
invocations (e.g. Bismillāh 'in the name of God'), a statement of
faith ("There is no god but God, and Muhammad is God's messen-
ger."), and prayers, including the Fātiḥa, the opening surah of
the Qur'an. Additional study of Islamic precepts requires memorization of further Arabic material, especially the Qur'an, and
ideally the mastery of Arabic to read the traditional works of
theology, jurisprudence, ethics, traditions of the Prophet, and
so on.

In Ethiopia there are great differences from one region
to another, one ethnic background to another, and one individual
to another, in the amount of Arabic a Muslim acquires for primarily religious reasons. The mastery of a few greetings and so on
is relatively insignificant in the total language economy of Ethiopia, but certain aspects of the religious use of the language deserve
special attention. In the first place, many thousands of Muslims
every year become literate in Arabic by studying with a traditional
teacher (muᶜallim) or attending some kind of traditional school
(madrasa); [3] typically this is their initial (or, in some cases,
only) acquisition of literacy since it normally takes place before
entry into a "modern" government or private school. Secondly,
there may be more than a hundred thousand Muslims in Ethiopia
who do not speak Arabic well but who make use of Arabic to the
extent of reciting long passages from Arabic works, carrying on
stereotyped conversational exchanges in a religious context, or
following to some extent a sermon or exhortation in Arabic.

4.3. Arabic as lingua franca

More important than the preceding two points, in terms
of extent of active use of Arabic in Ethiopia, is the widespread
use of Arabic as a means of oral communication between speakers
of different languages.   There is no doubt that Amharic is the most
important lingua franca in Ethiopia as a whole, but a number of
other languages serve as lingua francas in limited areas, not only
major languages like Tigrinya and Galla as mentioned in 2. above,
but even quite minor languages such as Wetawit (Berta) in the Beni
Shengul region of western Ethiopia.   The use of Arabic as a lingua
franca only partially follows regional lines; it tends to coincide
more with religious boundaries.   Arabic is used as a lingua franca
mostly among Muslims of various mother tongues.   Some indication of the range of use of Arabic as a lingua franca is given by
the questionnaire replies of twenty freshmen at Haile Sellassie I
University who claimed knowledge of Arabic (October, 1969).
These twenty students, of about 21 years of age, came from six
different provinces, and represented ten different mother tongues.
Twelve of the students claimed to speak Arabic "fluently", six
"with difficulty", and two "only a little".   While we cannot assume
that these findings are representative of the users of Arabic
throughout the country, they clearly show that Arabic can function
widely as a lingua franca.

There are of course many Muslims in Ethiopia who are
unable to converse in Arabic, so that the latter cannot be regarded
as a normal secondary language for Muslims, but it is probably
true that hundreds of thousands (as high as a million?) Muslims
in the country are able to use some kind of spoken Arabic as a
means of oral communication, whereas the number of non-Muslims
able to do so is very small.   The kind of Arabic spoken in this way
tends to cluster around "Yemeni" and "Sudanese" norms, but it
often fluctuates more than mother tongue Arabic, mixes regional
dialects, and incorporates features of Classical Arabic.   Finally,

we must take note of the fact that an indeterminate (although fairly
small) number of Muslims who cannot use Colloquial Arabic as a
means of conversation have learned enough Classical Arabic in
madrasa, mosque, radio and reading to be able to use it to a
limited extent as a lingua franca, and with some hesitation we may
add "w" also the "C" part of Arabic in the formula: Crlw:Vgw.

4.4. Arabic as trade jargon

Many of the Arabic-speaking immigrants to the Ethiopian
areas through the centuries have been merchants, and Arab traders,
shopkeepers, and small merchants can be found in many parts of
Ethiopia. In communication between Arab merchant and customer,
often a rudimentary, pidginized form of Arabic is used, and this use
of Arabic is not so strongly limited to Muslims as the more general
lingua franca use just described. Although there has been as yet
no systematic study of this kind of Arabic, impressionistic observation notes some of the usual features of pidginized Arabic, such
as the use of full forms of the numbers 3 - 10 with singular nouns,
use of the 3rd m.sg. for all persons of the verb, and so on. Some
indication of the use of Arabic in trade transactions is given in the
freshman student responses. Of the twenty students, eighteen
checked "usually use Arabic" or "may use Arabic" in the market,
in shops, or both (one student did not answer the question). Next
to religious use (prayers, preaching), the trade use (market,
shops) was most often checked in the "usually use Arabic" column
(religious use 12 checks, trade use 9).

4.5. Arabic in the Ethiopian formula

The material presented above on the types and functions
of Arabic in Ethiopia may be summarized by an entry for Arabic
in the national profile formula as
$$Crlw:Vgw(:Pt)$$

This formula is to be interpreted as follows: there is a Classical form of the language which serves religious and literary purposes and is in a diglossia relationship with vernacular varieties of the language the use of which serves as a mark of social group identity (i.e. Islam); both forms of the language, as well as the intermediate varieties characteristic of diglossic languages, serve as a lingua franca in the country. Less certain is the existence of a pidginized form of the language used primarily as a trade jargon.

5. Attitudes toward Arabic

We may assume that every community has some shared beliefs about language and attitudes toward language. In multilingual countries we can assume that some of these beliefs and attitudes will be about the appropriateness of the use of particular languages for different purposes as well as about esthetic and moral values inherent in one language and its uses in comparison with another. In order to understand fully the role of Arabic in Ethiopia it would be desirable to have information on the attitudes of Ethiopians toward Arabic and its use in comparison with their attitudes toward other languages.

Previous studies of attitudes toward Arabic (Ferguson 1959, Nader 1962) have been based on participant observation in communities of Arabic mother tongue, and studies of the role of Arabic in a multilingual society have been concerned with Arabic as a national language in relation to a European former colonial language (e.g. Gallagher 1968) or to a local minority language (e.g. Jernudd 1968). Accordingly, there is little precedent for a study of attitudes toward Arabic in a nation where it serves as a secondary lingua franca and religious language. A few predictions might be hazarded on the basis of the description in 4. above, but field investigation is required for any dependable conclusions.

Some meagre indications of the attitudes toward Arabic held by users of the language in Ethiopia can be found in the results of the questionnaire. To the question "What languages would you like your children to know?" the twenty university freshmen and the seventy Dire Dawa respondents gave overwhelming preference to English, Arabic, Amharic, and French (82, 81, 61, 57 votes respectively), the other languages named being mostly mother tongues. This at least testifies to the importance they attach to knowledge of Arabic. The responses to the questions about which languages seemed most pleasant and most unpleasant gave preference to Arabic and English as the most pleasant, and apart from 17 votes for Gurage gave no clear pattern of languages regarded as unpleasant (scattered votes or no language named). Again, this gives some indication of a favorable attitude toward Arabic.

The answer to the complex question (No. 7) on language preferences for different uses gives some slight additional information. Arabic was not consistently preferred to English, mother tongue, or Amharic for <u>any</u> use, although the largest number of top preference votes for Arabic was for talking about religion. This suggests that the use of Arabic as a lingua franca is not out of some kind of preference for that language, but because it is favored by the existing language competences of the people communicating. [4]

Finally, the answers to the questions about the use of Arabic in government schools and on the radio are of interest. The votes were overwhelmingly in favor of the teaching of Arabic as a subject in government schools, the use of Arabic in broadcasting to Ethiopians, and the recitation of the Qur'an over the Ethiopian radio. The vote was indecisive on the question of teaching the Qur'an in the schools (8 yes, 9 no, 3 no vote). Whatever else may be their attitudes about Arabic, the students seemed to want more use of Arabic under government auspices.

This very little bit of information about language attitudes
is tantalizing, and points to the need for a broader investigation
with other techniques. Even with fuller information on the attitudes of Ethiopians who use Arabic as a secondary language, any
attempt at characterizing the position of Arabic in the nation or
predicting future trends would fail without investigation of the
attitudes of those in the country who have Arabic as their mother
tongue as well as the attitudes of the vast majority of Ethiopians
who have little or no knowledge of Arabic at all.

NOTES

[1]This paper is in the nature of an interim report on one
subproject of the Language Survey of Ethiopia. The Survey is part
of the five-nation Survey of Language Use and Language Teaching
in Eastern Africa supported by the Ford Foundation. This paper
was presented in preliminary form at the Conference on Ethiopian
Languages held in Addis Ababa, October 1969. Even in its present
form it provides very little information not already well known to
many Arabists and specialists in Ethiopian affairs. What merit
it may have probably lies in the attempt to communicate this information in such a way that it can be readily assimilated by social
scientists, linguists, or interested laymen and can thereby serve
as the basis for more extended research or policy making.

[2]The entire range of linguistic variation in Arabic has bee:
studied chiefly by descriptions of "pure" varieties and studies of
local variation in a given dialect area. (For a summary of the
research see Abboud, in press.) Studies of variation in some kind
of social context have been extremely rare (e.g. Blanc 1960 and
1964, Mitchell, 1957). We are certainly far from having sociolinguistically sophisticated studies of verbal interaction of small
groups, studies of the sociolinguistic patterns of whole communities such as villages or social institutions, or large-scale studie:

of whole nations or the whole Arab world. It may be hoped that
the new generation of Arab linguists will undertake studies which
will utilize such fruitful sociolinguistic constructs as domain,
network, social situation, role relationship and interaction type
(Fishman 1968).

[3] Of twenty university freshmen who claimed knowledge
of Arabic (Addis Ababa, October 1969), all but three claimed some
reading knowledge. Fourteen reported having learned to read in a
madrasa, which they reported having attended for periods ranging
from 2 to 8 years (mean 5).

[4] The preferences for other languages are of some interest:
English was the most strongly preferred for the largest number of
uses: 15 out of the 20 gave it top preference for seeing movies
and reading books for fun, and 11 and 13 respectively for reading
newspapers and listening to news broadcasts. Amharic was not
consistently given preference above mother tongue or English for
any use, but was preferred by 5 respondents for talking during
sports or for writing letters. As might be expected the mother
tongue was strongly preferred for listening to songs; more surprising was the vote on talking about religion, in which mother
tongue preferences exceeded Arabic.

REFERENCES

Abboud, Peter F. Arabic dialects. Current Trends in Linguis-
       tics. 6. Linguistics in South West Asia and North Africa
       ed. by T. A. Sebeok et al.(The Hague: Mouton & Co.,
       in press).

Andrzejewski, B. W. Speech and writing dichotomy as the pattern
       of multilingualism in the Somali Republic. In Colloque
       sur le multilinguisme, Brazzaville, 1962 (London, 1964).

Bender, Marvin L. and Cooper, Robert L. The prediction of
      between-language intelligibility. Addis Ababa, 1969.
      (Mimeo.)

Blanc, Haim. Stylistic variations in Spoken Arabic: A sample of
      interdialectal educated conversation. In Contributions to
      Arabic Linguistics ed. by C.A. Ferguson (Cambridge,
      Massachusetts: Harvard University Press, 1964),
      pp. 79-161.

_____ Communal Dialects in Baghdad. Cambridge,
      Massachusetts: Harvard University Press, 1964.

Ferguson, Charles A. Diglossia. Word 15:325-40. 1959a.
      [Reprinted in Language in Culture and Society ed. by
      Dell Hymes (New York, 1964), pp. 429-439].

_____ The Arabic Koine. Language 35. 616-630. 1959b.

_____ Myths about Arabic. Georgetown University Mono-
      graph Series on Languages and Linguistics 12. 75-82.
      1959. [Reprinted in Readings in the Sociology of Language
      ed. by J.A. Fishman (The Hague: Mouton, 1968), pp.
      375-381].

_____ National sociolinguistic profile formulas. In Socio-
      linguistics ed. by W. Bright (The Hague: Mouton, 1966),
      pp. 309-324.

Fishman, Joshua A. Societal bilingualism: Stable and transi-
      tional. In Bilingualism in the Barrio. Washington:
      U.S. Office of Education, 1968a. Revised version of
      Bilingualism with and without diglossia; Diglossia with
      and without bilingualism. Journal of Social Issues
      23:2. 29-38. 1967.

Fishman, Joshua A. Sociolinguistic perspective on the study of
    bilingualism. In Bilingualism in the Barrio. Washington:
    U.S. Office of Education, 1968b.

_____   The relationship between micro- and macro- socio-
    linguistics in the study of who speaks what language to
    whom and when. In Directions in Sociolinguistics ed. by
    D. Hymes and J. J. Gumperz (New York, in press).

Gallagher, Charles F. North African problems or prospects:
    language and identity. In Language Problems of Deve-
    loping Nations ed. by J. A. Fishman et al. (New York:
    Wiley, 1968).

Gumperz, John J. Types of linguistic communities. Anthropolo-
    gical Linguistics 4:1. 28-40. 1962. [Reprinted in
    Readings in the Sociology of Language ed. by J. A. Fishman
    (The Hague: Mouton, 1968), pp. 460-472].

Heine, Berndt. Afrikanische Verkehrssprachen (INFRATEST
    Schriftenreihen zur empirischen Sozialforschung Bd.
    4. Köln, 1968.)

Jernudd, Björn. Linguistic integration and national development.
    In Language Problems of Developing Countries ed. by
    J. A. Fishman et al.(New York: Wiley, 1968).

Johnstone, T. M. Eastern Arabian Dialect Studies. London:
    Oxford University Press, 1967.

Leslau, Wolf. 1957. The phonetic treatment of the Arabic loan-
    words in Ethiopia. Word 13. 100-123. Arabic loan-
    words in Amharic BSOAS 19. 221-244. Arabic loan-
    words in Argobba JAOS 77. 36-39.

Lukas, J. The Linguistic situation in the Lake Chad area in
      Central Africa. Africa 9. 332-349. 1936.

Mitchell, T. F. 1957. The language of buying and selling in
      Cyrenaica; a situational statement. Hesperius 44.
      31-71.

Nader, Laura. A note on attitudes and the use of language.
      Anthropological Linguistics 4;6. 25-29. 1962. [Reprinte
      in Readings in the Sociology of Language ed. by J. A.
      Fishman (The Hague: Mouton, 1968), pp. 276-281].

Stewart, William A. A sociolinguistic typology for describing
      national multilingualism. In Readings in the Sociology
      of Language ed. by J. A. Fishman (The Hague: Mouton,
      1968), pp. 531-545. [Revised version of: An outline of
      linguistic typology for describing multilingualism. In
      Study of the Role of Second Languages in Asia, Africa,
      and Latin America ed. by Frank A. Rice (Washington,
      D. C.: Center for Applied Linguistics, 1962), pp. 34-53.]

Trimingham, J. Spencer. Islam in Ethiopia. London: Frank
      Cass. (2nd printing, 1965).

Uribe Villegas, Oscar. Instrumentos para la presentación de las
      situaciones sociolingüísticas. Revisto Mexicana de
      Sociología. 30. 863-884. 1968.

Bibliography of
Charles A. Ferguson's Works

Compiled by Anwar S. Dil

List of Abbreviations:

AA	American Anthropologist
HJAS	Harvard Journal of Asiatic Studies
JAF	Journal of American Folklore
JAOS	Journal of the American Oriental Society
LE&W	Literature East and West
Lg	Language
LR	The Linguistic Reporter
MEJ	The Middle East Journal
MSLL	Georgetown University Monograph Series on Languages and Linguistics
SIL	Studies in Linguistics

1944   The verb "to be" in Bengali. Paper presented at the Linguistic Society of America Annual Meeting, New York, December. (Unpublished).

1945 a. A chart of the Bengali verb. JAOS 65. 54-55.
      b. The phonology and morphology of Standard Collo-

quial Bengali. Unpublished Ph. D. dissertation,
University of Pennsylvania. Pp. 100.

c. "Short a" in Philadelphia English. Paper presented at the Linguistic Society of America Annual
Meeting, New York, December. (Unpublished).

1946 a. (With W. D. Preston). 107 Bengali proverbs.
JAF 59. 365-86.

b. (With W. D. Preston). Seven Bengali riddles.
JAOS 66. 299-303.

1947   (With Arnold Sattethwaite and B. V. Mukerjee).
Spoken Bengali. [Reproduced in part with
revisions by Joseph Reif, as Bengali Basic
Course Units 1-5. 1960]. Washington, D. C.:
Foreign Service Institute.

1948 a. Spoken Lebanese Arabic. Washington, D. C.:
Foreign Service Institute. (Mimeographed).
[Also reproduced by Army Language School].

b. A study in Arabic dialectology. Paper presented
at the Linguistic Society of America Annual
Meeting, New York, December. (Unpublished).

c. Review of Cours gradue d'arabé marocain, by
M. T. Buret. JAOS 68. 195-96.

1949   Review of Sudan colloquial Arabic, by J. S.
Trimingham. JAOS 69. 42-43.

1950   Review of A dictionary of non-classical vocables
in the spoken Arabic of Lebanon. [Mu'ǧamu
l'alfādi l'āmmiyyati fi Ilahǧati Ilubnāniyyah,
ǧama' ahā wafassarahā waraddahā 'ilā 'usūliha
'Anis Frayḥah], by A. Frayha. JAOS 70. 121.

1951 a. (With Henry Lee Smith). Language and Culture.

Washington, D. C. :   Foreign Service Institute.
(Mimeographed). Pp. 6.

b.   Choosing a native speaker for language study.
Washington, D. C. :   Foreign Service Institute.
(Mimeographed).

c.   Short courses in spoken Arabic— Iraqi, Lebanese,
Egyptian. Washington, D. C. :   Foreign Service
Institute. (Mimeographed materials for "the
Americans who want to learn a little Arabic to
be of practical use to them in the Near East").

d.   (With Frank A. Rice). Concord classes of
Arabic nouns. Paper presented at the Linguistic
Society of America Annual Meeting, New York.
(Unpublished).

e.   Review of Fonetika tadžikskogo jazyka, by V. S.
Sokolova. Word 7. 260-63.

f.   Review of Spoken Iraqi Arabic, by Morrill Y.
Van Wagoner. Word 7. 276-79.

g.   Bengali literature. Collier's Encyclopedia
4. 54-55 (-1969 edition).

h.   Bankim Chandra Chatterji. Collier's Encyclopedia
6. 14 (-1969 edition)

1952 a.   (With J. M. Echols). Critical bibliography of
spoken Arabic proverb literature. JAF
65. 67-84.

b.   Review of La strutturazione psicologica del
linguaggio studiata mediante l'analisi elettroacustica,
by A. Gemelli. SIL 10. 40-43.

c.   Review of The Persian language, by R. Levy.
AA 54.570.

1954 a.   French lessons; for the practical use of
Americans in the Near East. Beirut, Lebanon:
Foreign Service Institute Field School.
(Mimeographed). Pp. 55.

b.   Review of <u>Modern Lebanese proverbs, collected</u> <u>at Râs al-Matn, Lebanon</u>, by A. Frayha. <u>JAF</u> 67. 223-26.

c.   Review of <u>Arabisches Wörterbuch für die</u> <u>Schriftsprache der Gegenwart</u>, by H. Wehr. <u>Lg</u> 30. 174-77.

d.   Review of <u>Growth and structure of the Egyptian</u> <u>Arabic dialect</u>, by H. Birkeland. <u>Lg</u> 30. 558-64.

e.   Review of <u>Manuel élémentaire d'arabe oriental</u> (parler de Damas), by J. Cantineau. <u>Lg</u> 30. 564-70.

1955   a.   Syrian Arabic studies. <u>MEJ</u> 9:2. 187-94. (Reprinted with revisions in <u>Arabic dialect</u> <u>studies; a selected bibliography</u>, ed. by Harvey Sobleman (Washington, D.C.: Center for Applied Linguistics/ The Middle East Institute, 1962), pp. 1-17.

b.   Arabic politeness formulas. Paper presented at the Linguistic Institute, Washington, D.C. (Unpublished).

c.   Review of <u>The city of Beirut; a socio-</u> <u>economic survey</u>, by C. W. Churchill. <u>MEJ</u> 9. 198-200.

d.   Review of <u>Studies in north Palestinian Arabic,</u> <u>linguistic inquiries among the Druzas of western</u> <u>Galilee and Mt. Carmel</u>, by H. Blanc. <u>Word</u> 11. 343-47.

e.   Review of <u>A grammar of Pashto; a descriptive</u> <u>study of the dialect of Kandahar, Afghanistan,</u> by H. Penzl. <u>MEJ</u> 9. 464-65.

f.   Review of <u>A structural analysis of Uzbek</u>, by C. E. Bidwell. <u>MEJ</u> 9.464-65.

g.   Review of <u>Die klassisch-arabischen Sprich-</u> <u>wörtersammlungen insbesondere die des Abū</u> <u>'Ubaid</u>, by R. Selheim. <u>HJAS</u> 18. 455-56.

1956 a. Arabic baby talk. For Roman Jakobson, ed. by
          Morris Halle (The Hague: Mouton & Co., 1956),
          pp. 121-28.
      b. The emphatic l in Arabic. Lg 32. 446-52.
      c. The intensive methoc at FSI; essential factors.
          Washington, D.C.: Foreign Service Institute.
          (Mimeographed).
      d. Review of Stress patterns in Arabic, by H.
          Birkeland. Lg 32.384-87.
      e. Review of Dictionnaire arabe-français, by A.
          Barthelemy. Lg 32.555-56.
      f. Review of Language, thought and reality;
          selected writings of Benjamin Lee Whorf, ed.
          by J. B. Carroll. Literature East and West
          3.40-41.

1957 a. Word stress in Persian. Lg 33:2. 123-35.
      b. Two problems in Arabic phonology. Word
          13:3. 460-78.
      c. Languages of the Middle East. (Mimeographed).
          Pp. 9. [Multilithed with revisions, Ann Arbor,
          1960.]
      d. Bengali definitives. Lecture at the Yale
          Linguistic Club. (Unpublished).
      e. Review of Fonetika tureckogo literaturnogo
          jazyka, by E. V. Sevort'an. Lg 33.212-14.
      f. Review of A manual of phonological description
          [La description phonologique avec application au
          parler franco-provencal d'Hauteville (Savoie)],
          by A. Martinet. Word 13.335-45.
      g. Review of Studies in Arabic and general syntax,
          by M. M. Bravmann. JAOS 77.248-49.
      h. Review of Le parler arabe de Tripoli (Liban),
          by H. el-Hajje. Word 13.529-34.
      i. Review of Le parler arabe de Djidjelli (Nord

Constantinois, Algerie) Textes arabes de Djidjelli:
Introduction textes et transcription; traduction
glossaire, by P. Marcais. MEJ 10.214-15.

1958   Review of L'arabe classique: esquisse d'une
            structure linguistique, by H. Fleisch. Lg
            34.314-21.

1959 a.   Diglossia. Word 15:2. 325-40. [Reprinted
            in Language in Culture and Society,ed. by Dell
            Hymes (New York: Harper & Row, 1964),
            pp. 429-39].
      b.   The Arabic koine. Lg 35:4. 616-30.
      c.   Myths about Arabic. MSLL 12. 75-82. [Re-
            printed in Readings in the sociology of language,
            ed. by Joshua A. Fishman (The Hague: Mouton
            & Co., 1968), pp. 375-381].
      d.   Overcoming the Asia-American language barrier.
            LR 1:1.2-3, 8.
      e.   (With Raleigh Morgan, Jr.). Selected readings
            in applied linguistics. LR Supplement No. 2.
            1-4.
      f.   Problems of teaching Modern Standard Arabic.
            Report on a conference held at Harvard Univer-
            sity, August, 1958. Cambridge, Massachusetts:
            Center for Middle Eastern Studies. (Mimeographed).
            pp. 25.
      g.   (With Majed Sa'id). Lexical variants in Arabic
            dialects. (Multilith).
      h.   Arabic language. Encyclopaedia Britannica
            2. 182-84. (-1970 edition).
      i.   On the writing of grammars. Paper presented
            at the Linguistic Society of America Annual
            Meeting, Chicago, December. (Unpublished).

j.   Coloquio sobre la Enseñanza de al Lengua Arabe
     a los no Arabes. LR 1:5. 1, 3.
k.   Review of   Deutsch-Arabisches wörterbuch der
     umgangssprache in Palästina und ın Libanon, by
     L. Bauer. MEJ 13. 212-13.
l.   Review of Agyptisch-Arabischer Sprachführer,
     by K. Munzel. MEJ 13.212-13.
m.   Review of Syrisch-Arabischer Sprachführer, by
     E. Kuhnt. MEJ 13.212-13.
n.   Review of Arabic made easy, by M. Saheb-
     Ettaba. MEJ 13.471.

1960 a.   (With Munier Chowdhury). The phonemes of
          Bengali. Lg 36:1. 22-59.
     b.   (With John J. Gumperz). Introduction. Linguistic
          Diversity in South Asia, ed. by Charles A.
          Ferguson and John J. Gumperz (IJAL 26:3, Part
          II. = Publication 13 of the Indiana University
          Research Center in Anthropology, Folklore and
          Linguistics), pp. 1-18.
     c.   (Ed. with John J. Gumperz). Linguistic Diversity
          in South Asia. IJAL 26:3, Part II. Pp. vi, 118.
          [= Publication 13 of the Indiana University
          Research Center in Anthropology, Folklore and
          Linguistics].
     d.   (With Frank A. Rice). Iraqi children's rhymes.
          JAOS 80:4. 335-40.
     e.   (With Moukhtar Ani). Lessons in contemporary
          Arabic. Lessons 1-8. Washington, D.C.:
          Center for Applied Linguistics. Pp. vi, 160.
     f.   (Ed.). Contributions to Arabic linguistics.
          Cambridge, Massachusetts: Harvard University
          Press. Pp. v, 161. [Harvard Middle Eastern
          Monographs III].

g. (With Arnold Satterthwaite). <u>Bengali: basic course</u>. Washington, D. C.: Foreign Service Institute. (Mimeographed).

h. Number categories of the Arabic noun. Lecture at the Summer Linguistic Program, University of Michigan, Ann Arbor. (Unpublished).

i. Center has first anniversary. <u>LR</u> 2:2. 1, 3.

j. Congress of orientalists in Moscow brings linguists together. <u>LR</u> 2:5. 1-2.

k. Review of <u>Cuentos populares marroquies; folklore infantil de Gumara; diccionario de supersticiones y mitos marroquies</u>, by M. I. A. Haquim. <u>MEJ</u> 14.108.

1961 a. (With Moukhtar Ani and others). <u>Damascus Arabic</u>. Washington, D. C.: Center for Applied Linguistics. Pp. viii, 313.

b. Commonwealth holds English teaching conference. <u>LR</u> 3:1. 1-2.

c. Review of <u>Tell Toqaan: a Syrian village</u>, by L. Sweet. <u>MEJ</u> 15. 107-8.

1962 a. The language factor in national development. <u>AA</u> 4:1. 23-27. [Reprinted in <u>Study of the Role of Second Languages in Asia, Africa and Latin America</u>, ed. by Frank A. Rice (Washington, D. C.: Center for Applied Linguistics, 1962), pp. 8-14].

b. Linguistics in the preparation of language teachers. Seminar in Language Teachers Training and Supervision, Seattle, Washington. (Mimeographed). Pp. 10.

c. Quantity and quality in Iranian vowel systems. Paper presented at the Linguistic Society of America Summer Meeting, Seattle, Washington, July. (Unpublished).

d. (General ed.) Contrastive structure series: the sounds of English and German, by William G. Moulton; and, The grammatical structures of English and German, by Herbert L. Kufner. Chicago: University of Chicago Press.

e. Review of The sound pattern of Russian, by M. Halle. Lg 38.284-98.

f. Review of The sound structures of English and Bengali, by M. A. Hai and J. W. Ball. Lg 38.460-62.

g. Review of A dictionary cf modern written Arabic, by H. Wehr. MEJ 16.109.

h. Review of L'arabe moderne, by V. Monteil. MEJ 16.111.

i. Review of A textbook of the Arabic language, by A. A. Kovalev and G. S. Sharbatov. MEJ 16.110-11.

j. Nijmegen conference on second language teaching. LR 4:2.4.

1963 a. Problems of teaching languages with diglossia. MSLL 15. 165-77.

b. Linguistic theory and language learning. MSLL 16. 115-24.

c. Assumptions about nasals: a sample study in phonological universals. Universals of language, ed. by Joseph H. Greenberg (Cambridge, Massachusetts: The M.I.T. Press, 1963), pp. 53-60.

d. Clause negation in Bengali. Lecture at the Linguistic Institute, University of Washington, Seattle, Summer. [Revised version presented at the 26th International Congress of Orientalists, New Delhi.]

e. (Ed. with William A. Stewart). Linguistic read-

ing lists for teachers of modern languages.
Washington, D. C.: Center for Applied Linguistics.

f.   Review of Funciones gramaticales en el habla
infantil, by S. G. Gaya. Word 19:1.106-8.

1964 a.   Linguistic research in modern scholarship.
Pakistani linguistics 1963, ed. by Anwar S. Dil
(Lahore: Linguistic Research Group of Pakistan,
1964), pp. 169-75.

b.   Development of linguistic studies and research in
Pakistan. Pakistani Linguistics 1963, ed. by
Anwar S. Dil (Lahore: Linguistic Research
Group of Pakistan, 1964), pp. 248-56.

c.   The basic grammatical categories of Bengali.
Proceedings of the Ninth International Congress
of Linguists, ed. by Horace G. Lunt (The Hague:
Mouton & Co., 1964), pp. 881-90.

d.   Baby talk in six languages. The ethnography of
communication, ed. by John J. Gumperz and
Dell Hymes [= AA 66:6. Part 2], pp. 103-14.

e.   Teaching standard languages to dialect speakers.
Social dialects and language learning, ed. by
Roger W. Shuy (Champaign, Illinois: National
Council of Teachers of English, 1964), pp. 112-
17.

f.   On linguistic information. MSLL 17. 201-08.

g.   Information flow in linguistics. LR 6:2. 2-5.

h.   Glossary of terms relating to languages of the
Middle East. Washington, D. C.: Center for
Applied Linguistics. Pp. 11.

i.   Language study and the Middle East. The Annals
of the American Academy of Political and Social
Science 356. 76-85.

1965 a. Toward a typology of imperative systems.
          Paper presented at the Linguistic Society of
          America Annual Meeting, Chicago, December.
          (Unpublished).

      b. Holy Cross Day: a set of Lutheran propers.
          Response 6. 172-76.

      c. (General ed.). Contrastive structure series:
          The sounds of English and Italian, by F.B.
          Agard and R. J. DiPietro. The grammatical
          structures of English and Italian, by F. B.
          Agard and R. J. DiPietro. The sounds of
          English and Spanish, by R. P. Stockwell and
          J. D. Bowen. The grammatical structures of
          English and Spanish, by R. P. Stockwell, J. D.
          Bowen, and J. W. Martin. Chicago, Illinois:
          University of Chicago Press.

      d. (Associate ed. with Thomas A. Sebeok). Current
          trends in linguistics. 3. theoretical foundations.
          The Hague: Mouton and Co.

      e. Changing patterns in language study. Proceedings
          of the regional conference on the arts and
          humanities in college education. Los Angeles:
          University of California, 1965.

      f. Directions in sociolinguistics: report on an
          interdisciplinary seminar. Items 19: 1.1-4.

1966 a. The imperative system of Bengali. Shahidullah
          presentation volume, ed. by Anwar S. Dil
          (Lahore: Linguistic Research Group of Pakistan,
          1966), pp. 19-24.

      b. Sentence deviance and language teaching. A
          common purpose, ed. by James R. Squire
          (Champaign, Illinois: The National Council
          of Teachers of English, 1966), pp. 61-69.

c.   Applied linguistics. Language teaching: broader contexts, ed. by Robert G. Mead, Jr. (Menasha, Wisconsin: Northeast Conferences on the Teaching of Foreign Languages, 1966), pp. 50-58.

d.   Linguistic theory as behavioral theory. Brain function, ed. by E. C. Carterette (Los Angeles: University of California Press, 1966), pp. 249-61.

e.   On sociolinguistically oriented language surveys. LR 8: 4. 1-3.

f.   Saints' names in American Lutheran Church dedications. Names 14:2. 76-82.

g.   The language of faith. Stance 1:3. 1, 3. [Reprinted as "Should faith have a private language?" Lutheran Standard 7:2.13 (January 24, 1967)].

h.   Sociolinguistics for teachers of English to speakers of other languages. Selected conference papers of the Association of Teachers of English as a Second Language, 1966, ed. by Robert B. Kaplan (Los Angeles: University of Southern California Press, 1966), pp. 35-41. [= NAFSA Studies and Papers English Language Series No. 12].

i.   Review of The daily office, ed. by H. Lindemann. Response 8.55-56.

j.   Review of Linguistics, language and religion, by D. Crystal. Response 8.56-57.

k.   Review of Of this and that: essays by two sisters, by Saeqa Dil and Shaheen Dil. MEJ 20.558-59.

l.   Meditation on the Lord's Prayer (for a hospital patient). Stance 1:8.1, 6.

m.   Paul's letter to the Community of Christ. Stance 1:6. 1, 6.

n. New Brevaries: a review [Review of <u>The daily</u>
<u>office</u>, ed. by H. Lindemann. <u>Morning praise</u>
<u>and evensong</u>; <u>a book of common prayer</u>, ed. by
W. G. Stokey.] <u>Stance</u> 1:2. 3, 6.

1967 a. National sociolinguistic profile formulas. <u>Socio-</u>
<u>linguistics</u>, ed. by William Bright (The Hague:
Mouton & Co., 1967), pp. 309-24.

b. St. Stefan of Perm and applied linguistics. <u>To</u>
<u>honor Roman Jakobson</u>; <u>essays on the occasion</u>
<u>of his seventieth birthday</u>, <u>11 October 1966.</u>
Volume 1 (The Hague: Mouton & Co., 1967),
pp. 643-53.

c. Root-echo responses in Syrian Arabic politeness
formulas. <u>Linguistic studies in memory of</u>
<u>Richard Slade Harrel</u>, ed. by Don G. Stuart
(Washington, D.C.: Georgetown University
Press, 1967), pp. 35-45.

d. Review of <u>Saints and scholars</u>, by D. Knowles;
<u>Saints and sanctity</u>, by W. Benghardt; <u>Saints:</u>
<u>their place in the church</u>, by P. Molinari.
<u>Una Sancta</u> 24. 107-11.

e. The role of the Center for Applied Linguistics:
1959-67. <u>LR</u> 9:6. 1-4.

f. Letter to the nation [on Vietnam]. <u>Stance</u> 2:2.
2, 6.

g. Reflections on a victory. <u>Stance</u> 2:3. 3,6.

h. An Advent Psalm. <u>Stance</u> 2:4.4.

i. Report on sociolinguistics. <u>Items</u> 21:4.51-52.

1968 a. The domain of the language sciences. <u>Seminar</u>
<u>on computational linguistics</u>, October 6-7, 1966,
National Institute of Health, Bethesda, Madison
(Washington, D.C.: Public Health Publications

No. 1716, U.S. Department of Health, Education
& Welfare, 1968), pp. 4-8.

b.   Contrastive analysis and language development.
MSLL 21. 101-12.

c.   The morning suffrages in contemporary English.
Response 9:3. 131-38.

d.   Language development. Language problems of
developing nations, ed. by Joshua A. Fishman,
J. Das Gupta, Charles A. Ferguson (New York:
Wiley & Sons, 1968), pp. 27-35.

e.   (Ed. with Joshua A. Fishman and J. Das Gupta).
Language problems of developing nations. New
York: Wiley & Sons. Pp. xv, 521.

1969 a.   (Associate ed. with Thomas A. Sebeok). Current
trends in linguistics. 5. linguistics in South
Asia. The Hague: Mouton & Co.

b.   (With K. L. Cizikova). A bibliographical review
of Bengali studies. Current trends in linguistics.
5. linguistics in South Asia, ed. by Thomas
A. Sebeok (The Hague: Mouton & Co., 1969),
pp. 85-98.

1970 a.   Grammatical categories in data collection.
Working papers in language universals 4. F1-
F-15. Stanford, California: Language Universals
Project, Stanford University.

b.   The role of Arabic in Ethiopia: a sociolinguistic
perspective. MSLL 23. 355-70.

1971   Contrasting patterns of literacy acquisition in a
multilingual nation. Language use and social
change, ed. by W. H. Whiteley (London:
Oxford University Press), pp. 234-53.

In Press a. Regional language issues and studies: an overview. Current trends in linguistics. 6. linguistics in South West Asia and North Africa, ed. by Thomas A. Sebeok (The Hague: Mouton & Co.), pp. 667-70.

b. Absence of copula and the notion of simplicity: a study of normal speech, baby talk, foreigner talk, and pidgins. To appear in Social factors in pidginization and creolization, ed. by Dell Hymes. New York: Cambridge University Press.

c. Introduction. The learning of language; essays in honor of David H. Russell, ed. by Carroll E. Reed. Champaign, Illinois: National Council of Teachers of English.

d. The Ethiopian language area. To appear in Journal of Ethiopian Studies.

e. (Associate ed. with Thomas A. Sebeok). Current trends in linguistics. 6. linguistics in South West Asia and North Africa. The Hague: Mouton & Co.

f. (Ed. with Dan Slobin). Readings in child language acquisition. New York: Holt, Rinehart and Winston.

g. The / g/ in Syrian Arabic: filling a gap in a phonological pattern. Linguistic studies presented to Andre Martinet; on the occasion of his sixtieth birthday, ed. by Alphonse Juilland (London: The Linguistic Circle of New York), pp. 114-19.

h. 'Short a' in Philadelphia English. Revised and expanded version of 1945 paper. To appear in Studies in linguistics: essays in honor of George L. Trager, ed. by M. Estellia Smith (Westport, Connecticut: Greenwood Publishing Corporation).

Ferguson, Charles A   1921-
        Language structure and language use:
essays by Charles A. Ferguson. Selected and
introduced by Anwar S. Dil. Stanford, California:
Stanford University Press [1971]
        xvi, 328 p.   24cm.
(Language science and national development series,
Linguistic Research Group of Pakistan)
        Includes bibliography.

I. Dil, Anwar S., 1928-   ed
II. (Series) III. Linguistic Research C

DATE DUE

APR 2 0			